LANGUAGE AND GENDER IN AMERICAN FICTION
Howells, James, Wharton and Cather

Language and Gender in American Fiction

Howells, James, Wharton and Cather

Elsa Nettels

University Press of Virginia
Charlottesville

First published 1997 by Macmillan Press Ltd

First published 1997 in the United States of America
by the University Press of Virginia
Box 3608 University Station
Charlottesville, VA 22903

Library of Congress Cataloging-in-Publication Data
Nettels, Elsa.
    Language and gender in American fiction : Howells, James, Wharton
and Cather / Elsa Nettels.
        p.   cm.
    Includes index.
    ISBN 0-8139-1724-7 (cloth : alk. paper)
    1. American fiction—Men authors—History and criticism.   2. Sex
role in literature.   3. American fiction—Women authors—History and
criticism.   4. English language—United States—Sex differences.
5. Women and literature—United States—History.   6. Howells,
William Dean, 1837–1920—Language.   7. James, Henry, 1843–1916—
Language.   8. Wharton, Edith, 1862–1937—Language.   9. Cather,
Willa, 1873–1947—Language.   10. Authorship—Sex differences.
I. Title.
PS374.S46N48   1997
813'.409353—dc20   96–34294
                                                            CIP

Printed in Great Britain

Contents

Acknowledgements

My work has been substantially aided by the College of William and Mary, which awarded me a Faculty Research Assignment during 1987–88 and a summer grant in 1990. I am also grateful to the Commonwealth Center for the Study of American Culture for the award of a semester's research fellowship in 1990.

The expert work of Erika Monson, David Morrill, and Karen Veselits in preparing the final typescript was invaluable. I extend warm thanks to them and to other colleagues and friends: Jean Frantz Blackall, Donna Coyle, Marlene Davis, Susan Donaldson, Margaret Freeman, Terry Meyers, Deborah Morse and Kenneth Price. Their encouragement and assistance in reading parts of the project, lending books, and providing information are greatly appreciated.

Quotations from Edith Wharton's correspondence and Commonplace Book (Edith Wharton Collection #6909, Clifton Waller Barrett Library, Special Collections Department, University of Virginia Library) are published by permission of the University and the Watkins/Loomis Agency, agents for the Estate of Edith Wharton. Quotations from letters by Henry James to W.D. Howells, bMS Am 1784 (253), and to Mary Cadwalader Jones, bMS Am 1094 (756), are published by permission of the Houghton Library, Harvard University and Bay James, literary agent for the James family. Quotation from the letter by Ferris Greenslet to Willa Cather is by permission of the Houghton Library, Harvard University and the Houghton Mifflin Company. Quotation from the letter by Mildred Bennett to Dorothy Canfield Fisher is by permission of the University of Vermont, Special Collections.

List of Abbreviations

Chapter 1

MMW	*The Man-Made World*
RW	*The Revolution in Words*
WJ	*Woman's Journal*

Chapter 2

AH	*April Hopes*
MC	*The Minister's Charge*
RSL	*The Rise of Silas Lapham*
CP	*The Complete Plays of W. D. Howells*
VK	*The Vacation of the Kelwyns*
AK	*Annie Kilburn*
SRL	*The Son of Royal Langbrith*
HNF	*A Hazard of New Fortunes*
MF	*Mrs Farrell*
LLH	*The Landlord at Lion's Head*
DBP	*Doctor Breen's Practice*
SP	*The Story of a Play*
LA	*The Lady of the Aroostook*

Chapter 3

NN	*Notes on Novelists*
NR	*Notes and Reviews*
LRE	*Literary Reviews and Essays*
PP	*Partial Portraits*
FPN	*French Poets and Novelists*
ELE	*Essays in London and Elsewhere*
WW	*Watch and Ward*
CT	*The Collected Tales of Henry James*
E	*The Europeans*
B	*The Bostonians*

Chapter 4

BG	*A Backward Glance*
CC	*The Custom of the Country*

List of Abbreviations

AI	*The Age of Innocence*
TS	*Twilight Sleep*
HM	*The House of Mirth*
C	*The Children*
GM	*The Glimpses of the Moon*
SF	*A Son at the Front*
MR	*The Mother's Recompense*
HRB	*Hudson River Bracketed*
GA	*The Gods Arrive*
FWM	*French Ways and Their Meaning*
B	*The Buccaneers*

Chapter 5

KA	*The Kingdom of Art*
WP	*The World and the Parish*
SL	*The Song of the Lark*
UV	*Uncle Valentine and Other Stories*
CSF	*Willa Cather's Collected Short Fiction*
MA	*My Ántonia*
PH	*The Professor's House*
MME	*My Mortal Enemy*
SSG	*Sapphira and the Slave Girl*

Chapter 6

LB	*Looking Backward*
E	*Equality*
AR	*The Altrurian Romances*
GA	*The Gates Ajar*
GB	*The Gates Between*
BG	*Beyond the Gates*
CL	*Chapters from a Life*
H	*Herland*
WHO	*With Her in Ourland*
M	*Mizora*
UPR	*Unveiling a Parallel*
SS	*San Salvador*
AL	*Al-Modad*

Introduction

Between January 1880 and December 1889, *Harper's Monthly Magazine* published 263 works of fiction, including 19 serialized novels. Of the total, more than half, 132 novels and stories, are known to be by women or appear under a woman's name.[1] Four of the writers – George Eliot, Thomas Hardy, William Dean Howells and Henry James – have remained dominant figures in American and English literary history. Several others, including Sarah Orne Jewett, Thomas Nelson Page and Mary E. Wilkins, retained their status as regionalists. The majority, male and female, quickly passed into oblivion and have remained forgotten, their books long since out of print.

What is noteworthy is the near-parity of male and female writers. The contents of the *Century* and *Scribner's Magazine* show a similar balance. Judging by the popular mass-circulation magazines, women writers enjoyed equal opportunity, even an advantage, in the world of commercial publishing. But until the 1970s, the producers of reference works, literary histories, encyclopedia articles, and high school and college curricula made 'American literature' almost synonymous with male authorship. In the post-Civil War era, women could get their stories published; they wrote bestsellers and won prizes, but with few exceptions, the institutions that keep writers and their reputations alive did not choose to sustain them. The publication in recent years of monumental works such as *The Norton Anthology of Literature by Women* (1985) and *The Oxford Companion to Writing by Women* (1994) testifies to the long eclipse of scores of women writers.

For explanation of this phenomenon one need look no further than the pages of the magazines such as *Harper's*, so hospitable to fiction by women. Side by side with stories by Sarah Orne Jewett, Rebecca Harding Davis, Rose Terry Cooke and Constance Fenimore Woolson were articles and reviews expressing opinions of women's speech and language that cast women as inferior to men, defined their differences from male writers as deviations from an approved standard, and satirized or belittled qualities labelled

1

'feminine'. Most of this magazine journalism is of no literary conse-
quence. But taken all together, the mass of articles and reviews is
important; the magazines, described by one observer as 'the recognized gateway to the literary public',[2] disseminated ideas and
shaped and reflected public taste and belief.

As the first chapter of this study seeks to show, the influence of
the magazines was powerfully reinforced by others engaged in the
construction of gender: grammarians, linguists, philologists, socio-
logists, writers on manners and etiquette. Personally undistin-
guished though many of them were, together they constituted a
potent authority by which no writer or reader could remain un-
touched.

The chapters on William Dean Howells, Henry James, Edith
Wharton and Willa Cather examine the ways that these dominant
figures of the literary establishment helped perpetuate or subvert
their culture's ideology of language and gender. To see how these
four writers defined *masculine* and *feminine*, how they characterized
women's speech and language, how they distinguished male and
female discourse, where they invested authority in matters of
usage, is to gauge their response to the pervasive assumptions set
forth in the magazines that published their fiction.

Several facts dictated the choice of the four writers placed at the
centre of the study. All four had long careers of half a century or
more. Each produced a formidable body of work: together they
published more than 80 novels. Each writer wrote literary criticism
setting forth ideas and assumptions which can be compared with
the representations of language and gender in their fiction.

All four novelists were literary realists in that they assumed the
office of the historian as James defined it in *The Art of Fiction*: 'to
represent and illustrate the past', to produce 'the illusion of life', to
'catch the color, the relief, the expression, the surface, the substance
of the human spectacle'.[3] None of the writers can be confined by the
label 'novelist of manners' but as realists they represented the
culture of particular societies including the language and habits of
speech of men and women. None of the four proposed to create a
new language or attacked conventions perpetuating gender bias in
American English (for example the generic pronoun *he*, the feminine suffixes). But all four directly addressed issues exposing
vital connections between language and gender. The reader may
study the interactions of gender bias and social class in the novels
of Howells and Wharton; the association with women of colloquial

speech and oral narration in Cather's novels; the embodiment of linguistic authority in male characters of Howells and James; the representation of women as the preservers of culture in James's four-part essay 'The Speech of American Women'. All four novelists created first-person narrators of both sexes – diarists, letter-writers, storytellers, public speakers – thereby revealing their conceptions of the way men and women speak and write.

Finally, all four writers had lifelong connections to the dominant institutions of book and magazine publication in the United States. All four published their fiction and criticism in the leading periodicals – *Harper's Magazine*, the *Atlantic*, *Scribner's Magazine* and the *Century*. Howells and Cather were editors who, in choosing manuscripts and advising contributors, influenced the direction of other writers' careers and helped to shape public taste. All four writers had long-term close professional relationships with the most influential editors and publishers of the time.

The utopian novels treated in the final chapter offer another perspective on the realist fiction of the late nineteenth and early twentieth centuries. Did visions of societies socially and politically reformed dictate changes in language as well? Did the power of language to construct gender, to promote division and to circumscribe the lives of both men and women concern the authors of utopian fiction and their characters? Answering these questions we gain a measure by which to judge the potency of a culture's ideology and the capacity of writers of all persuasions to analyse its effects.

1

Language and Gender in Victorian America

I

The historian of issues debated in modern feminist criticism finds in American writing of the nineteenth century much that anticipates the discussions of scholars and critics today. In particular, the relation of literary style to gender became of increasing interest to Americans as women writers became ever more prominent in Victorian America. Reviewers and essayists of the post-Civil War years did not use modern terms such as 'patriarchal language', 'androgynous ideal' and 'phallocentric reading', but they debated questions to which critics and theorists today are seeking answers: Are there differences between the language of men and of women? Are there qualities of style that distinguish women's writing from men's? If there are differences, are they the result of cultural ideals and codes that are learned, or are they the result of inherent biological differences? Does literary style reflect mental processes or psychological traits that are distinctively feminine or masculine? In the most influential magazines of the late nineteenth century, such as *Harper's, Century, Atlantic, Scribner's, Cosmopolitan* and *Ladies' Home Journal*, writers directly or implicitly gave answers to these questions, answers which often reflect widely held views of the relation of the sexes and of the proper roles or spheres of men and women.

Like their predecessors, nineteenth-century critics and reviewers – most of whom were men – constructed literary gender by borrowing the grammarians' terms: *masculine* and *feminine* – 'perhaps the most culturally biased words in the language', according to the linguists Casey Miller and Kate Swift.[1] By the nineteenth century these words had already acquired powerful connotations sustained for several centuries. From the time of Edmund Spenser, *masculine* had signified the strong, the dominant, the superior; *feminine* the weak, the submissive, the inferior. Thus nineteenth-century writers called prose 'masculine' when they wished to praise it for strength,

5

vigour, precision and directness. James Russell Lowell, for instance, cited the Gettysburg Address – 'of a truly masculine English' – to identify Lincoln as a 'master' among writers.[2] A reviewer
in *Harper's Magazine* recommended Whateley's *Elements of Rhetoric*
for its precision, lucidity, and 'masculine good sense'.[3]

Strength and vigour combined with moral qualities such as
courage, candour and self-restraint produced a style to which
Victorians gave their word of highest praise – *manly*. Thomas
Wentworth Higginson found in nineteenth-century English prose
'an admirable vigour and heartiness, a direct and manly tone'.[4]
George William Curtis, the first occupant of the 'Editor's Easy
Chair' of *Harper's Magazine*, valued a 'manly reticence and re-
straint' in both conduct and art and preferred Tennyson's later to
his earlier poetry as being 'more manly' in style.[5] William Dean
Howells also liked a 'candid and manly style', praised the poetry of
Robert Frost for its 'manly power', and approved the 'manly hu-
manity' of Jacob Gould Schurman's speech opposing the war in the
Philippines.[6]

The most desirable elements that made a style *feminine* were
grace, delicacy, fastidiousness and ideality. A writer on 'Some Recent Women Poets' in *Scribner's Magazine* (1875) found women's
poetry 'sensitive', 'exquisitely spiritual', 'graceful' and 'mystical',
notable for an 'intense, indefinable aroma which could not have
been exhaled from any masculine mind'.[7] 'Purely feminine the
voice is', Howells said of Rose Hawthorne Lathrop's 'pretty book'
of poems, 'with an appealing, haunting quality that lingers, and
that thrills to heart-break'.[8] He did not use the word *feminine* in
analysing the 'rarity' and 'singular worth' of Emily Dickinson's
poetry but he detected 'something of the perfervid feminine flutter
in the emotional passages' of Mrs Humphry Ward's otherwise
admirable novel, *Robert Elsmere*.[9]

To nineteenth-century critics *masculine* and *feminine* not only connoted qualities differentiating the sexes but also signified realities immutable as night and day, more definitively bounded than
heat and cold or youth and age, as natural as the operation of the
heart and lungs by which Emerson in 'Compensation' illustrated
the 'inevitable dualism bisect[ing] nature'.[10] In 'Two Principles in
Recent American Fiction', for instance, the popular writer of genteel romances, James Lane Allen, subsumed all literature under
the rubric of gender, expanding the polarity into a series of match-
ing elements – the *masculine*: virility, strength, massiveness, large-

ness, obviousness and instinctive action, opposing the *feminine*: refinement, delicacy, grace, smallness, rarity and tact. When the masculine degenerates, he maintained, it becomes coarse, vulgar, and violent; when the feminine degenerates it becomes trivial, bloodless and decadent. These were timeless polarities 'whose history lies revealed as drawn unbrokenly across many centuries'.[11] Allen's classification anticipates Philip Rahv's well-known class-based division of American writers into 'two polar types': Palefaces, patrician and highbrow, identified by sensibility, 'philosophical depth' and refinement; and Redskins, plebeian and lowbrow, exhibiting energy, 'natural power' and 'gross riotous naturalism'.[12]

Nineteenth-century reviewers perceived that women writers did not all write alike, that the style of Mrs Southworth, described by Sarah J. Hale as 'wild and extravagant', was different from that of Mary Wilkins Freeman, commended for her 'short economical sentences'.[13] But reviewers generalized more readily than they discriminated, and so deeply ingrained was the masculine–feminine polarity that they attributed qualities of one sex to the other rather than dispense with the categories. Instead of allowing *feminine* to modify strength and vigour in a woman's style, they praised it for its *masculine* (but not manly) virtues. Mary Noailles Murfree, who wrote under the name 'Charles Egbert Craddock', was praised by one male reviewer for depicting 'with masculine force the minute, daily life of a scant civilization', by another for producing in her serial 'Where the Battle was Fought' a 'full-fledged novel of masculine strength'.[14] To the reviewer of Anne Douglas Sedgwick's novel *A Fountain Sealed*, the fineness of detail marked the book as that of a 'well-bred woman with a heritage of culture', but her use of extended metaphor seemed a 'point of excellence especially masculine'.[15] Julian Hawthorne praised Elizabeth Stoddard for not 'aping the masculine voice' in *The Morgesons* but found the 'virility, austerity, and . . . taciturnity' of her style even less suggestive of 'the conventional feminine tone'.[16]

In nineteenth-century criticism, the connotations of *masculine* were rarely negative, whereas *effeminacy* was always bad and *feminine* was at best graceful and delicate, at worst perfervid and shrill. Reviewers who found feminine qualities in the work of men they wished to praise usually qualified their statements. For instance, writers in the *North American Review* felt an 'almost feminine spitefulness' in Max Müller's criticism, saw in Howells's fiction 'the more than masculine, almost feminine touch', and wondered if 'feminine aid and counsel' might account for 'a delicacy of touch which does not belong to man'.[17]

Even when critics insisted on the presence of both the male and female principles in the greatest creative minds, they usually asserted the primacy of the male principle in the androgynous union. George Parsons Lathrop, in an essay on 'Audacity in Women Novelists' (1890), argued that 'every imaginative mind of the best and strongest sort must unite some of the elements of both sexes', but he accepted the traditional categories, implying that male strength was superior to female tenderness, sentiment and intuition. These feminine elements in Browning, for instance, 'do not for a moment hide the masculine nature of his mental action, the close-grained, robust muscularity of thought, which is one of his greatest traits'.[18] The novelist and essayist Grant Allen, who believed that 'the males are the race; the females are merely the sex told off to recruit and reproduce it', stated in an essay on 'Women's Intuition' (1890) that 'in the highest minds' the 'feminine element' commingles with 'the masculine element of pure reason' but only as 'a certain undercurrent' in genius which is essentially 'virile', as exemplified by his list of painters, musicians, statesmen and inventors, all of whom are men.[19] James Lane Allen attributed the stylistic excellence of American prose to the operation of the Feminine Principle but saw in the historical pattern of action and reaction a recurrent triumph for the Masculine Principle, not the Feminine, which 'the human spirit' has repeatedly rejected, 'having tried it and found it wanting'.[20]

A small minority of writers opposed the idea of innate differences which relegate men and women to separate spheres of mental activity. In response to Grant Allen's essay on 'Women's Intuition', the sociologist Lester F. Ward agreed that men have surpassed women in the arts but argued that men owe their success not to superior creative power but to a breadth of knowledge denied to women: 'man has displayed more genius than woman; largely because he has been in possession of a wider range of facts, a greater supply of the only material out of which genius can construct and create'.[21] James S. Metcalfe, in 'The Silent Revolution' (1890), attributed what he called 'the weaker characteristics of women' not to biology but to 'the errors of the centuries' which have perpetuated the belief that woman is inferior to man. No one can be certain, he declared, that once women are freed from the forces that compel their submission they will not be able to 'think and act with the vigour and force of man'.[22] All the writers quoted above judged women's accomplishments inferior to men's and held 'the vigour and force of man' as the ideal. A few writers anticipated certain modern feminist critics when they argued that the experiences, values and creative powers of women are essentially different from those of men but are of equal or greater value and importance. Women should therefore reject the standards promoted by men and assert the primacy of their own ideals. The essayist and novelist Helen H. Gardner implicitly urged women to become resisting readers and writers when she argued in 'The Immoral Influence of Women in Literature' (1890) that no novelists had represented life from women's standpoint, that 'even the woman character in fiction is what men fancy she is or ought to be'. Women writers had yet to free themselves from the 'established male critics' position' so powerful that even when literature portrays women, 'the *basis* of its morals, its standard of action and its motive, have remained masculine in conception and requirement'.[23] Her analysis counters the kind of argument made by a critic who opposed the special exhibit of books by women at the World's Fair in 1893, on the grounds that literary success depends on 'intrinsic merit', that only 'the genius of the writer' and 'the understanding of the people' will keep a book alive – as if 'merit', 'genius' and 'understanding' were universal ahistorical entities existing apart from human time-bound judgements.[24]

Those who believed that the creative powers of men and women were not essentially different likewise argued against classifying writers by sex. For instance, Helen Gray Cone, in an article on 'Woman in American Literature' (1890), urged that writers be categorized by 'method, local background, or any other basis of arrangement which is artistic rather than personal'. Arguing that faults described as 'womanish' are common to writers of both sexes, she rejected 'classification based upon sex' as 'necessarily misleading and inexact'. To her, the 'completely deceptive' mask of Charles Egbert Craddock proved the absurdity of 'the notion of ordained, invariable, and discernible differences between the literary work of men and that of women'.[25]

Implications of the premises in all these articles were explored by Charlotte Perkins Gilman in *The Man-Made World; or Our Androcentric Culture* (1911), the most comprehensive criticism of traditional concepts of gender to appear in America at that time. Rejecting the conventional polarity, Gilman argued for a third category, the *human*, to be distinguished from the *masculine* and the *feminine*, which comprise those functions (for example, procreation, giving birth) that belong to the male or female sexes of all species. The great wrong in modern society, she contended, was that women, their humanity denied, had been restricted to female functions while praiseworthy human powers and qualities such as courage and rationality were ascribed to men. 'What we have called "masculine" and admired as such, was in large part human, and should be applied to both sexes'.[26] Although she made the familiar identification of the masculine with combat, hunting and self-expression; the feminine with nurturing, building and connecting, she insisted that activities that create civilization, assumed to be 'man's work', belong to both sexes. 'Every handicraft, every profession, every science, every art, all normal amusements and recreations, all government, education, religion; the whole living world of human achievement: all this is human' (MMW, 25).

Gilman dedicated her book to Lester Ward, whose Gynaecocentric Theory she set forth in the Preface as the premise of her book: 'that the female is the race type, and the male, originally but a sex type, reaching a later equality with the female, and, in the human race, becoming her master for a considerable historic period'. But unlike Ward, who made male achievement his standard, asserting that women must be raised to the 'plane of intelligence' men have reached, that 'society should seek to make woman a companion for man',[27] Gilman argued that the 'unprecedented dominance of the male' had warped every institution and stunted the development of both men and women. Like Helen Gardner, she maintained that fiction, restricted to the male view of subjects most interesting to men (namely conquest and mating), ignored innumerable processes vital to human life and central to women's experience. 'Fiction, under our androcentric culture, has not given any true picture of woman's life, very little of human life, and a disproportioned section of man's life' (MMW, 102).

In language as well, Gilman saw reflected and perpetuated the ideology that identifies the man with the human and the normal, the woman with the deviant and the inferior. She noted that boys taught by women are said to become *effeminate* – a term of reproach. But no word denotes excessive masculine influence injurious to girls taught by men. 'Never has it occurred to the androcentric mind to conceive of such a thing as being *too* masculine. There is no such word!' (MMW, 149–50). Likewise, *emasculate*, denoting weakness, loss of vigour, has no analogue to suggest that one might suffer in lacking feminine qualities. To speak of literature as 'feminized' but never as 'masculized' is to acknowledge the masculine as the norm, the equivalent of human. 'We have not in our minds the concept, much less the word, for an over-masculized influence' (MMW, 89).

Gilman's book received favourable reviews in a number of magazines and newspapers,[28] but it did not effect changes in the language or diminish the power of the assumptions she challenged. The reviewer in the *Atlantic Monthly* who declared that 'the only quality which it is worthwhile for women to contribute to literature is . . . [the] feminine quality' spoke for more of his contemporaries than those who told readers of *Ladies' Home Journal* that 'there is no sex in brains' and that 'in the broad republic of letters there are no distinctions of sex and creed, class or condition, race or nationality'.[29] Unless 'are no distinctions' is read to mean 'should be no distinctions', the statement is controverted by the innumerable assertions that the masculine in literature is more worthy than the feminine.

One of the speakers in Henry James's dialogue, 'An Animated Conversation' (1889), declares that if women are 'the great consumers' of fiction today, they are 'still more the great producers . . . Literature is simply undergoing a transformation – it's becoming feminine. That's a portentous fact.' [30] Howells, too, cited the number of women novelists and readers as evidence of the 'process of feminization [that] is still going on, not in less but in greater degree'.[31] Such statements attest to the financial success of the growing number of women writers and to the dismay generated by such success, but so long as critics identified *feminine* with the subordinate and the inferior, their references to the 'feminization' of literature go to prove rather than disprove Helen Gardner's statement: 'the canons of literature have, so far, been laid down on strictly masculine lines'.[32]

II

To turn from literature to speech is to encounter sharper criticism of women and stronger insistence on behaviour that fixes the woman in her subordinate position, inferior in power and prestige to the man. Qualities defined as masculine were often praised in women's writing but were almost universally condemned in women's speech. From the fourteenth century to the twentieth, books of conduct and etiquette instructed women to speak in soft low voices, to refrain from gossip and scolding, and to leave strong language to men. As late as 1975, the *Emily Post Etiquette Book* informed readers: 'The expression "You know she is a lady as soon as she opens her mouth" is not an exaggeration. A pleasing voice is the first requirement for charm of speech. A low voice is always more appealing than one that comes out in a high squeak.'[33] This passage was dropped from the 1984 edition of the book.

St Paul's command 'Let your women keep silence in the churches' was but the most powerfully sanctioned of innumerable injunctions against public speaking by women. The ideal of womanly reticence was backed by the literary authority most revered – the plays of Shakespeare. King Lear gives the memorable expression of the ideal when he says of Cordelia: 'Her voice was ever soft, gentle, and low – an excellent thing in woman.' In *The Taming of the Shrew*, Shakespeare contrasts the ideal and its opposite: Bianca, the obedient daughter, mild, submissive, gentle, modest (and not very interesting); her sister Katharina or Kate, loud, rough, forward, waspish, 'renowned in Padua for her scolding tongue' until her husband tames her into wifely submission.

Young men in Shakespeare who give way to excessive emotion are chided for behaving like women at their worst. When Romeo bewails his fate and proposes to stab himself, Friar Lawrence demands: 'Art thou a Man? . . . Thye tears are womanish . . . Unseemly woman in a seeming man!' After Hotspur rails against his king for an entire scene in *Henry IV*, Part I, Northumberland exclaims:

> Why, what a wasp-stung and impatient fool
> Art thou to break into this woman's mood,
> Tying thine ear to no tongue but thine own!

Americans in the nineteenth century, according to their critics, most signally failed to achieve the ideal restraint because of their penchant for exaggeration in both speech and writing. Verbal inflation was the great American vice, which flourished everywhere – in polite society, in newspapers, in political oratory. Men were guilty of verbal extravagance, but women were even more guilty, according to scores of usage critics. Women were the ones to overuse intensifiers, to find everything 'perfectly lovely' or 'terribly clever' or 'absolutely ghastly'. 'Is there anything that a "gushing" young lady will not call sweet?' George Wakeman asked. Richard Grant White saw much to criticize in the language of both men and women but found 'the fair' more given than 'the stronger sex' to hyperbole: 'with most women now-adays everything that is satisfactory is splendid'. Frederic Bird admitted that men indulged in verbal inflation but regarded women as the chief offenders: 'boarding school misses' and 'feminine children of a larger growth'.[34] The patronizing tone of such statements disqualifies their authors as impartial analysts of women's speech. The Columbia-trained anthropologist Elsie Clews Parsons, who studied gender-based differences in cultures throughout the world, gives a more objective view in her chapter on 'Sex Dialects' in *The Old-Fashioned Woman* (1913), one of the earliest extended comparisons of male and female speech by an American. She contrasts women's tendency to overstatement (a fire is 'perfectly frightful') with men's habit of understatement (a fire is 'a pretty bad blaze'). But she finds men's words of praise – *great, fine, capital, stunning* – stronger than women's *nice, dear, lovely* and *just-too-sweet*, just as their terms of denunciation – *poor thing, minx* and *cat* – are weaker than men's *slob, skunk* and *shark*.[35]

Otto Jespersen illustrates similar differences in his chapter on 'The Woman' in *Language, Its Nature, Development and Origin* (1922). He contrasts women's 'gracious me' and 'dear me' with men's stronger exclamations – 'Great Scott' or 'Good heavens'. The man's 'infernal lie' is the woman's 'most dreadful fib'. Like earlier observers, he emphasized women's fondness for hyperbole, especially adverbs of intensity (*awfully, terribly, quite, so,* as in 'It is *so* lovely'). He compared the 'involute structures' of the periodic sentence he thought characteristic of men with the 'typical form of the feminine period', which links elements by *and*, like beads on a string. He diagnosed women's use of euphemisms to denote bodily functions and their habit of beginning but not completing exclamatory statements ('well, I never') as 'linguistic symptoms of a peculiarity of feminine psychology'.[36]

Social convention, not 'feminine psychology', was the most plausible, easily identifiable cause of differences between men's and women's language. Books of etiquette, essays on manners, and advice columns insisted on the impropriety in women of the bold or coarse expressions used by men. Elizabeth Stuart Phelps argued that women physicians were needed to counter 'a certain blunting of delicacy of speech' resulting from the treatment of women by male physicians.[37] 'Pure refined language is one of the many charms of noble womanhood', Amelia Barr instructed in an essay on 'Conversational Immoralities' (1890): 'Never is a woman so undignified and so unlovely as when uttering words of doubtful propriety'. But then she attacked women's use of euphemisms, such as 'fallen sister' and 'unfortunates', on the grounds that 'thus unnamable things have been made namable. It is a very significant breaking down of decent barriers'.[38] Clearly, the only solution was to forbid women not only the improper words but the subjects as well.

On the far side of 'decent barriers' was women's use of slang, which, according to Florence Kingsland in *Correct Social Usage*, 'may give point and piquancy to young men's conversation if kept within bounds, but used by young women is unpleasant to most people, and chiefly to those who hold them in highest estimation'.[39] Writers in *Ladies' Home Journal* advised girls to forbid the use of slang in their presence, to refrain from imitating their brothers' slang expressions ('Nothing so unsexes a woman as masculine ways'), and to form anti-slang clubs and fine themselves whenever they said 'You bet', or 'hold on', or 'give us a rest'.[40]

Jespersen believed that women's speech revealed 'an instinctive shrinking from coarse and gross expressions', a manifestation of 'feminine psychology'.[41] Parsons likewise attributed certain linguistic phenomena to 'difference in sex character and outlook in general'. But for her the primary determinants lay not in 'feminine psychology', but in the configurations of culture, in the operations of laws and codes that in societies on every continent subjected women to verbal taboos or forbade them to read the sacred texts of their religion or denied them knowledge of men's secret languages. Jespersen argued that men's vocabularies are larger than women's because men by nature 'take a greater interest in words as such'. Parsons attributed women's limited vocabularies to their exclusion from most of the spheres controlled by men – politics, business, finance, sport, war, law, statecraft and religious rites.[42]

Parsons's 'Sex Dialects' exposes the double-bind, no-win situation created by the critics of women's speech. Women were told to avoid boldness, coarseness and slang; one writer even asserted that 'strong' words such as *audacity* are 'repulsive to the instinctive delicacy of every true woman'.[43] Then women's writing was criticized as 'bloodless' and 'anemic' (when it was not 'perfervid') and women were chided for using genteelisms in the interests of 'false delicacy' by critics who feared the emasculating effects upon male writers of women's fondness for euphemism. In Jespersen's words, 'Men will certainly with great justice object that there is a danger of the language becoming languid and insipid if we are always to content ourselves with women's expressions, and that vigour and vividness count for something.'[44] Women were assured that 'their influence for purity is owing in large measure to their ignorance of the impure',[45] but as speakers and writers they were judged inferior because they lacked a man's range of knowledge. In short, women were criticized for the very qualities they were in structed to preserve.

III

Dennis Baron, in *Grammar and Gender* (1886), identifies the manifold ways by which linguists and grammarians from the Middle Ages to the twentieth century have perpetuated gender dichotomies and anti-feminist bias in their pronouncements on language. Etymologies that trace such words as *wife* and *woman* to unflattering origins; theories of the origin of language based on the Biblical accounts of Eve's creation from Adam's rib; analogies between grammatical gender and the roles in sexual reproduction assigned to the male (active) and the female (passive) – all these formulations, as Baron shows, purport to express truths that prove man's moral and intellectual superiority to woman and justify her subordinate position in societies controlled by men.[46] His book abundantly demonstrates that sex-bias expressed in language is not divinely ordained or inherent in the language but rather it reflects the interests, motives and assumptions of those who speak and write the language.

How successfully nineteenth-century Americans used language to construct gender and assert the worth of the masculine over the feminine is nowhere more clearly illustrated than in their grammars, particularly in sections on personification, which ascribe gender to so-called neutral nouns. For instance, Huber Gray Buehler's *A Modern English Grammar* (1900) instructs that 'things remarkable for size, power, strength or other manly qualities are referred to as masculine; things remarkable for beauty, gentleness, grace, or other womanly qualities are referred to as feminine'.[47] G. P. Quackenbos, in *An English Grammar* (1862), identified as masculine 'fierce, vast, and sublime objects' such as Anger, Time, and Revenge; he identified as feminine 'gentle, delicate, and beautiful objects' such as Hope, Evening, and Plenty.[48] Other attributes that customarily identified a noun as masculine included violence, majesty, courage, boldness and ruggedness. 'Womanly qualities' identifying the feminine generated even more modifiers: gentle, soft, submissive, timid, passive, fruitful, productive, graceful, peaceful, refined and lovely. Grammarians generally agreed that death, winter, war and the sun were masculine; nature, spring, peace, mercy and the moon were feminine.

Assigning gender to animals resulted in distinctions and dichotomies more clearly unfavourable to the feminine. According to Peter Bullions, in *Practical Grammar of the English Language* (1870), the pronoun *he* properly referred to animals such as the dog, horse and elephant noted for 'boldness, fidelity, generosity, size, strength'; *she* referred to animals such as the hare and the cat 'characterized by weakness and timidity'.[49] Simon Kerl, in *A Common-School Grammar of the English Language* (1868), illustrated his statement that 'sometimes animals are regarded as male and female, not from their sex but from their general character' with the following examples: 'The lion meets *his* foe boldly'; 'every ant minds *her* own business'. When one must choose a masculine or feminine noun to apply to both sexes, he noted, 'the masculine term is generally preferred' (for example *horses* rather than *mares*).[50]

Grammarians applied the same principle in dictating the use of *he* with pronouns such as *everyone* and *someone* and with nouns of 'common gender' such as *parent, child,* and *student. He,* like *man* and *mankind,* includes both men and women and should be used 'when the sex is not known or need not be emphasized'. William Chauncey Fowler differed from his contemporaries only in acknowledging the discrimination against the sex made invisible by the rule: '*He, his, him* may generally be allowed to stand for the common gender . . . ungallant as it may seem, we shall probably persist in refusing women their due here as stubbornly as Englishmen continue to offend the Scots by saying *England* instead of *Britain*'. Goold Brown in *The Institutes of English Grammar* (1863) stated bluntly what is implicit in his contemporaries' treatment of gender: 'in all languages, the masculine gender is considered the most worthy, and is generally employed when both sexes are included under one common term'.[51]

Protest against the use of *he* and *man* to refer to both men and women did not gather force or effect change until the 1960s. But many Americans in the nineteenth century felt the need of an epicene pronoun and proposed various alternatives to replace *he* when the antecedent was not necessarily male. While Howells was editor of *Atlantic*, several writers to the magazine's Contributors' Club called for a word of 'common gender' to serve for both *he* and *she*. One proposed a new word *hesh*, to be declined *hizer*, *himer*. Another offered *che*, *cher's* and *cher*. A third proposed using *they*, *them* and *their* as both singular and plural.[52] One coinage, *thon* (a contraction of *that one*), proposed by the lawyer and composer Charles Converse survived long enough to be included in Funk and Wagnall's New Standard Dictionary from 1898 to 1964. Contributors to a discussion of pronouns carried on for two years in *The Writer* (1889–91) proposed *ons*, *e* and *em*, and *they*. Charles Converse reminded readers of *thon*.[53]

Sustained opposition to any alternative to the generic *he* came from many sources. Grammarians generally rejected the proposal that *they* and *them* be used with singular antecedents, counselled against the use of 'his or her', and supported 'the sound rule of rhetoric which recognizes the masculine pronoun as dominant'.[54] A writer in *Appleton's* ridiculed the critics of the generic *he* by attacking it so violently, as 'an outrage upon the dignity and an encroachment upon the rights of women', and by proposing to 'hand this duty of amending the language over to Mrs Stanton and Miss Anthony'.[55] Richard Grant White saw no need for a new pronoun, finding *he*, like *man* and *mankind*, perfectly satisfactory in reference to women. If there were really a need for a new pronoun, he concluded, 'we should have had one long ere this'. In any case, pronouns, of all words, were the most 'tenacious of hold, the most difficult to plant, the most nearly impossible to transplant'.[56] The fate of the more than fifty coinages to replace the generic *he* proves the truth of this last contention.

As White's *Words and Their Uses* proves, commentators on usage were not always consistent. White and most of his contemporaries unquestioningly accepted *he* and *man* as generic terms that included women, but they approved feminine forms such as *poetess*, *authoress* and *doctress* for women engaged in activities outside the domestic sphere. The desire to distinguish women from men produced hundreds of gender-marked words: according to Edwin B. Dike, more than five hundred feminine terms appeared in *The New English Dictionary* between 1888 and 1933.[57] Some coinages, such as *clowness* and *neighbouress*, quickly became obsolete. Others, notably *poetess, authoress* and *actress*, were sturdy survivors that recent critics have attacked on the grounds that they trivialize or stigmatize women, implying a standard from which women are a deviation.[58]

Nineteenth-century defenders of feminine suffixes did not, of course, say that they wished to deprive women of the dignity conveyed by the masculine forms, although humorists such as Artemus Ward and Petroleum V. Nasby obviously intended to ridicule women by such words as *nabobess, sharpshootress,* and *rebeless*.[59] Richard Grant White in *Words and Their Uses* invoked the authority of centuries-old precedent in insisting, erroneously, that 'the distinction of the female from the male by the termination *-ess* is one of the oldest and best-established usages of English speech'. A reviewer of White's book agreed that *poetess* and *authoress* were unlovely but necessary words, to be preferred when 'we have to choose' between them and 'female author' and 'female poet'. The necessity of choosing was taken for granted.[60]

Others rejected the suffix *-ess* as pedantic and affected, an encumbrance characteristic of 'school marmish' hypercorrectness, according to Gilbert Tucker, in *Our Common Speech* (1895). (Making the pedant a schoolmarm instead of a schoolmaster was commonplace.) Tucker considered *actress* useful, *poetess* unnecessary. Simon Kerl ruled that *poets* can refer to a group of both sexes, as in 'the poets of America', but a woman's name requires the feminine form: for example 'the poetess Sappho'. Preserving the aura of masculine privilege that surrounded the literary genre most highly esteemed, Philip Krapp decreed that 'one may speak of a female writer as an *author*, but hardly of a female writer of verse as a *poet*'. In *Good English* (1867) Edward Gould rejected as a 'false assumption' the idea that *poets* signifies only men and declared both *poetess* and *authoress* 'philologically absurd'. 'Nothing, in either word, indicates sex; and everybody knows that the functions of both poets and authors are common to both sexes.'[61]

Such unequivocal rejection of anti-feminist bias by a nineteenth-century grammarian was fairly rare. Arbiters of the language were more likely to pronounce on language in ways that enforced traditional gender roles and confirmed the subordinate status of women. White, for instance, writing on the 'misuse' of *marry*, stated that a man 'marries' a woman but a woman 'is married' to the man.

> It is her name that is lost in his, not his in hers; she becomes a member of his family, not he of hers; it is her life that is merged, or supposed to be merged, in his, not his in hers . . . so long, at least, as man is the larger, the stronger, the more individually important . . . it is the woman who is married to the man.

Although White thought that *poetess* and *authoress* had 'the right to a place in the language' that 'cannot be denied', he considered *widower* (one of the few words, like *bridegroom*, derived from the feminine form) a 'monstrosity', given the 'preposterousness' of its formation. He argued that the masculine form must have come long after the feminine, for 'among no people would a peculiar name be first given to a man who was deprived of a woman'.[62] Austin Phelps, Professor of Rhetoric in the Andover Seminary and the father of the novelist, illustrated the power of *woman* to debase a modifier by his example of an English word with divergent meanings: 'we speak . . . of a "nervous writer" meaning a strong writer; we speak of a "nervous woman" meaning a weak woman'.[63]

Lindley Murray, whose grammars sold more widely than any others, exemplifies the construction of gender identity in illustrating the rules of syntax by the following pairs:

> He loves his studies.
> She performs her duties.

> Some men think exceeding clearly, and reason exceeding forcibly.
> She appeared on this occasion, exceeding lovely.

> He is eager to learn.
> She is worthy to be loved.[64]

Grammars not only set forth rules to be learned but instructed pupils to apply the rules in exercises. Thomas W. Harvey, in *An Elementary Grammar of the English Language* (1869), inculcates the idea of the man as the actor, the woman as the receiver of action, in the following exercise: 'Write five sentences, using *masculine* nouns as subjects.' 'Write five sentences, using *feminine* nouns as objects.'

Kittredge and Arnold's grammar, *The Mother Tongue* (1900), encourages students to observe the traditional gender dichotomies in instructing them to provide a noun or pronoun for the following sentences, 'tell its gender and give your reason':

1. The poet had written — last song.
2. — swept the hearth and mended the fire.[65]

Polarization extended from the smallest units of language to the languages themselves. For centuries, vowels, characterized as soft, delicate and liquid, were identified as feminine; consonants, perceived as harsh, sturdy and solid, were masculine. English, a consonantal language, was masculine; the Romance languages, in which vowels predominated, were feminine.[66] The presumed superiority of the 'masculine' English language to the 'feminine' French was a commonplace in the nineteenth century. In Max Müller's formulation, English, characterized by 'a manly, sharp, and definite articulation' of vowels and consonants, was more worthy than the 'effeminate, vague, and indistinct utterance' produced by speakers of the Romance languages, who 'shrink from the effort of articulating each consonant and vowel', and thereby cause 'phonetic degeneracy in language'.[67] James Russell Lowell applauded Longfellow's translation of Dante's *Divine Comedy* into English and explained why Dante could not be translated into French. 'The most virile of poets cannot be adequately rendered in the most feminine of languages.'[68] (Apparently, the use in Italy of the vernacular for literature, which Dante ascribed to the influence of women ignorant of Latin, did not keep him from being 'the most virile of poets'.)

The gendered virtues of English continued to have their champions in the twentieth century. Jespersen extolled English as 'positively and expressly *masculine*, it is the language of a grown-up man and has very little childish or feminine about it'.[69] A writer on language in the fourth edition of *The Literary History of the United States* (1974) pronounced General American as the best form of English because it 'shows a clear if somewhat metallic pronunciation, gives all necessary consonants their true values, keeps to simple and narrow speech tunes, and is vigorous and masculine'.[70]

Grammarians and linguists believed their rules and definitions to express truth grounded in natural fact. This belief collided with the idea of language as a human creation subject to human control – an idea accepted by most turn-of-the-century writers, who often likened words to money or weapons or builder's tools. In Thomas Lounsbury's words, language 'is an instrument which will be just what those who use it choose to make it'.[71] If rules of grammar and usage are determined not by natural law but by human will, then the gender bias inscribed in language is revealed as the product of human purpose and belief, and Lounsbury's pronouncement becomes the premise enabling the subversion of his own authority.

IV

Compared to the hundreds of articles and books on sex-biased language published in the 1970s and 1980s, attacks in the nineteenth century on man-made English seem scattered and fragmentary. Feminists who wrote and lectured for the causes of women's rights were the most numerous and widely published of the critics, but anti-feminism in language was only one of many issues that absorbed their energies. Nevertheless they showed as keen an awareness as critics a century later of gender stereotypes and bias inscribed in the language.

The range of their concerns is readily seen in *The Revolution*,[72] a newspaper supporting women's rights begun in 1868 by Elizabeth Cady Stanton and Susan B. Anthony, with the financial backing of George Francis Train. During its three years of publication, contributors of both sexes protested the use of language to discriminate against women. George Train's claim that *The Revolution* 'is coining a new vocabulary' (RW, 167) was not realized, but contributors proposed new words and objected to the use of current ones. One suggested 'cock-pecked wife' for a woman who drudges for her husband (RW, 167); another proposed *Alma Pater* for colleges that refused to admit women (RW, 165). Protests against the use of *he* and *man* to refer to women were common. One correspondent criticized ministers who addressed as *brethren* congregations composed mainly of women (RW, 182). Another objected to the use of *female* as in 'Troy Female Seminary' when one does not say 'Harvard Male University' (RW, 177).

The identification of positive qualities with men, negative ones with women, inspired repeated protest. One contributor objected to *womanish* to describe timidity or cowardice in men: 'Courage . . . is no special attribute of any one sex' (RW, 179). Stanton inveighed against the negative connotations of *woman* (as in 'a woman's logic') 'as if all incapacity and inefficiency were of the feminine gender' (RW, 129). *The Revolution* published the 'Reclamation' written by the French feminist and editor Jenny P. d'Héricourt to protest the praising of a woman's literary style as *virile*: 'To-day strong women do not wish to be compared to men. They understand that they owe themselves to their sex, and if anything about them is honored, this honor should reflect on their whole sex . . . ' (RW, 186).

The *Woman's Journal*, a weekly newspaper founded in 1870 by Lucy Stone and her husband Henry Blackwell, for nearly fifty years provided another forum for the debate of issues, including gender-marked language, central to the cause of women's rights.[73] Correspondents wrote to protest the stigmatizing of the independent-minded woman by calling her *masculine* (WJ, 5:201); to propose that a title be devised to distinguish the married man from the bachelor (WJ, 8:42); to argue for the woman's right to keep her own name in marriage (WJ, 8:42); to defend public speaking by women who have the 'noble elements of true eloquence' belonging to both sexes (WJ, 9:142). One correspondent quoted Webster's definition of *man*: 'mankind, man, a woman', to argue that the Constitution in giving *man* the vote thereby includes women in the suffrage (WJ, 5:43). Both men and women wrote to reject the proposal of a male correspondent who thought women physicians should be called *doctras* because 'the vowel sound of "*a*" as in ah! is feminine and properly expresses female things and aspects' (WJ, 9:23). One of the most controversial letters proposed a new category, the 'third sex', to identify women who had no desire to marry and chose to devote their lives to a vocation (WJ, 5:371). Opponents argued that no third sex exists because married and unmarried women have the same desires (WJ, 6:8); that the phrase 'third sex' implies that women are unsexed if they do not marry (WJ, 5:397); that 'third sex' logically requires a 'fourth sex' for men who do not marry (WJ, 6:8).

Critics made their most sustained attacks on certain words and phrases in which the ideology of a whole culture was encoded. Frances Willard cited *illegitimate child* as one of the words she would scourge from 'the dictionary of common speech'. It is not the innocent child who is illegitimate, she declared, but the father who 'endures nothing' while the mother and child are stigmatized and rejected.[74] Many men joined women in declaring the noun *female* a vulgarism that relegated women to the company of the cow and the sow. In Richard Grant White's words, 'when a woman calls herself a female, she merely shares her sex with all her fellow females throughout the brute creation'. Mark Twain regarded Cooper's reference to *females*, 'as he always calls women', as one of his literary offences. Thomas Lounsbury, however, in one of his articles on language for *Harper's Magazine*, argued that the prejudice against *female* was 'purely artificial' and referred sarcastically to 'the delicate feminine perceptions' of women whose objections to being called a *female* and an *authoress* were incomprehensible to one of his 'dull masculine apprehension'.[75]

The stigmatizing power of 'old maid' made that label one of the most opprobrious to feminists, who sought to nullify its effect by portraying the unmarried woman as an attractive figure. The novelist Fanny Fern (Sara Payson Willis Parton) defined the modern 'old maid' as a vigorous accomplished woman happy and fulfilled in her independence (RW, 166–7). Howells dismissed the stigma attached to the phrase 'old maid' as a vulgar and foolish tradition harboured in 'empty minds' and asked why a woman more than a man should be accounted a failure for not marrying. But his character he repeatedly designates 'the old maid', Adeline Northwick in *The Quality of Mercy*, conforms to the unattractive stereotype with her emaciated frame, chill bony knuckles, and fits of hysterics and whimpering self-pity. He pleaded with Elizabeth Jordan, the editor of his projected multi-authored novel, *The Whole Family*, to reject Mary Wilkins Freeman's chapter on 'The Maiden Aunt', which transformed the elderly supernumerary Howells had in mind into an attractive woman of 35 whom the young hero chooses over her niece.[76] Thanks to the kind of efforts Howells resisted and Jordan supported (she accepted Freeman's chapter), the old maid is probably no longer regarded as the 'most calamitous Creature in Nature', as she appears in *The Ladies' Calling* (1673).[77] But two centuries later the phrase in standard dictionaries still has its negative connotations of prudery, fussiness and unattractive spinsterhood.

Against the power of gender ideology, backed by all the institutions of nineteenth-century society, critics of anti-feminist bias in language could accomplish certain limited objectives, such as discouraging the use of -ess in titles, removing *female* from the names of women's colleges, and discrediting *female* as a synonym for *woman*. But thus far eloquence has been powerless to remove the stigma from gender-marked words such as *old maid, womanish* and *effeminate,* proving that it is easier to expel opprobrious words from the vocabulary of polite society than to elevate terms of reproach.

V

Grammarians, essayists, editors and arbiters of manners in Victorian America united in asserting the supremacy of the masculine over the feminine. But at no time in American history have these authorities attached more cultural importance to women's speech. American women in the post-Civil War era were repeatedly told that they were 'guardians of the language', that upon them depended the correctness and purity of English speech. Introducing the series 'Hints on Language' (1871–72) in *Godey's Lady's Book,* the editor emphasized the importance of women's having 'complete mastery' of the arts of speaking and writing their mother tongue. 'To teach the young to use their native language correctly and elegantly is a special and recognized point of women's work.' According to the *Ladies' Home Journal,* 'much of [the] work of cultivation' required to lower 'the high-pitched nasal tone' common in American voices 'properly falls into the mother's hands'.[78]

In genteel society as in the well-conducted nursery, upholding the standards of decorum, including propriety in speech, was assumed to be the woman's responsibility. Presumed to have more leisure and finer moral natures than men, women were charged with the obligation to maintain 'the high social tone' of their society, 'to be the leaders and stimulators of the best conversation'. The social critic Eugene Benson maintained that conversation was a 'lost art' in America because men were so seldom in the society of women, 'our natural civilizers', in contrast to Frenchmen of the seventeenth and eighteenth centuries in whose society women were 'absolute social agents'. Women talking by themselves, he stated, could not achieve 'the dignity of conversation', but men alone could not recapture the lost art. 'We can only realize an agreeable society by giving full play to the feminine element.'[79]

Benson in his essay observed what later writers such as Howells, Wharton, Santayana and Henry James likewise perceived as a debilitating split in American society, in which men were absorbed in the business of making money, leaving to women the pursuit of culture in the stores, museums, galleries, theatres, lecture halls and reading clubs. As early as 1856, an editor of *Harper's Magazine* attested to the social power of women: 'A large part of our social system is under their control and they legislate for our dress, etiquette, and manners without a fear of a veto.'[80] According to the unwritten half of the equation, men controlled the institutions of politics, business and the law that sustained the social system.

Fifty years later, Henry James made the same observation in his four-part essay, 'The Speech of American Women' (1906), published in *Harper's Bazar*. In America, only the speech of women is 'discussable', he argued, for in America women, not men, are the social arbiters. Whereas in England and France, 'the men have invented the standard and set the tone', in America, women are the authorities; the 'whole of the social initiative is theirs'. But American women had failed to exercise their power, he continued; women and men alike not only lacked any standard of cultivated speech; they recognized no need for such a standard. In the most highly civilized European societies, he observed, the distinguishing mark of a lady is not beauty or wit but cultivated speech – 'the sovereign stamp of the well-conditioned woman'. Americans, however, gave no attention, either in home or in school, to careful enunciation, control of tone, or cultivation of an agreeable speaking voice. Children and adults alike muttered, grunted, mumbled and shrieked without fear of correction. The result was 'an inimitable union of looseness and flatness'.[81]

James stated that the absence of criticism of women's speech was complete. But his essay was preceded by scores of adverse judgements upon American speech, particularly women's speech, published in American magazines in the late nineteenth century. Prominent in the critics' gallery of women who, like Mrs Malaprop, abused the English language were the affected speakers – women who returned from England saying 'weally' and 'coals'; clubwomen who united to broaden their *a*'s; girls and women fond of overemphasis called by one critic a 'silly twist'; 'well-meaning ladies' teaching 'precise and orthoëpical speech' to their students of 'voice culture'. At the other extreme were the underbred speakers given to whining, mumbling, unmodulated 'social screaming' and sonorous laughter.[82]

The defects upon which speech critics dwelt most persistently – volubility, affectation, exaggeration and shrillness – were those they ascribed to women and believed to be typical of feminine nature. And yet women were expected to educate the young in

proper speech and introduce into society the art of agreeable conversation which men could not accomplish on their own. In other
words, women were charged with duties they were apparently
incapable of performing.

The inconsistency is real but the functions assigned to women did
not elevate their status or threaten masculine authority. Women
who taught children the established rules of grammar and usage
were not subverting the ideology of gender but collaborating in a
process of education that inculcated the idea of male superiority.
The ideal society envisioned by James and Benson and others does
not extend women's influence or do away with separate spheres; it
simply creates a space between them where men and women can
join in civilized converse to the benefit of all. Nor did everyone's
ideal of good conversation imply greater prominence for women.
No doubt many shared the sentiments of the man who thought
conversation was best when women were passive and who longed
for the time 'when women, whose talents were not insignificant,
would sit, apparently interested and certainly respectful listeners,
if a subject were started among men of parts, and would wait to
mingle in the discussion until they were appealed to' (WJ, 8:130).

Passages assembled from newspapers and magazines might suggest clear-cut conflicts between single-minded advocates of change
and defenders of the status quo. But many individual writers were
divided in their sympathies, opposed to some established practices
and in favour of others. All the novelists to be considered in the
following chapters embraced conflicting ideas about gender as
shown in their treatment of language. Their representations of
character in fiction may contradict statements in their criticism and
letters; within a novel the impression created by characters and
their words may be at odds with what the narrator says about them;
figurative language may support assumptions the writer explicitly
rejects elsewhere. To begin with Howells starts with the writer who
most fully embodies the struggle of conflicting impulses, the writer
who declared himself a 'heretic about women', and maintained that
'this question of the sex of the novelist can be safely disregarded in
the study of the novel',[83] but whose fiction consistently supports
the conventional assumptions about gender that he repudiated in
his interviews and criticism.

2

The Voices of Men and Women in Howells's Fiction and Drama

I

When Robert Frost acknowledged his 'great debt' to William Dean Howells for teaching him that 'the loveliest theme of poetry was the voices of people', he claimed for Howells powers of representation that the novelist himself prized most highly. 'No one ever had a more observing ear or clearer imagination for the tones of those voices', Frost wrote of Howells. 'He recorded them equally with actions, indeed as if they were actions (and I think they are).'[1] In his criticism of fiction and drama, Howells rarely failed to judge the representation of characters' speech. The novelists and dramatists he most valued, such as Turgenev and Ibsen and Björnson, were those who wrote in language renewed by the 'never-failing springs of the common speech'.[2] He championed the realist who put aside literary models and tried instead to 'report the phrase and carriage of every-day life . . . to tell just how he has heard men talk and seen them look'.[3]

Howells might well have instructed writers to tell how they had heard 'men and women' talk. In most of his own novels, women are as prominent as men, and the speech of men and women, he believed, exhibited differences that writers should strive to represent. He made the point most explicitly in his criticism of Robert Browning's *Inn Album*: 'The women are in no wise distinguished from the men by anything feminine in their phrase in this story, as they are in real life and real drama, and no one is characterized by any mental or other peculiarity not plainly attributive.'[4]

In his own fiction, Howells as narrator often noted habits of speech, particularly those of the female characters, that he believed to reflect differences between the sexes. He represented these differences in the dialogues of his novels and plays, and his characters comment on the social codes that govern when and how they speak. In novel after novel, he showed how the relations of men and women in courtship and marriage are defined by gender-based differences in speech that reflect and reinforce traditional structures of authority and power. Thus Howells made the representation of male and female speech a defining principle of realism, vital to his portrayal of women and men in Victorian America.

II

By the 1870s, when Howells began to publish novels and plays, the contradictory assumptions about women's speech were commonplace. Countless Americans had counselled women against using slang and coarse expressions, expressed disapproval of women engaged in public speaking, and reiterated the centuries-old complaints that women talked too much, exaggerated, exclaimed, and scolded in loud shrill voices. At the same time, critics of women's speech placed upon women the responsibility for teaching children the proper use of their mother tongue and for preserving (or creating) the standards of polite discourse in their societies.

The apparent contradiction is abundantly illustrated in Howells's novels and essays. On the one hand, he repeatedly declared American women superior to American men in taste and culture. Mr Homos, the traveller from Altruria, notes that his hostess, Mrs Makeley, is 'infinitely superior to her husband in cultivation, as is commonly the case here'.[5] According to Bromfield Corey, another of Howells's fictional analysts of American society, women naturally assume the role of social arbiters because in America women alone enjoy the 'patrician leisure' that in Europe both sexes enjoy. Therefore, American women are a 'natural female aristocracy' that establishes the 'forms, usages, places, and times of society'.[6] In 'Our Daily Speech', Howells assigned to women the task of correcting the defects of American speech, declared that reform 'must begin at home', with 'the child at its mother's knee', and told 'the fable of two mothers' to teach the consequences of negligence and the rewards of care.[7]

On the other hand, in his novels and plays, Howells portrayed women, the presumed social arbiters and guardians of the language, as subordinate and inferior to men in matters of language.

Although he asserted that the speech of American men is 'worse' than women's speech and will improve only when 'their mothers and wives reform',[8] his female characters look to male characters for guidance in points of usage, and their speech exhibits defects such as exaggeration, affectation and undue emphasis that Howells and his contemporaries attributed primarily to women. Not only do his characters, male and female, value man's speech above woman's; in his reviews and essays, Howells consistently wrote as a man addressing men. 'We speak in superlatives like women', he complained in a *Nation* essay.[9] Fifty years later, in an 'Easy Chair' paper, he cast himself as the Elderly Essayist conversing with women who persist in using 'lady's words', such as *lovely*, *sweet* and *gotten*, despite his tactful correction.[10] In another essay, he is the 'Veteran Novelist' informed by his great-niece, presumably speaking for his female audience, that his books lack fire and passion, that instead of 'saying the most distinguished things in the simplest way', he should 'say even the simplest things in a distinguished way' and be *virile, epigrammatic* and *passionate*.[11] Although Howells appears to deny his authority by posing as the rueful outmoded writer swept aside by the tide of current fashion, his irony reflects his sense of superiority to the female speaker.

Howells's statements about women suggest conflicting answers to the central question: how did he account for the defects he represented in their speech? His references to the 'Eternal Womanly' and the 'Ever-Womanly' imply belief in a universal female nature to which women's virtues and deficiencies can be referred.[12] But in an interview in 1895 he insisted that most of the commonly noted differences between men and women were artificial, the result of education and upbringing which allowed greater freedom to boys than to girls. Girls were the victims, not of their sex, but of the restrictions imposed by society on their mental and physical activity – 'our version of the Chinese foot-binding'. He concluded: 'There is a little difference between men's and women's characters that is real, but it has been very much exaggerated.'[13] In an interview nine years later, he seemed to shift his ground, claiming that 'our women are superior to our men' because their education allows them 'better opportunities for self-cultivation'. But again he stressed the sense of deprivation and inferiority suffered by women isolated from men's business and professional lives.[14]

Given the importance Howells placed on language as an index of a character's social conditioning, we might expect his fiction to offer a clear-cut representation of women's speech as the product of their background and training. But often his narratives convey a strong sense of women as an alien sex inherently different from his own. Indeed, from the beginning, Howells overtly distanced himself from his female characters by identifying himself as a man viewing them from a man's perspective. An early sketch, 'A Perfect Goose', published in April 1859, when he was 22, is remarkable evidence of his lifelong preoccupation with women's speech as a phenomenon baffling to men. 'We have been endeavoring to master their vocabulary, but so far with but meager success', the narrator observes. He then seizes on one 'purely feminine' expression, 'a perfect goose', and in half a dozen vignettes illustrating its different meanings he proves 'a beautiful versatility in the appreciation of the phrase'.[15]

In its view of women as other, their language a mystery, this sketch foreshadows the novels, in which the distance between male narrators and female characters is reinforced in a number of ways. Frequent references in his novels to 'our sex' and 'their sex' set women apart from men in a world in which, as Alfred Habegger notes, 'the two sexes are nations'.[16] Howells further detaches himself from his female characters by tagging their speech ('as she would have said') and by identifying certain words as those only women would use. The narrator of *The Rise of Silas Lapham* (1885) elevates himself above women when he notes that they call Tom Corey *sweet*, 'a word of theirs which conveys otherwise indefinable excellences'.[17] In *An Imperative Duty* (1892), the protagonist, Dr Olney, is distanced from the two women he counsels when the narrator conveys the doctor's reflection that Rhoda Aldgate and her aunt 'were formed to wear upon each other, as the ladies say'.[18] The implication is that the man exemplifies the standard, from which women deviate. Even in giving stage directions, Howells could not resist a dig at women's words that turns a pun into social criticism. In the opening scene of *Out of the Question* (1877) appear 'two young ladies with what they call work in their hands and laps'.[19]

On occasion, Howells's narrator generalizes the speech of one character as typical of the whole female sex. He notes that Helen Harkness (*A Woman's Reason* [1883]) 'hasten[ed] to spoil her point, as women will, with hysterical insistence'.[20] After recording the speech of one of the most intelligent women in *April Hopes* (1888), the narrator notes 'the necessity her sex has for putting its superlatives before its positives' (AH, 338). When Elmer Kelwyn loses the self-restraint that Howells identified with masculine speech, the narrator observes that Kelwyn spoke 'with a volubility worthy of a woman'.[21]

The attitude implicit in the narrators' comments is made explicit in Howells's portrayal of male characters said to enjoy the vocal manifestations of the Ever-Womanly that indicate her need of a man's protection and guidance. Dr Morrell, talking with Annie Kilburn, whom he later marries, 'laughed with enjoyment of her convulsive emphasis' and takes pleasure 'in the feminine excess of her demand'.[22] In the story, 'At the Sign of the Savage', Colonel Kenton 'prized beyond measure the feminine inadequacy and excess of [his wife's] sayings'.[23] Male characters also pointedly disso ciate themselves from 'feminine excess', as Dr Anther does in *The Son of Royal Langbrith* (1904), when he quotes to his friend, Judge Garley, the words of the widow, Amelia Langbrith, who has asked Anther what he thinks of 'a man who takes the life of another's soul'. Anther then feels compelled to add, 'it was a woman's expression', whereupon the judge 'smiled intelligently' and says, 'I should imagine'.[24] In none of these scenes does Howells undermine the figures of male authority – a colonel, a judge, and two doctors – by implying any criticism of their attitudes.

In Howells's novels and plays, women of all ages, married and unmarried, betray what the novelist calls 'the histrionic intention of [their] sex'.[25] But he grounds the 'histrionic intention' in certain social conditions, making hyperbole and intensity most characteristic of one group – sheltered girls of well-to-do city families. Genteel young women from upper-class Boston signal their superior social status by what Howells called 'young-lady American'[26] – speech abounding in breathless intensifiers: *terribly, perfectly, horribly*. 'Your young lady talk is marvellous', Henry James wrote to Howells of his play, *Out of the Question*: 'It's as if the devil himself were sitting in your inkstand. *He* only could have made you know that one girl would say that another's walking from the station was ghastly.'[27] The speaker, Maggie Wallace, who also says of her friend, Leslie Bellingham, 'she's so refined and cultivated, you can't live' (CP, 35), is a feather-brain, but Leslie herself, portrayed as more intelligent and sensible than her friends, talks as they do, exclaiming of a grove of birches, 'how perfectly divine' (CP, 44); of her snobbish aunt's tone, 'It was outrageous, atrocious, hideous' (CP, 38); of the loss of an earring, 'I've met with *such* a calamity!' (CP, 40).

In *Out of the Question*, the snobbery of Leslie's mother and aunt is the main target of Howells's criticism. By contrast, the 'young-lady American' of Leslie and her friend seems relatively harmless. But in *April Hopes*, his most relentless attack on conventional ideas of romantic love, Howells shows the excesses of women's speech to have injurious consequences and pernicious roots in the ideology of a culture that conduces to false judgement and self-deception in both women and men. Hyperbole and intensity enable the central female character, Alice Pasmer, to convince herself of the perfect purity of her motives and to nourish her ego in socially acceptable ways, by displays of sacrificial ardour and self-abnegation expressed in the conventional superlatives. When her suitor, Dan Mavering, forbids her to accuse herself of being wicked, she exclaims, 'How lovely you are! Oh! I *like* to be commanded by you!' (AH, 160). Their engagement moves her to exaltation: 'We must try to live for eternity' (AH, 162). When Dan equivocates, she declares, 'the least grain of deceit . . . spoils everything' (AH, 280) and breaks their engagement. Later she acknowledges her culpability in self-inflating visions of the supreme atonement: 'I feel as if I could make my whole *life* a reparation' (AH, 344).

In his way, Dan is as immature and irresponsible as Alice, as much the romantic egoist as she is, but after her breathless effusions, his 'masculine American',[28] invigorated by slang and colloquialisms, seems the guarantee of common sense. When Alice declares that as lovers she and Dan must be an example to the world of 'how people *ought* to care', he deflates her with his homely phrase: people would 'only think we were spoons on each other' (AH, 262). Dan, in turn, is checked by his anti-romantic college friend, Boardman, who comments, 'I didn't suppose it was so much of a mash' (AH, 140), when Dan seeks him out in the throes of despair after Alice rejects his proposal of marriage. Restored to his more manly self, Dan answers in the same idiom: 'I hadn't the sand to stick to it like a man' (AH, 141). After attempting to sustain himself on Alice's lofty plane, he is always relieved to 'drop down and touch earth in Boardy' (AH, 261).

As confidant and adviser, Boardman is a salutary influence, as is Falk, whose collegiate slang, in *The Son of Royal Langbrith*, punctures the self-dramatizing speeches of his Harvard friend and classmate, James Langbrith. Like the young men, Howells's young women have friends of their own sex in whom they confide. But none of the confidantes acts as a corrective influence; all of them appeal to the weakest, not the strongest, side of the other woman's nature. In all the pairs – Alice Pasmer and Miss Cotton (*April Hopes*), Grace Breen and Miss Gleason (*Doctor Breen's Practice* [1888]), Leslie Bellingham and Maggie Wallace (*Out of the Question*), Helen Harkness and Marian Butler Ray (*A Woman's Reason*), Bessie Lynde and Mary Enderby (*The Landlord at Lion's Head* [1897]) – the confidante is more foolish and romantic, more given to hyperbole and sentimental clichés, than the woman she idolizes.

That all these female characters belong to the same genteel class suggests that their speech is learned, not instinctive, the product of their social conditioning. Of course, individual temperament plays its part, too. Alice Pasmer's speech reflects personality traits not inflicted on every girl in her circumstances. Her rival, Julia Anderson, as well-bred as Alice, is notable for her sturdy common sense and her 'bold, deep voice, with tones like a man's in it' (AH, 68). But Julia, a New Yorker, has escaped the influence of Puritanism in which Howells roots Alice's degenerate idealism. Alice's inherited tendencies to morbid egoism are then powerfully reinforced by her limited education, her lack of serious occupation, and her indulgence in romantic novels that create false ideas about love and marriage. In her 'wild impulses' and 'mistaken ideals' the narrator sees the effects of 'disordered nerves, ill-advised reading, and the erroneous perspective of inexperience' (AH, 246).

In his portrayal of country women, Howells made his clearest case for environment and upbringing as the determining forces that mould traits of character revealed in speech. The hyperbole of fashionable girls and women from Boston is foreign to the whole class of taciturn women like Mrs Woodward (*Mrs Farrell* [1875]) and Mrs Durgin (*The Landlord at Lion's Head*), who labour on barren farms in rural New England and serve the city women when they come there as summer guests. Country girls like Rachel Woodward (*Mrs Farrell*), Lydia Blood (*The Lady of the Aroöstook* [1879]), and Cynthia Whitwell (*The Landlord at Lion's Head*) likewise reflect their lives of toil and deprivation in their chariness with words. One of the (male) summer guests in *Mrs Farrell* marvels that Rachel always thinks before she speaks and chooses 'just the words that shall give her mind with scriptural scruple against superfluity'.[29] Mrs Durgin reveals the gulf between her and her summer guests when she calls the women 'tonguey' and tells the painter, Westover, 'They'll be *wild*, as they call it, when they know you're in the house.'[30]

Habitual use of superlatives and intensifiers thus appears to be the prerogative of women and girls with the power to spend money freely, the leisure to read romantic novels, and no professional responsibilities that would require them to weigh their words and hold themselves accountable for what they say. Their unexpended energy requires some kind of verbal outlet that men, but not women of their class, find in slang. Lacking real power in the world outside their homes, women perhaps betray in the excesses of their speech the need to assert themselves and make their presence felt.

In his novels and plays, Howells pictures no alternatives for women bred to the restrictions of polite society. To girls in families like the Coreys and the Bellinghams, the opportunities for intellectual growth afforded their brothers at Harvard apparently seem so remote, girls do not even imagine or desire them for themselves. No upper-class woman portrayed by Howells achieves success in a profession, and well-bred women like Annie Kilburn and Margaret Vance (*A Hazard of New Fortunes* [1890]), moved by the laudable desire to put their money and their leisure at the service of the poor, blame themselves for doing more harm than good. Socially conscious male characters likewise fail to effect reforms, but in their professional capacities as ministers or journalists or magazine editors they can reach the public through the written and spoken word. Unlike Henry James, however, Howells portrayed no professional women writers or public speakers in his fiction. Helen Harkness fails miserably in her one attempt to write book reviews, and there are no women journalists – no Henrietta Stackpoles or Maud Blandys. As an editor and literary critic, Howells was the most influential supporter of women writers in America in the nineteenth century, but in his fiction, literature is the man's domain.

It is difficult to determine at every point whether Howells excluded his women characters from a wider sphere in order to highlight the barriers to professional success that women in America faced and the injurious effects of their exclusion; or whether he was unable or unwilling to portray in his fiction a woman able to achieve success and fulfilment in a career outside her home and marriage. His fiction shows the workings of both the reformist intention and the impulse in conflict with it. In such novels as *A Woman's Reason*, *The Rise of Silas Lapham* and *April Hopes*, he portrays the corrupting effects upon the whole society of an ideology that confines the sexes to separate spheres and deprives women of purposeful work in the world. But the criticism is subverted by narrators who uncritically voice assumptions about women that, if true, justify inferior status and, whether true or not, buttress the ideology Howells proposed to attack. His treatment of women's speech betrays a need to secure male characters in the favoured position, even as he exposes the inequities that assure their advantage.[31]

III

Country women like Mrs Durgin and Mrs Woodward, whose labour supports their families, dominate in households where a feeble and ineffectual husband yields to the superior energy and intelligence of his wife. But in the marriages of those who belong, or aspire to belong, to polite society in towns and cities, the man is usually the ruling partner. Although Howells claimed that women 'as a rule, are better and nobler than men',[32] in his novels he almost always gives to the husband, not the wife, the firmer sense of principle and the stronger powers of reason, as if to defend the traditional relation of the sexes in marriage. When one partner in a genteel Howells marriage acts as the moral guide, it is almost always the man who holds the office (for example the Athertons, Sewells, Marches, Enderbys).

The moral authority Howells vests in male characters has its counterpart in their supremacy as masters of the language whose authority women acknowledge. Not only does Howells cast his narrators and male characters as critics of women's speech; he fortifies the man's privileged position by portraying female characters who act to affirm it. In fact, the more highly bred the woman, the more prone she is to regard men as her superiors in force and precision of statement and to defer to them in the choice of words. After Dr Grace Breen has used her suitor's slang word *bobbish*, which she would never have introduced herself, the narrator states: 'A woman respects the word a man uses, not because she would have chosen it, but because she thinks that he has an exact intention in it, which could not be reconveyed in a more feminine phrase.'[33] Grace Breen's impulse is consistent with a similar pronouncement in *April Hopes*: 'The mind of a man is the court of final appeal for the wisest women. Till some man has pronounced upon their wisdom, they do not know whether it is wisdom or not' (AH, 80).

Women's often noted ignorance of the language of politics, business, sport and war is amply illustrated in Howells's novels, in which men must explain to women the meaning of the words they use, including the jargon of their professions. The wife of the playwright Brice Maxwell, in *The Story of a Play* (1898), learns from her husband that 'trying it on a dog' means trying out a new play in the country, and 'playing to paper' means performing for an audience holding free tickets.[34] Mrs March, in *A Hazard of New Fortunes*, has to ask her husband what Fulkerson means when he talks of 'coming in on the divvy' (HNF, 202). The minister's wife, Mrs Enderby, in *The Son of Royal Langbrith*, asks her husband whether 'to tally' is slang and says, 'I oughtn't to use it if it is, in a place like this' (SRL, 133). Parthenope Brook, in *The Vacation of the Kelwyns* (1920), does not know what her suitor, Emerance, means by calling himself 'a mere empiricist' (VK, 236). In *The Day of Their Wedding* (1896), after the young Shaker, Lorenzo, has been for several days in the 'world outside', he speaks to the girl he is to marry in words 'that she had never heard before, and he used familiar phrases in a new sense'.[35]

The descendants of Mrs Malaprop are almost always genteel women. Mrs Enderby refers to her husband's 'sociological' instead of 'socialistic' tendencies (SRL, 130). Miss Garrett, in the farce-tragedy *Self-Sacrifice*, is not sure whether her friend, Miss Ramsay, should do something 'static' or something 'drastic' (CP, 632). A rare instance of male malapropism appears when a hotel clerk in *Ragged Lady* (1899) describes a fellow employee as 'so aesthetic' when he means 'ascetic'. But his mistake is easily explained: 'his own education had ended at a commercial college'.[36]

Women's ignorance of the meaning of words is traceable to their restricted experience. But Howells arbitrarily assigned to women deficiencies presumably shared by both sexes. For no apparent reason, he identified bad spelling as a woman's failing. 'Probably the man, and certainly the woman, does not live who has never felt a doubt as to his or her spelling of some word', he claimed. 'The best, the loveliest of women are notoriously bad spellers.'[37] Characters in Howells's fiction who write letters filled with misspelled words are women – Lottie Kenton (*The Kentons* [1902]), Imogene Graham (*Indian Summer*), and Mrs Saunders (*The Coast of Bohemia* [1899]). None of the male characters, even the most ungrammatical, mutilate words in this fashion. The letters of Abner J. Baysley (*Letters Home* [1903]) are filled with solecisms ('hain't', 'he done', 'we set there', 'for wife and I'), but all his words, including *grippe*, *collision* and *acquaintance*, are spelled correctly.

Uneducated men like Silas Lapham mispronounce words but Howells shows only women doubly betraying themselves by expressing doubts about pronunciation. Miss Ramsay in *Self-Sacrifice, A Farce Tragedy*, asks Miss Garrett whether she should say '*primarily*' or '*primarily*', but her friend is equally in the dark, confessing, 'I never know. I only use it in writing' (CP, 630). That women are concerned about such matters indicates their care to speak correctly (if not to spell correctly), but in doubting themselves they reveal a sense of insecurity and inadequacy Howells rarely attributes to his male characters. Even Lemuel Barker, the young man from the provinces who learns to speak well in *The Minister's Charge* (1887), is not pictured seeking guidance or self-consciously imitating the speech of others.

Howells's sense of propriety forbade his allowing any but his half-bred male characters, such as Bartley Hubbard (*A Modern Instance* [1882]) and Hicks (*The Lady of the Aroostook*), to lapse into the slurred speech of the intoxicated. But only his female characters assume the affected speech of the socially ambitious who strive to elevate themselves by imitating the manners of a higher class. None of his male characters behaves like Mrs Erwin (*The Lady of the Aroostook*) or Marian Butler Ray (*A Woman's Reason*) or Mrs Roberts (*A Letter of Introduction*), who make themselves comic by scorning Americanisms and aping the speech of the English upper class. When male characters experiment with new words, they signal their superior status and sense of security by imitating what they consider below, not above, their own parlance. Bromfield Corey enjoys using 'a bit of the new slang' (MC, 320). Englishmen such as Lord Rainford (*A Woman's Reason*) and Mr Erwin (*The Lady of the Aroostook*) amuse themselves by experimenting with American colloquialisms and slang.

On occasion, Howells's sensitivity to words showed itself in a sudden awareness of gender bias in language. 'I must husband (why not wife?) my poor strength', he wrote to his sister, Annie Fréchette (11 June 1905), explaining why he could not visit her.[38] In *Self-Sacrifice*, Miss Garrett declares that she will not kiss her friend goodbye because 'it might unman you, and you need all your strength', then reflects, 'Unman isn't the word, exactly, but you can't say ungirl, can you? It would be ridiculous. Though girls are as brave as men when it comes to duty' (CP, 632).

To perceive inequities inscribed in the language is to take a step towards eradicating them, but Howells does not pursue this path. Other than Miss Garrett, hardly a militant foe of sexist speech, Howells's characters accept without question language that signals the inferior status of women. For instance, Susan Gilbert, the most discerning woman in *Mrs Farrell*, sees nothing anomalous in her praise of Rachel and Mrs Woodward: 'You're the manliest girl, and your mother's the manliest woman I know of – and I can't say anything better!' (MF, 108). No one reflects on the impossibility of praising a man by calling him womanly.

Howells does not portray women as blind to the unequal status of the sexes or unable to resist expressions of masculine assertion when they feel threatened by them. The self-mistrust and deference to male authority that Howells imputes to Grace Breen do not prevent her from pronouncing Dr Mulbridge a tyrant who despises women and wants 'a slave, not a wife' (DBP, 254) when he forces on her his proposal of marriage, on the grounds that only united to a man can a woman succeed as a doctor. Grace Breen can quell Howells's most overbearing male chauvinist, however, only by announcing her engagement to another man. Unless a woman delivers the crushing blow of rejecting her suitor's proposal of marriage, Howells implies, in a struggle of wills the man will dominate if both man and woman have been conditioned by a society that vests authority in men and better equips men, psychologically if not intellectually, to manipulate words to their own ends.

Such is the advantage of Dr Morrell in a telling exchange with Annie Kilburn during a conversation about morality and justice that occurs early in their friendship. She allows his humour to deflect her earnestness until he subjects her to his 'professional scrutiny' while he fingers the blade of 'a large ivory paper-knife which he was in the habit of playing with in his visits' (AK, 260). Then she requests him to stop: 'When you get that knife and that look, I feel a little too much as if you were diagnosing me'.

Commanded to put down one weapon, he seeks another: he questions her word. ' "Diagnosticating", suggested the doctor.'

She is not ready to yield. 'I always supposed it was diagnosing. But it doesn't matter. It wasn't the name I was objecting to.'

Each has touched a nerve in the other. He obeys her: 'He put the knife back and changed his posture'. But he turns her word against her by implying that she has an ailment. 'Very well, then; you shall diagnose yourself.'

She taunts him: 'Diagnosticate, please.'

He continues to spar with her. 'Oh, I thought you preferred the other.'

Annie is right to prefer *diagnose*, 'more seemly', H. L. Mencken thought, than the 'bizarre' *diagnosticate*.[39] But she capitulates, although with a delicate irony he doesn't seem to perceive. Her word, she says, 'sounds undignified, now that I know there's a larger word' (AK, 260). The scene ends as he notes her 'perfervid concentration', reasserts his authority as her physician by proposing to send her 'a little more of that tonic' he had prescribed earlier, and departs, leaving her 'looking wistfully at the door he had passed through' (AK, 266).

IV

In portraying male characters in possession of knowledge, authority and powers of influence denied to female characters, Howells expressed his sense of the advantages he believed that American men did in fact enjoy. His sympathetic awareness of the effects on women of their less enviable position, however, was not accompanied by a wish to see men dispossessed of their advantages or their authority undermined. Whether he traced differences in speech and inequalities of position to natural or social causes, he put his powers of selection at the service of the privileged position of his male characters, not only creating scenes that enhance their authority but sparing them certain situations that might diminish it.

One evidence of Howells's desire to protect the status of his male characters is his unwillingness to subject their speech to correction by female characters. Men in his novels freely criticize women's speech and note their lapses, but scarcely ever do women even mentally note errors that men make. Bessie Lynde's sly mockery of the Harvard 'jay', Jeff Durgin, for calling his people his 'folks' is a rare instance of a woman's assertion of superiority, but her ill-bred impulse to humiliate him diminishes her, not him. When other provincial male characters, such as Silas Lapham and Lemuel Barker, deviate from standard English, their errors are noted by the narrator or other male characters – Bartley Hubbard and Tom

Corey in *The Rise of Silas Lapham*, David Sewell and Bromfield Corey in *The Minister's Charge*.

Women in Howells's novels may be employed by wealthy men to tutor their daughters in the arts of letter writing and polite conversation. Frances Dennam in *Letters Home* is engaged to correct the spelling of America Ralson's letters. Mrs Mandel in *A Hazard of New Fortunes* is brought by Fulkerson to the Dryfoos household to instruct Christine and Mela Dryfoos in the rudiments of grammar and genteel behaviour. Lillias Bellard (*Miss Bellard's Inspiration* [1905]) teaches in 'the department of oratory' in an 'upper-grade school', where, she admits, her real subject is 'applied conduct', although she 'pretend[s] to teach the niceties of speech and pronunciation only'.[40] But in no scene does Howells show a woman instructing a male pupil or a suitor or husband in correct usage. Nor does he portray relationships like those in James's *The Europeans* and *The Ambassadors*, in which a sophisticated woman undertakes to mould a shapeless young man into a member of good society. In Howells's one novel, *Ragged Lady*, in which a woman proposes to refine the speech and form the manners of a younger person, her charge is a country girl, the 'lady' of the title.

Howells's refusal to compromise the standing and authority of male characters is also evident in his portrayal of the marriage of characters of different social classes. Here again he favoured men, making men, but not always women, linguistically equal or superior to their mates. When a man marries a genteel woman above him on the social scale (usually a woman of the Boston Brahmin caste), his speech is as grammatically correct as hers. Emerance, the teacher who marries Parthenope Brook in *The Vacation of the Kelwyns*, is 'entirely middle class', and according to her aunt, Mrs Kelwyn, 'hasn't the least notion of society as we know it' (VK, 214). But the Kelwyns' tenant rightly observes that 'he's full as well educated as they be. He talks as correct' (VK, 99). Leslie Bellingham, who wishes to marry a western inventor without antecedents in *Out of the Question*, assures her mother, who opposes the marriage, that 'he used words more refined and considerate than I ever dreamt of . . . he talked splendidly'. Her brother defends her choice: her suitor is not only a 'natural gentleman'; he has 'the most sympathetic voice in the world' (CP, 61, 62). Mrs Hilary, a Bostonian with the social traditions of Mrs Bellingham, objects to the marriage of her daughter, Louise, to an impoverished journalist who 'was undoubtedly of a different origin and breeding' (SP, 39). She can better tolerate the marriage because the young man has refined features and 'the neat accent and quiet tone' of a gentleman.[41]

When a woman marries a man of a higher social class than her own, she may reveal her inferior status in her speech. A number of Howells's female characters who marry social superiors fall from the standard of their suitors when they betray their provincial origins in solecisms the men do not fail to notice. At their first meeting, Lydia Blood shocks the patrician Bostonian, Staniford, whom she will later marry, by exclaiming, 'I want to know' in response to his observation about the weather. Until he falls in love with her, she and he seem to him 'hardly of the same race'.[42] Cynthia Whitwell, a farmer's daughter, who says 'don't know as' and 'don't want you should', causes her fastidious suitor, Westover, to reflect on the eve of his proposal of marriage that between them 'there were many disparities, and that there would be certain disadvantages which could never be quite overcome' (LLH, 456). Edmund Ludlow, in *The Coast of Bohemia*, falls in love with his fellow artist, Cornelia Saunders, but wishes that she said 'don't know *that* instead of *as*'; then he reflects that 'ninety Americans out of a hundred, lettered or unlettered, would have said the same'.[43]

Staniford, Westover, and Ludlow all seem inferior in vitality to the women they marry – as Ben Halleck, Bromfield Corey and David Sewell lack the force and energy of the provincial men (Bartley Hubbard, Silas Lapham and Lemuel Barker) whom they patronize. But the importance that genteel speakers attach to their superior use of the language can assuage any sense of deficiency, although masculine energy alone does not compensate for linguistic impropriety, as the fate of Silas Lapham proves. Fulkerson, in *A Hazard of New Fortunes*, appears to violate the rule that women may but men never fall below the standard of a 'genteel and grammatical' mate.[44] But the exuberant and slangy Fulkerson, inconceivable as the husband of a Corey or a Bellingham, can marry a well-bred woman like Madison Woodburn, whose Southern accent places her apart from, if not below, the standard and dilutes the effect of Fulkerson's grammatical lapses. Otherwise, poor journalists and teachers, western inventors and aspiring writers (like Howells himself) who marry into the Eastern upper class command both the energy of the vernacular speakers and the best English of genteel Boston.

V

Although male characters are favoured, the advantage is not always with the man in Howells's novels. Among his most effectively drawn figures are young women remarkable for their powers of expression: Kitty Ellison (*A Chance Acquaintance*), Penelope Lapham (*The Rise of Silas Lapham*), Alma Leighton (*A Hazard of New Fortunes*) and Hope Hawberk (*The Son of Royal Langbrith*). In originality and liveliness of mind they surpass their suitors, who seem rather stiff or stodgy by comparison. To Kitty Ellison, a westerner with antecedents like Howells's, the novelist gave not only the gift of flawless English but his own powers as a writer of urbane and witty letters. Penelope Lapham charms Tom Corey by her storytelling filled with droll humour such as he has never heard in a woman's conversation before.[45] Hope Hawberk is that rare figure in Howells, a woman who surpasses in common sense and moral insight the man she marries – a 'beautiful guardian', in Elizabeth Prioleau's phrase,[46] who frees James Langbrith from bondage to illusions and guides him to maturity.

Howells liked these heroines, just as he liked the witty and spirited Elizabeth Bennet in *Pride and Prejudice*. But none of Howells's young women enjoys the kind of conclusive triumph that Elizabeth enjoys in her verbal contest with the odious Lady Catherine. In the world of Howells's fiction, women are actively discouraged from being witty or clever in conversation. Mrs Corey censures what she calls 'pertness' in Penelope Lapham and judges her a 'thoroughly disagreeable young woman' who 'says things to puzzle you and put you out' (RSL, 169). Mrs Enderby cautions Hope Hawberk before her marriage to James Langbrith: 'he's not as quick as you . . . You must be careful of that keen little tongue of yours' (SRL, 120). Such is the power of traditional codes that members of the sex most restricted by them are often the most vocal in upholding them.

Howells created his most important exception to the prevailing pattern of male dominance in the portrayal of Alma Leighton, the aspiring painter from Maine in *A Hazard of New Fortunes* who begins a promising career as an illustrator in New York. In each of her five scenes with an egoistic suitor, Angus Beaton, a painter who had courted her, urged her to study art in New York, and then ignored her for half a year, Alma dominates the conversation, setting the tone and balking his every attempt to assume control.

When he finally comes to call on her in New York after months of silence, she dons a 'mask of radiant cordiality' (HNF, 131) to hide her resentment and disarms him by burlesquing the kind of speech for which women were criticized: her volubility and emphases are as overpowering as the 'crushing handshake' accompanying her greeting: 'How *very* kind of you to come to see us . . . how *have* you been since we last saw you?' (HNF, 131).

Her strategy, to feign ignorance of everything Beaton has told her of himself, throws him off balance at once. When she asks him why *he* doesn't come to New York too, he falters, 'I – I live in New York.'

Unwittingly, her mother abets her, speaking as if on cue in a script her daughter writes. 'Surely Alma, . . . you remember Mr Beaton's telling us he lived in New York' (HNF, 131).

Alma continues to provoke him, pretending to forget that he had recommended her art teacher. 'Oh, *do* you know Mr Wetmore?'

Again her mother helpfully reminds her: 'Why, Alma . . . it was Mr Beaton who *told* you of Mr Wetmore' (HNF, 132).

Impregnable in her 'shining ease and steely sprightliness' (HNF, 132), she bombards her hapless visitor with 'women's words': of Mr Wetmore: 'Isn't he delightful?'; of Miss Woodburn: 'She's perfectly lovely'; of her Southern accent: 'Isn't it fascinating?' She plays the scene to the end, leaving Beaton 'sensible of being manipulated, operated, but . . . helpless to escape the performer or to fathom her motives'. (HNF, 133).

Alma not only converts typically 'feminine' behaviour into aggressive self-defence; she is quick to reject the stereotypes that perpetuate unthinking acceptance of socially prescribed attitudes and assumptions. When her timidly conventional mother advises her to encourage Beaton and demands: 'Don't you expect to get married? Do you intend to be an old maid?' Alma counters, 'I intend being a young one for a few years yet', and adds, 'I shall pick and choose, as a man does; I won't merely be picked and chosen' (HNF, 477).

Alma's rejection of Beaton in their penultimate scene is also a rejection of the romantic clichés (for example 'you have the secret of my happiness') by which he proposes to win her. All the while Alma is exposing the banality of his sentiments, in a reversal of roles she makes her suitor the object of her gaze as she sketches him in his new fur-lined overcoat (reminiscent of the coat Howells confessed to buying, the symbol of his complicity in the established order). Under Alma's scrutiny, Beaton, helpless in his egotism, repeatedly sets himself up to be cut down.

'You think I can't be sincere with anybody', he challenges her. She leads him on. 'Oh, no, I don't.'

He takes the bait. 'What do you think?'

She captures him with a 'victorious laugh.' 'That you can't – try' (HNF, 383).

He tries flattery and self-abasement. 'If I were one-tenth as good as you are, Alma, I should have a lighter heart than I have now. I know I'm fickle, but I'm not false, as you think I am.'

She catches him up. 'Who said I thought you were false?'

He tries to inflate himself by proposing that she is consumed by her disapproval of him. 'It isn't necessary, when you look it – live it.'

She punctures this effort to cast her in a sentimental role. 'Oh, dear! I didn't know I devoted my whole time to the subject' (HNF, 385).

Alma's function in this, the most unconventional proposal scene Howells wrote, is not simply to discredit the clichés of sentimental romance but to attack the idea that a woman can find fulfilment only in marriage; to ask: 'Why do men think life can be only the one thing to women?' (HNF, 388). Unlike Grace Breen, Alma need not counter an unwelcome proposal by declaring herself already engaged. Her dedication to her art and her faith in her talent enable her to tell Beaton: 'A life of art, and of art alone – that's what I've made up my mind to' (HNF, 387).

The voice of his culture's ideology makes the familiar claim: 'A woman that's made up her mind to that has no heart to hinder her!'

Is the same charge to be made of a man? she asks. 'Would a man have that had done so [sic]?'

He evades her logic by taking refuge in conventional lover's talk. She need not sacrifice her art to him; he will sacrifice himself to it and to her. 'I would be its willing slave, and yours, heaven knows.'

She does not suggest that a man who vows to be a woman's slave actually wants to be her master, but she exclaims, 'I don't want any slave – nor any slavery. I want to be free – always' (HNF, 387).

In her candour, intelligence and self-respect, Alma Leighton is an attractive example of the new woman. She is also Howells's only character to refuse outright 'the negative part assigned to women in life' that the narrator of *The Lady of the Aroostook* identifies as a woman's fate (LA, 52). Of course, none of Howells's female characters is simply a passive spectator of a man's deeds or a mere receptacle for his ideas. A novelist like Howells who proposes to reveal the shifting tensions of relationships through dialogue, as a dramatist does, must give his female characters an active role in conversations, whoever initiates and controls them. If situations are to have dramatic interest, women, like men, must have a point of view, must be able to express it and engage in the give and take that creates the momentum of a scene.

It is also true that Howells's male characters, as well as the female, make errors in speaking, and that many of his women speak as flawlessly as the men. But women in his novels and plays are shown to be handicapped in ways that confirm their place below men. Restricted in their observation and knowledge of the world, they must confess ignorance of the words men use, and they adopt a man's words as better than their own. Men can criticize and correct women's speech with impunity, but, of the women, only Alma Leighton enjoys the privilege of criticizing a man's speech without putting herself in the wrong. Narrators make generalizations about women's speech and language, but not about men's. Women of all ages misuse and misspell words, fall into affectation and extravagance, and use words and phrases which men stigmatize as 'women's expressions'. Women are denied the immunity from error that protects men who court and marry women socially above them. Women with social authority, like Mrs Corey, seek to suppress bold speaking in younger women and thus they put their power to establish 'forms and usages' at the service of those forces that divide the culture on the line of gender as well as class, that place not only patricians above plebeians, but men above women.

Howells's treatment of language and gender illustrates his complex view of women that a number of critics have analysed. He accepted conventional ideas of sex-based differences in speech but he also exposed the deficiencies of the society that perpetuated these ideas. His preoccupation with the defects of women's speech is central to his social purpose, emphasized by Edwin Cady and Sidney Bremer, to improve the condition of women by dramatizing the injurious effects of their defective education, their restricted experience of the world, and the perverted idealism fostered by their reading of romantic novels (which male characters like Bartley Hubbard and Angus Beaton plunder for phrases to use in manipulating the feelings of women).[47]

Howells's detachment from his female characters, reinforced by references to 'their sex' and by the tagging of their words, betrays the suppressed hostility towards women that John Crowley and Gail Parker have detected in his work.[48] But Howells's portrayal of such characters as Penelope Lapham, Kitty Ellison and Hope Hawberk shows his strong sympathy for women of courage and independent spirit whom snobbish social arbiters like Miles Arbuton and Mrs Corey misjudge or condemn. It is true that Howells constructed his plots and fashioned the speech of his characters to fortify the dominant position of men in the societies he portrayed. Women like Hope and Kitty and Alma Leighton, who outshine the men who court them, are not rebels who wish to dominate men or who imagine a social order different from the one they know. But one identifies in Howells not only the man of his times who accepted the traditional roles of men and women and who wrote from a man's perspective of a sex that often seemed alien, if not inferior; one also recognizes the social critic who exposed conditions that cripple both men and women; and the novelist whose enduring interest in the nature and circumstances of women grants them a place of prominence, often surpassing that of men, in the world of his fiction and drama.

3

Masculine and *Feminine* in James's Criticism and Fiction

When Henry James delivered his commencement address, 'The Question of Our Speech', at Bryn Mawr College in 1905, he spoke on a subject that had preoccupied him from the beginning of his career. For 40 years, in England and America, he was an inveterate observer of cultural signs, including language. At clubs, hotels, dinner parties and country houses he listened to men and women talk; he noted the habits of speech of different social classes and made studies of American colloquialisms and Cockney dialect that guided him in portraying the characters of his 20 novels and more than a hundred short stories and novellas. The title of his four-part essay, 'The Speech of American Women', identifies what he considered the infallible index of a person's culture. Speech that reveals the presence or absence of the moral and social virtues – restraint, self-control, modesty, powers of perception and imagination – shows in James's fiction, as in Howells's, the degree to which language reinforces or reflects the kinds of power men and women exercise in their private relationships and within the social order. Finally, James's lifelong concern to define what is masculine and what is feminine in speech and writing reflects the preoccupation with the nature of sexual identity that informs his fiction and criticism throughout his career.

Fascinated though James was by the nature of gender in the characters he created and the writers he analysed, his practice as a novelist diverged from his practice as a critic. According to Howells, James was unrivalled in his portrayal of female characters. When compared with James, male novelists writing in English 'seem not to have written of women at all'. (Howells's deprecation of his own achievement is characteristic.) Women writers such as Jane Austen, George Eliot and the Brontës had created a few heroines to rival James's, he acknowledged, but none could equal the 'rich amplitude' produced by James, creator of 'more, and more finely, yet strongly differenced heroines than any novelist of his time'.[1] The reader may protest that the creators of Becky Sharp and Tess of the D'Urbervilles cannot be dismissed so readily, but still acknowledge that James created some of the strongest, most memorable heroines in nineteenth-century fiction, that characters such as Isabel Archer, the Princess Casamassima, Kate Croy and Milly Theale make a more lasting impression on the reader than the men who surround them.

In his literary criticism, however, James seems to resist, even to fear, the promise of female variety and strength he embodied in his heroines. Early and late in his criticism he made the conventional associations of the masculine with strength and reason, the feminine with weakness and emotion, thereby confirming the inferior status of what he called the 'subordinate sex'.[2] Thus James reversed the position of Howells, whose fiction subverts ideals of the equality of the sexes that he championed in his essays and interviews. In his fiction, James portrayed women who surpass men in the power to initiate and control action; in his criticism, he maintains the masculine–feminine polarity to guarantee the supremacy of the male artist.

I

James's early reviews, which he began writing for the *Nation* and the *North American Review* in 1864–65 when he was 21, are notable for their range of reference, satiric wit and incisive formulation of principle. Their tone is that of a critic, assured, authoritative, untroubled by self-doubt, confident in his powers of judgement. The youthful critic also purveys the conventional assumptions about gender differences as uncritically as the most commonplace of literary hacks whom he scorned. Like countless long-forgotten reviewers who asserted the superiority of the masculine to the feminine, James accepted the male sex as the norm from which women, a subclass, should be distinguished; men's writing as the standard by which women's writing should be judged. At the same time, he viewed women, but not men, as a monolith, imputing one writer's qualities (usually undesirable ones) to the whole sex. 'Like all women, she has a turn for color', he wrote of Mary Elizabeth Braddon, author of the sensationally popular *Lady Audley's Secret*, but her possession of 'a woman's *finesse*' assured neither 'moral delicacy' nor 'intellectual strength'.[3] Harriet Prescott Spofford likewise was typical in her defects: 'like the majority of female writers . . . she possesses in excess the fatal gift of fluency' (NR, 28). The domestic realism of Elizabeth Charles's *The Chronicles of the Schön-berg-Cotta Family* proved to James that 'if women are unable to draw, they notoriously can at all events paint' (NR, 79) – an early expression of his lifelong conviction that women excelled at detail but lacked a sense of form. A pun given positive value by modern feminist scholars appears in James's review: the *Chronicles*, set during the Reformation, had little history, James asserted, but 'a great deal of what has been very wittily called "*her story*" ' (NR, 80). James did not spare male novelists such as Trollope and Hardy his biting wit and withering irony but he did not characterize their defects as 'masculine' or as typical of 'all men'. Praiseworthy qualities, however, such as the realism, logic and precision of Dumas's *Affaire Clemenceau*, in which 'not a word . . . is accidental', were gender-marked virtues: 'Such writing is reading for men' (NR, 227).

The most frequent target in James's criticism of women writers was the 'woman's man', a compound of clichés, such as those in Alcott's *Moods* – the 'quiet smile', the 'masterful soul', the 'commanding eye' (NR, 50–51) – properties of 'those impossible heroes, whom lady novelists concoct half out of their own erratic fancies and half out of those of other lady novelists' (NR, 41). When James praised the depiction of a male character in a novel by a woman, he made the male writer the standard of excellence, as in his review of Gaskell's *Wives and Daughters*: 'It is good praise of these strongly marked, masculine, middle-aged men to say that they are as forcibly drawn as if a masculine hand had drawn them' (NR, 159). He did not suggest that a man's successful portrait of a woman might have been drawn by a wise feminine hand, nor did he propose a class to correspond to a 'woman's man', to contain heroines such as Bathsheba Everdene and Trollope's Alice Vavasar that he considered artistic failures. 'A man's woman', as the title of Frank Norris's novel indicates, denotes the woman who satisfies a man's requirements.

James did not call George Eliot an 'authoress' or a 'lady novelist', terms he reserved for the women writers he disparaged – but in praising her he again made the male his standard. One strength of 'The Spanish Gypsy' was the hero's 'rich, masculine nature'.[4] *Felix*

Holt showed 'a much broader perception of human incongruities than belongs to many a masculine humorist' (NR, 202). But although 'a certain masculine comprehensiveness' distinguished her from Jane Austen and Maria Edgeworth, George Eliot, too, was 'a delightfully feminine writer' whose miniaturist virtues – 'microscopic observation' and 'exquisitely good taste on a small scale' that distinguish 'the feminine mind' – apparently precluded the 'heat' and 'inspiration' that produce masterpieces (NR, 207).

In his view of language, James was a conservative who invested in tradition a power and authority masculine in nature that women were more likely than men to defy. He counselled Harriet Prescott to respect 'such good old English words as we possess, words instinct with the meaning of centuries . . . which long use has invested with almost absolute force of expression' (NR, 29). He offered as the corrective to her verbal excesses the example of Gautier, whose 'occasional liberty with the French language' was always governed by 'a policy of studious respect even for her most irritating forms of conservatism' (NR, 28). Although the French language is feminine, the power of the French Academy assures that it be 'paternally governed' (NR, 28). With or without institutional control, a writer should submit himself to the discipline of the familiar figure of male authority: 'A true artist should be as sternly just as a Roman father' (NR, 29).

By the time James published his first book of criticism, *French Poets and Novelists*, in 1878, he had modified his style and method of criticism. No longer a reviewer obliged to deal with books he considered worthless, he ceased to expose weakness by frontal attack or to patronize writers by lecturing them. Instead of sarcasm and wounding irony he cultivated urbanity. For denunciation and satire he substituted the irony of understatement and self-deprecation. But his criticism, informed by the premises of the early reviews, expressed no fundamental change in his view of women writers, no doubt of the eternal reality of the masculine and the feminine. He remained convinced that women, 'ever gracefully, comfortably, enviably unconscious . . . of the requirements of form' (NN, 91), could excel only in short works, that they lacked the power to organize large masses of material. Even Edith Wharton's masterpiece and bestseller, *The House of Mirth*, he declared 'too loose and too confused'.[5] In commending George Eliot for 'proving how few limitations are of necessity implied in the feminine organism',[6] he assumed the inevitable existence of some limitations. His spokesman Constantius in 'Daniel Deronda: A Conversation' is not praising George Eliot when he describes her as 'delightfully, almost touchingly, feminine' in her idealistic portrayal of the title character, whom a man 'would certainly have made . . . more peccable' (PP, 81). James honoured Constance Fenimore Woolson by including her in *Partial Portraits* but diminished her in defining her almost solely by gender-marked traits: 'tenderness of feeling', 'a remarkable minuteness of observation', a 'sympathy altogether feminine', restriction of interest to the 'love-story' in contrast to greater range of reference in even the simplest novels by men (PP, 179, 180, 189).

James's essay on Woolson exemplifies his habitual practice (so much more persistent than with Howells) of judging women writers according to the conventional constructs of masculine and feminine. How firmly his mind was held by the age-old dichotomy is most apparent in his criticism of George Sand, the writer to whom he devoted the most essays and reviews (nine), the one woman he called *master* (NN, 160), 'the greatest of all women of letters' (NN, 214), who most resisted his classification by the traditional categories. What most fascinated him – the androgynous nature of her genius – emerges in his first criticism of her fiction, his review (1868) of *Mademoiselle Merquem*, in which he judged her style superior to that of Dickens and Thackeray, her imagination 'restless, nervous, and capricious . . . in short, the imagination of a woman' (LRE, 126). He continued to find feminine, that is, inferior, qualities coexisting with masculine ones. Her genius was 'masculine' in its 'force, and mass, and energy', but because she was a woman 'the laxity of the feminine intellect could not fail to claim its part in her'.[7] Her greatest literary gift – her 'noble and imperturbable style' (FPN, 153) – was weakened by 'all a woman's loquacity' although never by a 'woman's shrillness' (FPN, 167). In later years, the 'exemplary eloquence' (NN, 207) itself signified weakness, symptomatic of the sense of fluidity 'fatal to the sense of particular truth' that he believed endemic to women's writing (NN, 192).

What most interested James in his last essays about George Sand was not the work but the novelist herself: 'the career and the character are the real thing' (NN, 193). Above all he was concerned to analyse her sexual identity, to determine whether masculine or feminine attributes defined her. In *French Poets and Novelists* he had found her 'more masculine than any man she might have married' (FPN, 160); 'very masculine' (FPN, 155) in her appetite for wide experience and yet 'our final impression of her always is that she is a woman and a Frenchwoman' (FPN, 155). Twenty years later, however, she seemed to James 'a woman quite by accident' (NN, 178), to have 'more of the inward and outward of the other sex than of her own' (NN, 178). The woman survived in her fiction only in 'the feminine streak' produced by an occasional 'excess of volubility' (NN, 212) and by 'her immense plausibility' (NN, 178).

James might seem to propose George Sand as an example for feminists, the woman who more than any other shifted 'the emphasis from the idea of woman's weakness to the idea of her strength' (NN, 221). But the 'strength', as James defined it, left the power structure of the man-made world intact. Instead of rejecting the idea of domination of one sex by the other, George Sand simply reversed the usual pattern, dealing with her lovers 'exactly after the fashion in which numberless celebrated men have contributed to their reputation . . . by dealing with women' (NN, 224).

If retributive justice is the goal, George Sand was successful in her life: 'the history of her personal passions reads singularly like a chronicle of the ravages of some male celebrity . . . It is very much the same large list, the same story of free appropriation and consumption' (NN, 178). But James perceived that the heroines of her novels, in defying convention, act not for their own sex but for the pleasure of men; they are liberated 'up to a point at which men may most gain and least lose by the liberation' (NN, 223).

Whether James found one sex's ravages more disturbing than the other's, whether he was more troubled by the plight of George Sand's quasi-liberated heroines or by the sufferings of her lovers, notably Musset and Chopin, is debatable. His sympathies with the women in his own fiction who suffer under the laws and codes that give men power over women is undeniable. But in his letters and criticism he viewed what he termed 'the revolution taking place in the position and outlook of women'[8] with ambivalent, if not openly hostile, feelings. His essay on Mrs Humphry Ward (1892), which takes her highly acclaimed novel *Robert Elsmere* as the sign of women's triumph in the world of literature, treats their success as a condition to be lamented, not an achievement to be celebrated. Their dominance he attributes not to their own merits but to the failure of men to recognize and seize upon 'a possible form of resistance'.[9] (He does not say what this might be.) Because of men's 'predestined weakness', women writers 'may justly *pretend* that they have at last made the English novel speak their language'

(ELE, 255; emphasis added). He belittles women's writing either by exaggerated claims or reductive satire. Women writers in England and America have no cause to complain of 'the intolerance of man' for in the literary world they 'have been admitted, with all the honours, on a perfectly equal footing' (PP, 177). The result is debasement of rational discourse: the 'feminine voice', so long silent, now 'makes its ingenious hum the very ground-tone of the uproar in which the conditions of its interference are discussed' (ELE, 254).

Belwood, one of the male speakers in 'An Animated Conversation', posits the 'essential, latent antagonism of the sexes', prophesying that the 'armed opposed array of men and women founded on irreconcilable interests' will eventually produce conflict overshadowing all others. Darcy, James's spokesman for moderation and reconciliation, denies the inevitability of sexual warfare and insists that 'we *must* be united'.[10] But in his criticism James repeatedly envisioned the literary world as a battleground where men and women, like natural enemies, struggled for supremacy. He described women's literary success in military terms as a conquest, 'a well-fought battle' in which women 'have again and again returned to the charge' and 'have carried the defenses line by line' (ELE, 254–5). George Sand, the supreme warrior, owed her powers of psychological survival, superior to her lovers', to the 'sustaining force' of her eloquence (NN, 182): 'In the citadel of style . . . she continues to hold out' (NN, 169). She annexed male identity as a victorious general annexes a defeated country. Her love letters written to the doctor who attended her lover Alfred de Musset in Venice were 'pontoon bridges which a force engaged in an active campaign holds itself ready at any time to throw across a river' (NN, 208).

The potency of George Sand's psychological weapons ensured her dominance over men in intimate relations but did not give her literary supremacy. James's pronouncement that 'she had the greatest instinct of expression ever conferred on a woman' (NN, 165) limits her to a class small enough to make such judgements possible. In James's view, she was great enough to sustain comparison with Goethe – in *French Poets and Novelists*, he compared her 'L'Histoire de ma Vie' to Goethe's 'Dichtung und Wahrheit' – but comparison revealed her the inferior: 'she was to have all the distinction but not all the perfection . . . she confirms us, masculine as she is, in believing that it takes a still greater masculinity to have both' (NN, 191). One wonders whether James had his own family in mind when he universalized George Sand's case to illustrate

> precisely the difference even in the most brilliant families be-
> tween sisters and brothers. She was to have the family spirit, but
> she was to receive from the fairies who attended at her cradle the
> silver cup, not the gold. She was to write a hundred books but she
> was not to write 'Faust'. (NN, 191)

In George Sand James the critic met the greatest challenge to his traditional ideas of gender. But he rejected neither the concept of polarity nor the conventional definitions of masculine and fe-minine. By deploying them to analyse the writer who, more than any other, controverted them, he would affirm their enduring re-ality.

II

James's imagination imbued the characters of his fiction with energies more resistant to definition than were the writers he constructed in his criticism. Nevertheless, the gender-based as-sumptions of the criticism operate in his fiction in a variety of ways. The narrative text may enunciate them, illustrate them, qualify or subvert them. How language functions to affirm male authority is most apparent in James's portrayal of the teacher–pupil relation-ship, the subject of his first novel, *Watch and Ward* (1871).

The protagonist, Roger Lawrence, a wealthy bachelor whose pro-posal of marriage is rejected in the first chapter, adopts a 12-year-old orphan, Nora Lambert, intending to educate her to be the perfect wife. In James's version of the Pygmalion story, language is the creator's primary concern. Roger's first task is to instruct his ward, the child of rootless adventurers, in proper diction and grammar, to rid her vocabulary of the 'various impolite words' she had learned in her neglected infancy. She is a model of obedience. 'When once Roger had straightened out her phrase she was careful to preserve its shape; and when he had decimated her vocabulary she made its surviving particles suffice.'[11] A woman of society who meets Nora years later praises Roger for giving voice to the voiceless: 'She is a deaf-mute whom you have rendered vocal' (WW, 99). To which Roger replies, 'I have reason to be proud of my work' (WW, 99).

To create the perfect wife is also to create the ideal reader and a text to be read. Roger mentally addresses his diary to Nora, 'she being implied throughout as reader and auditor' (WW, 36). He sees his fashioning of Nora as analogous to the composing of a narrative with a dénouement 'not yet written' (WW, 49). His story, he tells Nora, will be different from the conventional love stories which 'are nothing to what I can fancy' (WW, 49). He does not tell her how his story will differ, but he himself, so unlike the masterful hero of popular romance, most clearly confounds the conventions of popular fiction. In choosing Roger over her more dashing suitors, Nora marries a man without beauty or sexual magnetism, defined by qualities traditionally described as feminine. He is a victim of 'incurable personal shyness' and speaks in a 'mild deferential tenor' (WW, 4), but he is blessed with a 'heart full of tenderness' (WW, 26), and 'a loving turn of mind' (WW, 29). Far from being the brooding master of romance who would treat his ward 'as Rochester treats Jane Eyre' (WW, 48), he despairs of being worthy of Nora, fears in her 'a deeper penetration than his own' (WW, 47), feels his lack of 'that omniscience, that a woman demands of her lover' (WW, 47), and concludes that to teach Nora, he himself must be a student; 'to educate her, he should first educate himself' (WW, 35).

Roger's humility, however, does not lessen his authority as her teacher and the guardian of proper speech. Correspondingly, Nora perfectly conforms to the traditional ideal of the woman submissive to male authority, created to be the helpmeet of the man she loves, exhibiting behaviour traditionally identified as feminine. When she grows up she comes 'into her woman's heritage of garrulity . . . she rattled and prattled uneasingly upon all the swarming little school interests' (WW, 33). When in Rome for the first time, she writes to Roger's cousin about a German woman – 'a marvel of learning and communicativeness' (WW, 111) but concludes that 'only a man can talk really to the point of this manliest of cities' (WW, 111). Whether or not she believes what she writes, her words are calculated to please her male reader. The goal of her education and the success of Roger's teaching are revealed when the charming, well-shaped letters he has enabled her to write determine him to leave a beautiful woman with whom he has dallied in Peru and return to his ward.

In his criticism, James attacked the kind of romantic novels Nora enjoys – she reads *The Heir of Redclyffe* and a story about a Protestant minister who converts a Roman Catholic woman to his own religion before he marries her. But James approves in Nora the deference to male authority reinforced by the novels he disparaged. He shows Nora achieving happiness when she recognizes herself as Galatea, totally dependent on the supervision of her creator, Roger Lawrence: 'He was her world, her strength, her fate! He had made her life; she needed him still to watch his work' (WW, 119). Neither Nora nor the narrator even imagines woman's escape from what Margaret Fuller called 'blind pupilage', destined to endure until 'Woman lay aside all thought; such as she habitually cherishes, of being taught and led by men'.[12]

In Roger Lawrence and Nora, James portrayed a relationship typical in Victorian fiction, between a young girl and a man who teaches and guides her and may ultimately marry her. One thinks of Emma Woodhouse and Knightley, Esther Summerson and Mr Jarndyce, Jane Eyre and Rochester, M. Paul and Lucy Snow, Savonarola and Romola, Dorothea and Casaubon, Daniel Deronda and Gwendolen. In James's fiction, Roger Lawrence is followed by a succession of men who advise young women for better or worse – Rowland Mallet, Winterbourne, Gilbert Osmond, Basil Ransom, Peter Sherringham. James's treatment of the teacher–pupil attachment differs from that of the English novelists in his greater emphasis on the speech and voices of his characters and in the greater moral ambiguity attaching to the guides and teachers. Roger Lawrence is the first of many characters to produce conflicting impressions and inspire diverse responses among readers. A few critics see him as a man of integrity and noble ideals, with whom James sympathizes. Others see a dark underside to the benevolence of the man who sometimes regards his ward as an object to be possessed and manipulated – a flower with petals to be 'playfully forced apart' (WW, 58), a 'superior doll, a thing wound up with a key' (WW, 37).[13]

Feminist criticism has made the objectifying male gaze inherently suspect. But James did not take a uniformly negative view of his teacher-patrons although all on occasion see their protegés as objects – instruments to be played, texts to be written or read, material to be shaped. Speech is one index to the morality of the teacher and his tutelage, as James perceived it. Whatever prurient and lustful impulses lurk in Roger's view of Nora as soil to be 'gently tickled' by other suitors before his own 'vertical rays' penetrate it (WW, 58), James represents his gift to Nora of the speech of a lady as wholly positive, essential to the ideal development of the young woman.

Roger also gains in contrast to Nora's other suitors, who are condemned by their voices and their speech. Roger's cousin, the minister Hubert Lawrence, is exposed as a duplicitous actor by his
rhetorically polished sermons delivered in a voice 'modulated with
infinite art' that charms the young Nora into thinking his words
'the perfection of eloquence' (WW, 92). Nora's cousin Fenton seems
to embody the masculinity Roger envies, but Fenton's 'colourless
monotone' and his 'thin, drawling, almost feminine voice' (WW,
56) betray his inferiority. Although Roger lacks the masculine as-
sertiveness of his rivals, the stigmatizing word *feminine* is never
attached to him.

Like Roger Lawrence, Rowland Mallet, the protagonist of James's
second novel, *Roderick Hudson* (1875), assumes responsibility for
another person's development, when he launches the title character
on his career as a sculptor in Rome.[14] As his surname *Mallet* suggests, Rowland sees his protegé, 'my gifted pupil' (I, 49), as plastic
material to be shaped. The office of patron and adviser fills him
with 'an almost creative ardour' (I, 48). But unlike Nora, Roderick
so stubbornly resists guidance and resents supervision that Rowland wishes that 'the paste of Roderick's composition had had a
certain softer ductility' (I, 234).

When Roderick degenerates after yielding to temptations against
which Rowland had warned him, Roderick blames his patron. But
in the second chapter Roderick's fatal weakness is signalled to the
reader, if not to Rowland, by Roderick's voice: 'a soft and not
altogether masculine organ', often pitched 'in a plaintive and pet-
tish key' (I, 21). He has the habits of speech that traditionally
construct women as inferior: upon first meeting Rowland, he 'rattled away for an hour'; his talk 'abounded in the superlative and
the sweeping' (I, 24). In Europe, his 'childish unmodulated voice'
signifies his failure to mature, to learn self-control and restraint.
Late in the novel, Christina Light, the first of James's alluring
women and a shrewd judge of character despite her caprices, tells
Roderick, 'Your voice condemns you . . . I always wondered at it;
it's not the voice of a conqueror' (I, 261).

Rowland sees Roderick as a blood-horse to be ridden, a machine
to be operated, a boat to be launched. These images of domination
and control taint Rowland's benevolence, which not only serves
Roderick's interests but gives Rowland companionship and occupation. But James solicits approval of Rowland by insisting upon
his kindness, self-restraint, modesty and sympathy ('his vision of

the case for others' (I, 424), expressed repeatedly by his speech. In contrast to Roderick, who in his 'flights of eloquence' (I, 232) 'said more than he meant' (I, 232), Rowland is 'a temperate talker' (I, 24) whose sincerity gives his voice 'an extraordinary amenity' (I, 223). Christina Light identifies Rowland as the friend who will speak truthfully, welcomes his 'hearty directness' (I, 209), when the compliments of other men bore her, and asks him to recommend books for her to read.

Although Rowland alters the lives of several characters, despite his 'almost creative ardour' he does not change the essential nature of anyone. The character in James who comes closest to creating a person is Gilbert Osmond, who in *The Portrait of a Lady* (1881) so completely controls the development of his daughter Pansy that when she is only 14 she seems 'formed and finished for her tiny place in the world' (III, 401). The results of Osmond's domination, reinforced by the sisters of the convent where Pansy is educated, are not wholly unfortunate. Her manners are impeccable, her conversational poise unfailing: she 'might have given lessons in deportment' to her voluble aunt (IV, 85). Repressive training has not spoiled Pansy's sweet and generous spirit. But the pernicious nature of Osmond's 'system' is evident in her passivity, in her almost total inability to assert herself, to defy paternal authority, even in order to marry the man she loves.

Osmond is condemned by his actions – his callous disregard of Pansy's feelings, his suppression of Isabel Archer's spontaneity and 'quick eagerness' once he marries her, his proposal that Isabel in effect prostitute herself to procure Lord Warburton for Pansy. Osmond is condemned as well by his motives, caring nothing for any one's well-being apart from the person's ability to enhance his reputation and self-esteem. He participates in dialogues and produces responses: by his words he seduces Isabel, cows Pansy, humiliates Ned Rosier, confounds Casper Goodwood, and reduces Madame Merle to despair. But what he seeks in conversation is not the exchange of ideas or the stimulation of another's wit but the flattering reproduction of his own thoughts. In a brilliant image, James represents the egotism of a man who converses with others that he may feed more pleasurably on his own substance. Isabel's mind will be a 'silver plate . . . that he might heap up with ripe fruits, to which it would give a decorative value, so that talk might become *for him* a sort of served dessert' (IV, 79; emphasis added).

Women in the novel, by their acquiescence, reinforce the patriarchal power Osmond typifies. Initially Isabel is not averse to service
as the silver plate. She is pleased to see herself as an object suitable
for Osmond's collection, 'worth more', after her travels, 'like some
curious piece in an antiquary's collection' (IV, 42). Osmond compares women to books, but Isabel compares Pansy to 'a sheet of
blank paper' and 'hoped that so fair and smooth a page would be
covered with an edifying text' (III, 401). The familiar image, seemingly at odds with the idea of Pansy 'formed and finished', is
revealed as sexual. Pansy is blank because virginal; her aunt the
Countess Gemini, who has had many lovers, is 'by no means a
blank sheet; she had been written over in a variety of hands' (III,
401). Isabel declares to her rejected suitor Caspar Goodwood that
she wishes to 'choose [her] fate' (III, 229), but the figurative language of the narrator and the characters implies that a woman does
not write her own story; she waits, a blank page, to receive a text
composed by men.

Fittingly, the last of James's male guides and teachers helps to
form a character whose success frees her from all dependence on
teachers and guides. Like Roderick, Miriam Rooth in *The Tragic
Muse* (1890) is an artist awaiting financial backing and opportunities. Unlike Roderick, she initially shows little promise beyond
grim determination to become an actress. She is simply raw material waiting to be fashioned into an artist. The celebrated actress
Madame Carré, who at their first meeting hears Miriam render
French and English poetry in a 'solemn droning dragging measure'
(VII, 130) can only imagine that she has a voice 'somewhere or
other' and tells her, 'We must try and put our hand on it' (VII, 127).

Madame Carré teaches Miriam the art of her profession and in-
stils in her the traditions of the ancient *Comédie Française*. Peter
Sherringham, a rising young diplomat, appoints himself Miriam's
tutor in English. After insisting that she eradicate the 'little queer-
nesses and impurities in [her] English' (VII, 202), she readily adopts
him as her model ('I like the way you speak', VII, 202). Seeing her
as 'a kind of challenge . . . a subject for enquiry, a problem, an
explorable tract' (VII, 136), Sherringham undertakes to form her
taste and enlarge her knowledge of European culture. He sets
passages from Wordsworth and Swinburne for her to learn and
recite to him, believing that lyric poetry will teach her 'the mysteries of rhythm, the communicableness of style, the latent
music of the language' (VII, 225). He enables her to understand

Shakespeare's *King John*, which they read and discuss together, and thus he contributes to her first dramatic triumph, an 'ample and powerful' recitation of Constance's passionate lament in Act III, before him and Madame Carré.

Sherringham's interest extends beyond Miriam to the English stage, which he longs to help regenerate. He exhorts her to 'do something for the standard', and, speaking here for James, he complains that 'purity of speech, on our stage, doesn't exist', thanks to the 'abominable dialects and individual tricks' abounding everywhere (VII, 203).[15] Miriam is his means to an end 'since she was the instrument . . . that had come to his hand' (VII, 226). Having helped to fashion the artist, he falls in love with the woman. But here the transformation of the teacher into the husband effected in *Watch and Ward* is frustrated by the very success of the teacher's tutelage, which contributes to the consummate success the actress is unwilling to sacrifice for marriage.

In *The Tragic Muse* James looked to an actress to raise the standard of speech on the English stage. But his fiction controverts the widely held assumption, advanced by *Godey's Lady's Book*, that women were fit instructors of children in the proper use of their language. In James's fiction, governesses are invariably inadequate as teachers of the young, especially their male pupils. The self-effacing governess of 'Master Eustace' confesses feeling 'dreadfully below the mark' when she attempts to entertain and instruct her precocious charge, whom she recognizes as 'very much wiser than myself'.[16] The governess-narrator of 'The Turn of the Screw' soon perceives that her preternaturally intelligent pupils, Miles and Flora, easily '[soar] quite out of *my* feeble range' (XII, 268) and describes as 'fiction' the notion that she can teach them anything. The disparity between teacher and pupil requires Miles in particular to engage in 'tacit little tricks' to relieve the governess of the effort to 'meet him on the ground of his true capacity' (XII, 294). Of all James's governesses, Mrs Wix (*What Maisie Knew*) is the most ignorant. Rather than give instruction in 'subjects', she 'took refuge on the firm ground of fiction', telling Maisie stories from popular romances 'all about love and beauty and countesses and wickedness' (XI, 27).

To one group of women, however, James believed the office of instruction to be rightly assigned. Sophisticated, widely travelled women, usually married but separated from their husbands, were the natural preceptors of callow young American men, whose manners had yet to be formed, their speech refined. The outline of this cosmopolitan figure first appears in 'Eugene Pickering', in the widowed Madame Blumenthal, the author of trivial novels (so judged by the male narrator), who initiates the title character into the artifices and mysteries of European society, then betrays the love she has inspired in him.

The mature cosmopolitan woman is more fully drawn in *The Europeans*, James's fourth novel. Eugenia, the Baroness Münster, who comes with her brother Felix to visit her cousins the Wentworths, living near Boston, is complex both in the impressions she receives and in those she produces in others. Unlike the one-dimensional Madame Blumenthal, she can be wounded as well as wounding. But until the end, when her cautious suitor Robert Acton fails to call on her when she expects him, she dominates situations, commanding power, not through beauty, but through conversation, her 'strong point'.[17] Her social accomplishments, Felix believes, qualify her to be the teacher of Clifford Wentworth, a clumsy inarticulate youth who the Europeans believe should be trained and educated to take his place as a gentleman and a man of importance in his society. Felix urges Mr Wentworth to send Clifford to Eugenia, who will 'exercise a civilizing influence' (E, 147) and 'inspire him with a taste for conversation' (E, 149). Eugenia assures Clifford: 'there is no agreeable man who has not, at some moment, been to school to a clever woman' (E, 181).

James might have been speaking through Eugenia from his own experience. We know from his correspondence and from Leon Edel's biography that James as a young man living abroad enjoyed friendships with a number of socially prominent women, such as Mrs Charles Sumner, Mrs Edward Boit and Mrs Owen Wister.[18] In James's fiction, however, the relationship of the young man and the older accomplished woman is always flawed by deficiencies in one or both of the characters. Madame Blumenthal is manipulative and heartless; Eugenia is compromised by self-interest; and Clifford is impervious to her advice and admonitions.

Even James's supreme example, the metamorphosis of Chad Newsome in *The Ambassadors* (1903), is not the marvel it seems at first. To the protagonist Lambert Strether, sent by Chad's mother to Paris to rescue her son from what is presumed to be a degrading liaison, the change in the young man from a loutish adolescent to a suave man of the world seems a phenomenon almost magical, 'a case of transformation unsurpassed' (XXI, 137), the 'sharp rupture of an identity' (XXI, 137), 'the alteration of the entire man' (XXI, 167). But the language which registers Strether's dazzled vision indicates that the change in Chad is essentially superficial: the process of transformation has given Chad 'an inscrutable new face' with features retouched; has 'toned his voice, established his accent'; has given him 'a form and a surface, almost a design', making him smooth to the sense, as is 'the taste of a sauce' (XXI, 152). The reader is therefore not surprised to discover little depth in Chad. He makes graceful introductions at parties, deploys metaphors skilfully and utters French phrases with ease – accomplishments not to be scorned in James's world, but Chad says nothing memorable, offers no moral insights, and generates no ideas. Strether eventually perceives that the polished young man is still 'only Chad' (XXIV, 284); Strether makes the telling indictment when he tells Chad, 'you have, I verily believe, no imagination' (XXII, 225).

As if sensing Chad's inert spirit, Strether from the beginning instinctively sees Chad as passive, 'made over' by external forces, shapeless substance 'put into a firm mould and turned successfully out' (XXI, 152). Seeing Chad as a product, Strether naturally seeks the producer, whom he identifies when he himself is charmed by Madame de Vionnet, whose intimacy with Chad he almost wilfully refuses to recognize, even as he defines her as 'the prime producing cause' of Chad's transformation. Other characters – Maria Gostrey, little Bilham, Miss Barrace and Sarah Pocock – tacitly acknowledge the primary importance of Madame de Vionnet in Chad's development, and she herself assures Strether that 'to a great extent' she is responsible for the reformed Chad. But her means of education, unlike those of the male teachers, are never specified and so must be imagined by the reader.

Each of James's teacher–pupil relationships is distinctive, but together they form a basis for generalization. The standard upheld by the mentors, male and female, is the same: disciplined behaviour and conduct, in which cultivated speech is an essential part. Some of James's characters pervert the standard, many fall below it or never even recognize it, but James allows none to subvert the ideal of urbane gentility, or to suggest that a better alternative exists.

Men outnumber women as teachers of the unformed and untutored, but neither sex has a monopoly on success. Because women in James's Victorian world are conditioned to submit to male authority, however, young girls such as Nora and Pansy are more malleable, more promising subjects for moulding, than self-willed young men like Roderick Hudson and Clifford Wentworth, encouraged by female deference to resist authority.

In James's fiction, when a man is transformed by a woman, narrator and characters assume that a sexual intimacy has effected a mysterious transfer of energy, leaving the woman depleted, drained of vital energies. When characters at the Newmarch house party in *The Sacred Fount* (1901) observe the remarkable transformation of Gilbert Long from a stupid boor to an agreeable companion with the 'gift of talk' they start looking for his 'sacred fount', the woman who has 'given him a mind and a tongue' and lost her own wits in the process.[19] In her final appearance, Madame de Vionnet, destined to lose the man she has 'made over,' bitterly describes herself as 'old and abject and hideous', certain only that 'I shall be the loser in the end' (XXII, 288).

In none of his novels did James portray men without women. The histories of his leading male characters are always histories of their relations to women. But whether women are the teachers of men or taught by men, they effect no change in the structures of society which institutionalize the relation of the sexes. Even Miriam Rooth, whose personal success makes her independent of both her teachers, remains subject to the power of the patriarchy in Victorian England, which decrees that the actress on the English stage shall play parts written by male dramatists in theatres owned and controlled by men.

III

James's characters not only teach and are taught; they write diaries, letters and stories of their own and others' experience. Of James's 52 first-person narratives, 11 are presented as written documents. The majority of writer-narrators are male, but the most famous is a woman, the governess in 'The Turn of the Screw'. Three women and three men produce the correspondence in each of the two epistolary stories, 'A Bundle of Letters' and 'The Point of View'.

The polarization of writers on gender lines is less marked in James's first-person narratives than in his criticism. Male and female narrators alike exhibit James's wit, rhetorical skill and perception of likeness in difference. Women as well as men develop metaphors, construct epigrams, balance words and phrases and achieve shadings of irony. Unlike Howells, James allowed none of his narrators to deface their pages with misspelled words, grammatical errors or malapropisms. Female narrators make fewer references and allusions to literature than do the men but otherwise their culture equals that of the male narrators.

Nor does James spare either sex in his satire on human folly and weakness. All the correspondents, male and female, in the epistolary stories reveal themselves deficient – pompous, self-important, smug, affected, frivolous, self-deluded or naive. The male letter-writers are the more broadly satirized than the women by their style: the aesthete Louis Leverett by affectation ('as they say here') and hollow emphasis ('the great thing is to *live*'); the German scientist Rudolf Straub by pretentious dehumanizing abstraction ('the premature vitiation of the American population'); the Honourable Edward Antrobus, MP by pompous circumlocution ('a mysterious being of another sex') (XIV, 496, 530, 573). To avoid the appearance of male bias, James lets a female correspondent, the 50-year-old spinster Miss Sturdy in 'The Point of View', enumerate the defects of American women's speech: they interrupt, 'make too many vague exclamations', and lack 'repose'. English girls 'know how to speak but don't know how to talk'; American girls can talk but they can't speak (XIV, 564, 570). But it is an American girl, Miranda Hope, of all letter-writers the most forthright and unaffected, who recognizes the power that linguistic mastery confers and so seeks to acquire it. She alone takes private lessons in French, seeking to 'gain an insight' through study of the language. She remains an artless tourist who at the end plans to 'visit some new country' but hasn't decided which one (XIV, 532). But she is the only correspondent whose idiom changes to reflect a growing consciousness of form. As one reader has noted, the simple unstudied ending of her first letter – 'Dear mother, my money holds out very well, and it *is* real interesting' (XIV, 483) metamorphoses in the final letter into a more distanced mannered conclusion: 'Dearest mother, my money holds out, and it *is* most interesting!' (XIV, 533).[20]

The impulses that move characters to write are best studied in the narratives of four diarists: Locksley of 'A Landscape Painter' (1866); Maximus Austin of 'A Light Man' (1869); the unnamed Englishman of 'The Diary of a Man of Fifty' (1879); and Catherine Condit of 'Impressions of a Cousin' (1883). Three are Americans back from long sojourns in Europe. The Englishman, the 'man of fifty', foreshadowing Lambert Strether, has returned to Florence, where long ago he refused the love of an Italian countess and now discovers his 'own young identity' (CT, IV, 399) in an Englishman in love with the countess's daughter. Older than the other diarists, the Englishman, assailed by wonder of 'what *might* have been' (CT, IV, 390), not only keeps a diary but sees his past life as a text, like a letter written in 'sympathetic ink' that memory will make visible again (CT, IV, 389).

Locksley and Catherine Condit are painters; Austin and the Englishman are connoisseurs, habitués of galleries and museums who speak familiarly of favourite paintings and statues. All four draw upon the painter's vocabulary of *tones, hues, colours, texture* and *shades* to create verbal portraits of other characters, whose faces they study with the intentness of artists scrutinizing their subjects. The artist's perspective encourages their natural tendency to see persons closest to them as more simple and less sophisticated than they themselves are. Foreign travel, awareness of superior intelligence, the proximity of the relative or friend who seems innocent and naive, combine to produce in the diarists a tone of sceptical detachment, at times blasé, sardonic or cynical.

All four narrators confess in their diaries to thoughts and feelings they cannot express elsewhere, but gender operates as a constraint only on the female diarist. Austin and Locksley are compelled to silence and dissimulation by roles they themselves have chosen to play. Locksley is posing as a poor man and congratulates himself on 'play[ing] my little part pretty well' (CT, I, 114). Austin, a self-confessed adventurer, ingratiates himself with a rich and aged sybarite, Mr Sloane, until his success disgusts him and he refuses the old man's request to destroy the will drawn in Austin's friend Theodore's favour.

Likewise, Catherine Condit must conceal her impressions and judgements, but not because she has chosen to deceive others. Rather, she feels herself silenced by convention in a society that disapproves of candid speaking in women. 'I suppose a she-critic is a kind of monster; women should only be criticized. That's why I keep it all to myself – myself being this little book' (CT, V, 117). Her position in society, as the poor relation dependent on the generosity of a rich cousin, makes all the more urgent her need to break silence in her diary. 'I am so horribly tongue-tied that I must at least relieve myself here' (CT, V, 168).

For all the diarists, writing is compensatory, a form of self-defense and self-assertion. But only the female diarist feels compelled to explain and justify herself for keeping a diary. Because Catherine is an unmarried woman in a society that devalues the spinster, especially 'an unloved and unlovable third-cousin', as Catherine is pleased to see herself (CT, V, 112), she must take her pleasure where she can, in 'the luxury of recorded observation' (CT, V, 117). 'If one is poor, plain, proud – and in this very private place I may add, clever – there are certain necessary revenges' (CT, V, 117–18). The male diarists never feel obliged to defend themselves for the way they write, but the female diarist is conscious that she might be criticized. 'I suppose my superior tone would seem very pretentious if anybody were to read this shameless record of personal emotion' (CT, V, 111).

In an unpublished review quoted by Leon Edel, James, then aged 21, reflected on the difficulty of assuming the identity of one's antithesis. 'To project yourself into the consciousness of a person essentially your opposite requires the audacity of great genius' (CT, II, 8). Few critics have acknowledged James's success in creating the voice of his opposite, Catherine Condit. Gorley Putt alone has hailed the story as a work of 'unusual skill', 'a remarkable *tour de force* for a male author'.[21] The reader of Alice James's writings may wonder whether James had his sister in mind when he wrote 'Impressions of a Cousin'. The diary of Alice James is remarkably similar to Catherine Condit's diary in its ironic, occasionally acid tone, hard-edged observations, and persistent detachment from even the most painful feelings. Alice James began writing her diary six years after 'Impressions of a Cousin' was published, but for more than ten years before then James, living in France and England, had received letters from his sister at home in Cambridge. The correspondent who wrote to her brother of 'an ultra-refined parlor-maid who has mastered the mysteries of the nominative case after the verb *to be*, but whose desire for "Sabbath privileges" . . . will interfere too much, I am afraid with our noonday alimentation'[22] might have been a model for the diarist who paints a portrait of a foolish woman that is 'not bad enough to please her' and reflects on the 'difficulty in representing an expression which consisted so completely of the absence of that article' (CT, V, 116).

The language of James's male and female narrators differs most strikingly in his ghostly tales. Both men and women see or believe they see ghosts, but among the first-person narrators only the women feel themselves menaced or terrified and express themselves accordingly. The diary which tells the story of 'The Friends of the Friends', described by the first narrator as 'fearfully indiscreet', is a confessional into which a guilt-ridden woman pours her jealousy, suspicions and horror in gushes of superlatives and intensifiers. She arranges a meeting between her fiancé and a woman who, like him, has reported seeing the ghost of a dying parent; then the diarist succumbs to 'a momentary madness', a 'sudden panic', and wires the fiancé not to come at the appointed hour (XVII, 337, 340). The friend arrives, the diarist feels 'a really piercing pang of pity and remorse', and that night she confesses to her fiancé her 'iniquity and the miserable reason of it' (XVII, 342). The next day she learns that her friend has died and she enters 'the dim and dreadful chamber' where the friend 'lay locked up in death' (XVII, 346). 'Superstitiously, insanely', the narrator blames herself, but the doctor, 'superlatively wise and clear', assures her that heart disease of long standing was the cause of death (XVII, 344, 346). When the fiancé insists that the friend came to his room the night of her death, the diarist accuses him of telling a story 'positively monstrous', admits that her jealousy, 'fed by suspicions unspeakable', has 'lividly survived', and accuses him of being 'abjectly in love' with the dead woman, 'sick almost to death with the joy of what she gives you' (XVII, 349, 359, 363). The diarist then breaks their engagement and leaves him to 'his inconceivable communion' (XVII, 364).

Several of James's male characters – notably John Marcher in 'The Beast in the Jungle' and Spencer Brydon in 'The Jolly Corner' – are undone by fear and horror in the presence of the uncanny and unspeakable. But their stories are narrated in the third person; they are not the recorders of their experience. When male characters narrate their own stories of ghostly encounters they present themselves in control of their eerie sensations, which they describe with scientific detachment. The male diarist who records his encounters with the supernatural in 'Sir Edmund Orme' is typically self-contained and undaunted, fearful only that the girl he loves will see the apparition who appears to him and her mother. He is not alarmed when the girl's mother, Mrs Marden, haunted by the ghost of the man she jilted, hints at a portentous fate reserved for the narrator. 'I wondered more than I shuddered.' He confesses himself 'wonderfully at sea', refers humorously to 'the mystic initiation that was in store for me', and deliberately overstates, creating effects not horrific but mock-heroic. He declares himself 'terribly frightened' but admits to himself 'I exaggerated on purpose' (XVII, 376). Meeting the gaze of the apparition, the narrator admits to 'feeling rather cold and wishing he would say something' (XVII, 385), but dread gives way to a 'sense of pleasure' and to pride in his being chosen to experience such 'mystic enlargement of vision' (XVII, 390). He reflects complacently that ghosts 'were much less alarming and much more amusing than was commonly supposed' (XVII, 390). The narrator heightens the effect of cool detachment by his presentation of Mrs Marden, who in one scene speaks with 'intensest excitement' and 'passionate decision' and looks at the narrator 'in quite an extraordinary manner' (XVII, 379, 380).

Five stories alone may not support a generalization, but it is noteworthy that only in the ghostly tales narrated by women does irresolvable ambiguity attach to uncanny events. By the end of the male-narrated tales, the mysteries are explained and the line between the natural and the supernatural is clearly drawn. A ghostly presence proves to be a real woman ('The Ghostly Rental'); other characters share the narrator's vision of an authentic ghost ('Sir Edmund Orme'); supernatural appearances and absences are established as fantasy at the beginning ('The Private Life'). Even in the problematic, exhaustively analysed novel, *The Sacred Fount*, described by James as 'fanciful, fantastic . . . calculated to minister to curiosity',[23] a number of characters observe the seemingly miraculous changes that move the narrator to formulate a theory about his fellow guests at a country-house party. In contrast, 'The Friends of the Friends' never conclusively establishes whether the fiancé saw the living woman, as he insists, or her ghost, as the narrator believes. Whether the communion of the living and the dead occurs in actuality or only in the inflamed imagination of the narrator can never be known.

The most tantalizing Jamesian ambiguities of course occur in 'The Turn of the Screw', which has impelled several hundred critics to address the unanswerable questions: are the figures described by the governess apparitions, hallucinations, or living persons? Have the figures the motives that the governess imputes to them? Are the children, Miles and Flora, aware of any presences, and if so have they been corrupted by contact with them? What causes the death of Miles at the end? One can't imagine James giving this story to a male narrator – a tutor at Bly for instance. The tradition of the Gothic novel, evoked by the allusions to *Jane Eyre* and *The Mysteries of Udolpho* (XII, 179), requires that the narrator be a woman. Moreover, for James (if not for his predecessor Edgar Allan Poe), the vocabulary of the unspeakable that conveys effects of unutterable horror demands that the narrator be a woman.

But to simply label the governess's style 'feminine' is to ignore the different effects created by her language, depending on whether she is describing her own actions and sensations or evoking realms of the unseen and unimaginable. Her responses to what she hears and sees (or thinks she sees) suggest someone out of control at the time, given to exaggeration in retrospect. 'I almost shrieked' (XII, 192); 'A portentous clearness now possessed me' (XII, 194); 'I had to smother a kind of howl' (XII, 197); 'I fairly threw myself into her arms' (XII, 203); 'I looked prodigious things' (XII, 203); 'I sobbed in despair' (XII, 208); 'I flung myself about' (XII, 245) – such overwrought expression has no doubt contributed to many readers' impression of the governess as hysterical, neurotic, unbalanced, predisposed to delusions and hallucinations. But as Elizabeth A. Sheppard points out, the excesses of the governess's style are similar to those of Jane Eyre as she gives way to grief and horror. 'In his governess, James is simply representing, on indications supplied by Charlotte Brontë, an early Victorian young woman in a state of excitement and alarm . . . to a reader of, say, *The Old Curiosity Shop*, the portrait would not seem overdrawn.' (Sheppard also describes as feminine the governess's habit of deprecating her capacities by exaggeration: 'My mere infernal imagination', 'My dreadful liability to impressions'.)[24]

But when the governess struggles to express the inexpressible, to render in words the realm of the soundless, voiceless and wordless, her language transcends traditional gender categories. Her first vision of Quint, which turns the park into a solitude and for the 'unspeakable minute' silenced all living sounds (XII, 176); her sense near the end of 'taking a new plunge into the hideous obscure' (XII, 296), then floating 'into a darker obscure' (XII, 307), recalls, not Jane Eyre, but Conrad's Marlow, who in 'Heart of Darkness' journeys up an 'empty stream', through a 'great silence', feels 'the stillness of an implacable force brooding over an inscrutable intention' (48–9), imagines 'unspeakable rites', feels himself 'buried in a vast grave full of unspeakable secrets' (78), verges on the 'threshold of the invisible' (87) and draws back.[25]

Like Marlow, who despairs of conveying in words 'the life-sensation of any given epoch of one's existence', the governess is a self-reflexive narrator who repeatedly disclaims the power to render her experience. Her first sight of Quint, on the tower, induces a 'bewilderment of vision' of which 'there is no living view that I can hope to give' (XII, 176). After learning that Quint is dead, she confesses: 'I scarce know how to put my story into words that shall be a credible picture of my state of mind' (XII, 198). She struggles to convey her sense of the ghostly presences as they pass unseen: 'the strange dizzy lift or swim (I try for terms!) into a stillness, a pause of all life' (XII, 245–6). Bly becomes 'a setting of beauty and misery that no words can translate' (XII, 268).

Thus James reminds the reader that the governess has written her narrative and that the 'authority' he noted in his preface as having given to her, comprehends the office of author. The first words of her narrative, 'I remember', create the perspective: she re-creates the events at Bly in all their immediacy as she relives them years later when she writes the manuscript. Unlike Esther Summerson in *Bleak House*, who is requested to write her story, the governess apparently has chosen to write her manuscript without prompting from anyone else.

Her task requires her to do more than translate memories into words. She must seek meaning in events that confound the understanding. She does not simply see a man on a tower but, like an author creating a character, she imputes intentions to him: he has come for Miles. Symmetry requires that the ghostly woman in black seek Flora. Like exhibitionists the two ghostly figures, the governess decides, want to 'appear' to the children. The process of creation James described in his notebooks is similar to the governess's creation of the plot from which she proposes to save the children. As James recognized the germ of a subject in an anecdote, evoked characters and ascribed motives to them, multiplied developments, pondered alternatives and watched ideas generate more ideas in his imagination, so the governess, in conversations with Mrs Grose that serve the function of the notebook, converts the events into a narrative. The governess 'sees' a woman in black; she declares that the woman is the former governess Miss Jessel: 'I had thought it all out' (XII, 204). Prompted by Mrs Grose's questions, the governess accounts for Flora: the child gave no sign of seeing anything because she determined to conceal from her governess her knowledge of Miss Jessel's intention 'to get a hold of her' (XII, 206). As James in his notebooks wrote of one subject: 'All sorts of possibilities vaguely occur to one as latent in it'; of another, 'there seems to me much in this . . . to be gouged out',[26] so the governess declares excitedly to Mrs Grose: '. . . there are depth, depths! The more I go over it the more I see in it, and the more I see in it the more I fear' (XII, 204).

Several critics have noted that the governess in constructing a narrative assumes the functions of a novelist, that 'in crafting her story she is like the writer in her efforts'.[27] But most critics see her novelizing as evidence of neurotic instability, or at least proof that she is an unreliable narrator. One critic even regards her as James's 'most sinister vision of the power of the maker of the tale'.[28] At the other extreme, a sceptic doubtful of the governess's ability to write her own story suggests the possibility of a ghost writer, as Freud wrote the story of Miss Lucy.[29]

The critical fate of the governess assumes added significance when compared with critical responses to the male narrator of *The Sacred Fount*, published three years after 'The Turn of the Screw'. Like the governess, the male narrator of the novel reads meaning into appearances, posits supernatural forces to explain otherwise inexplicable events, and converts appearances into evidence that supports his premises. He, too, encounters denial and disbelief in the woman who had been his confederate. But critics have been far more disposed to see the narrator of *The Sacred Fount* as an artist or an artist *manqué* or a surrogate of Henry James than to credit the governess with creative powers. Tony Tanner makes the conventional distinction, attributing the governess's vision to 'an intense disordered imagination' but ascribing to the narrator of *The Sacred Fount* 'the artistic instinct' and 'the power of [the] creative imagination to bring events to pass'.[30] The governess, when perceived as a creator, usually represents to critics the dark destructive side of the artist's imagination.

The governess is directly implicated in the breakdown of Flora and the death of Miles; no one dies in *The Sacred Fount*, and the narrator's notion that characters act at the bidding of his 'creative intelligence' seems a harmless fancy since no one apparently is seriously affected by his speculations. But the different responses elicited by the female narrator and the male narrator – both unnamed, both obsessed, both fabricators of meaning – suggest a positive answer to the question raised by Jean Frantz Blackall: 'Do matters of gender, the characters' sexual identities, their relative status in the social hierarchy, and their power relative to that status affect the authority with which these characters address the reader?'[31]

IV

Even more conclusively than James's first-person narrators, the
professional writers in his fiction are differentiated by their sex. It
is true that both his male and female journalists are insensitive
violators of others' private lives, but the male journalists (for
example George Flack, Mathias Pardon) are more aggressive and
crass than female journalists such as Henrietta Stackpole and Ade-
laide Wenham. The obverse is true of the woman novelists, who are
invariably inferior to the men. The more financially successful the
women writers are, the more abysmally they' fail as artists. The
popular romances they write to divert the philistines in 'the age of
trash triumphant' not only violate the principles of realism but
debase the English language. According to the male narrator-critic
of 'Greville Fane', the title character, who depicts 'passion in high
life' (XVI, 114) in the Victorian equivalent of the Harlequin Romance, is incapable of writing 'a page of English' or contributing 'a
sentence to the language' (XVI, 113). The narrator represents himself as her friend but ungallantly compares her to 'an old sausage
mill' that grinds out 'any poor verbal scrap that had been dropped
into her' (XVI, 116).

Greville Fane at least can claim to be an honest hack: 'she made no
pretence of producing works of art' (XVI, 116). 'Amy Evans', the
pretentious female novelist in 'The Velvet Glove' – suggestive of
Edith Wharton in her appellation 'the Princess', the title of her
novel *The Top of the Tree*, her motor car, and her palatial residence
in Paris – is exposed by a passage from her novel encrusted with
adjectives and mythology which begins: 'The loveliness of the face,
which was that of the glorious period in which Pheidias reigned
supreme. . . .' (CT, XII, 249). At the other extreme, Miss Amy Frush
('The Third Person'), author of 'a novel that had been anonymously
published and a play that had been strikingly type-copied' (CT, XI,
136), has no literary identity at all. The only female writer James
does not satirize is Mrs Harvey ('Broken Wings') who has the merit
of having lost her popularity after publishing 'eight or ten' 'su-
premely happy novels' (CT, XI, 234). In the story, she expects to be
fired from her current position on a provincial newspaper for
which she writes a 'London Letter' for three and ninepence.

As consistently as James mocked and patronized female novelists, he elevated male novelists, endowing them with intelligence,
imagination, and a sense of style and form so lacking in the female

writers. Beginning with Mark Ambient in 'The Author of Beltraffio' (1884) James created more than a dozen novelists cast from the same mould. They are mature consummate artists, in James's words 'enamoured of perfection', 'of high aesthetic temper' (XV, viii, x). They are almost always portrayed through the eyes of an adoring young male disciple, who more often than not is himself an aspiring novelist or literary critic and the narrator of the tale. He thus relieves James of responsibility for proclaiming the greatness of the idolized writer. The reader must take it from the narrator that Mark Ambient is 'a man of genius' (XVI, 7), that Clare Vawdrey ('The Private Life') is 'the greatest (in the opinion of many) of literary glories' (XVII, 217), that the work of Neil Paraday ('The Death of the Lion') is distinguished by 'fine maturities', and themes 'singularly rich' and 'infinitely noble' (XV, 106, 107).

James countered the criticism that he had idealized his artists, saying in effect: if such artists did not exist, they should be imagined as a protest 'against the rule of the cheap and easy' (XV, x). Through his 'supersubtle fry' as he called them (XV, ix), James also expressed his pained awareness that he himself failed to achieve the popular success (and large royalties) enjoyed by writers he scorned. Despite their greatness, the male novelists of his fiction are figures of pathos, either exploited and lionized by a public that never understands or even reads their work ('The Death of the Lion', 'The Figure in the Carpet') or unappreciated and unrecognized save by a few discriminating readers ('John Delavoy', 'The Middle Years'). Several novelists, exhausted by their unremitting, unrewarded labour, fall ill and die before the tale ends ('The Death of the Lion', 'The Middle Years', 'The Next Time', 'The Figure in the Carpet').

James represents the stricken male novelists as victims of a gross mercenary society in which a striking feature, 'the masculinization of women' – as a French female critic termed it – exemplified for him 'the great modern collapse of all the forms and "superstitions" and respects'. He saw the process of masculinization, in which he recognized 'a big comprehensive subject', primarily as a system of economic exploitation. Women had become masculinized, he believed, not because they wished to be like men but because 'in many departments and directions the cheap work they can easily do is more and more all the "public wants".'[32] If one reads the operative word *cheap* to mean shoddy, produced and enjoyed with little mental effort, the statement applies to women novelists as

James portrayed them – workers producing the commodity that sells best.

In 'The Death of the Lion', James carried the process a step further: women are so successful in the marketplace that male novelists assume female identities. At a country-house party attended by the narrator and Neil Paraday, the 'lion' of the moment, the guests include not only 'Guy Walsingham', in reality, Miss Collop, but also 'Dora Forbes', in reality 'an indubitable male' (XV, 116) with a red moustache. The narrator reflects that 'in the age we live in one gets lost among the genders and the pronouns' (XV, 144). But once a male writer takes a woman's name, he apparently loses his masculine superiority. Nothing suggests that 'Dora Forbes' is any better than 'Guy Walsingham'. They seem interchangeable except that the male 'Dora Forbes', according to a journalist, has the advantage of generating 'a great deal of interest' by writing as a woman. 'There's every prospect of its being widely imitated' (XV, 116). Possible models for 'Dora Forbes', who is never named, include William Sharp, who published under the name Fiona McLeod, and Henry Adams, the author of *Esther* by Frances Snow Compton.

James made his most extended transposition of gender roles in 'The Next Time', in which a male narrator, a literary critic of refined perceptions and little income, contrasts the ironic fates of a male and a female novelist. The woman, Jane Highmore, longs desperately to write a literary masterpiece, 'to do something artistic', something 'subtle' and 'exquisite' (XV, 158, 160). But she cannot escape 'the hard doom of popularity' (XV, 160) and can only produce one trashy bestseller after another. Her novels bring in so much money, however, that she, not her husband, is the supporter of the family.

Her brother-in-law, Ray Limbert, also a novelist, longs desperately to write a bestseller; he declares, 'I want to sell . . . I must cultivate the market' (XV, 188) and proposes to study his sister-in-law's methods. But despite his efforts to be 'obvious' and 'popular' (XV, 188), he can produce only one unsaleable masterpiece after another. Like the narrator of 'John Delavoy', he fails to satisfy an editor who demands literary notes that are chatty and personal. Limbert asserts that his work is 'the very worst he can do for the money' (XV, 171) – James's words to the editor of the *Herald Tribune*, who terminated James's assignment to write 'Letters from Paris'. Limbert loses an editorial position when he refuses to replace the narrator's essays with the 'screaming sketches' of Minnie Meadows, 'the new lady-humorist every one seems talking about' (XV, 200).

The narrator's moral is clear: 'you can't make a sow's ear of a silk purse' (XV, 204), but the masculine and feminine roles are not so neatly reversed. Ray Limbert is so unsuccessful in the marketplace that he must accept money from his sister-in-law to pay his bills. Her efforts to transform him into a virile money-maker – 'she cocked up his hat, she pricked up his prudence' (XV, 181) – are doomed to fail. Limbert's unwanted masterpieces are described as *exquisite, subtle* and *charming* – words commonly associated with the feminine style in literature. The narrator compares Limbert to the parent who longs for boys but can father only girls. Every novel he publishes he hopes will be a bestseller, 'a bouncing boy', but every novel disappoints him by being yet 'another female child' (XV, 214). (Apparently the traditional notion that the male is the preferred sex in babies is more potent than the identification of bestsellers with female authorship.) Limbert's female child novels, however, are not only 'charming with all his charm', but 'powerful with all his power' (XV, 194). The 'shyer secrets' that Limbert's novels reveal on a second reading resemble not only those of 'a beautiful woman more denuded' but those of an art traditionally considered masculine – 'a great symphony on a new hearing' (XV, 196). At the end, Limbert dies of fever before completing a novel titled 'Derogation'. But he has written books that will live and he has fathered five children to bear his name. Jane Highmore survives in robust health, but her only children are her novels – 'a little family, in sets of triplets' (XV, 164), each destined to perish with the season.

The polarized novelists in 'The Next Time' might suggest that James saw art and commerce as opposing, mutually exclusive realms, but in fact he accepted their unbreakable connection from the beginning of his professional career when he negotiated the sale of his first stories. In his fiction, all his writers – male and female – want their work to be published and paid for. But James treats his writers differently in their relation to the marketplace. His narrator satirizes Greville Fane and Mrs Highmore, but he does not mock Ray Limbert for trying to emulate them, partly because James wants to make it clear that Limbert will fail to be obvious and popular.

But if a male novelist writes a bestselling book, his success in the marketplace does not compromise or corrupt him. John Berridge

('The Velvet Glove'), whose popular novel and play *Heart of Gold* makes his critical opinion worth money, proves himself a man of principle when he refuses to write a preface for the latest romance of the pseudonymous 'Amy Evans'. She betrays her mercenary motives when she proposes to trade the promise of her sexual favour for praise that will sell her novel.

In James's fiction, only male writers of high culture can operate in the marketplace yet remain above it. His female writers who, like the men, aspire to be artists and also sell their stories, are doubly exposed to the satirist's wit. James derides Susan Stringham, the companion of Milly Theale in *The Wings of the Dove*, both in her commercial success and in her cultural aspirations. He patronizes her as a 'contributor to the best magazines', who 'fondly believed she had her "note", the art of showing New England without showing it wholly in the kitchen' (XIX, 107); he mocks her adulation of 'masters, models, celebrities, mainly foreign . . . in whose light she ingeniously laboured' (XIX, 107). He pictures her 'little life' as a structure with 'narrow walls' and 'rather dim windows' through which she sees the fabulously wealthy Milly Theale as a princess in a 'legend . . . of romantic isolation' (XIX, 104, 106). That James is using her to help create the romantic aura he himself wished to surround his doomed heroine does not mitigate his derisive view of her romanticism.[33]

Greville Fane, who has to learn from her son 'about City slang and the way men talk at clubs' (XVI, 125), tells the narrator that 'she had found her sex a dreadful drawback' (XVI, 120). She is laughable in thinking that by wearing trousers as George Sand did, 'she could have written as well as that lady' (XVI, 121). But she is right in her main point. A woman writer in the Victorian society James represents is restricted by her inability to go where men go. She labours in a marketplace where all the organs of publication – magazines, books, newspapers – are controlled by men. Finally, in James's view, she is handicapped from the start by limitations he believed inherent in her sex.

V

Given James's elevation of his male novelists over their female competitors, one would expect a similar bias to determine his portrayal of public speakers. But the male–female polarity all but collapses when his characters become orators. Unlike Howells, James never exalts the pulpit or the platform as a site of male authority and mastery. His fiction reveals a lifelong aversion to public exhortation, and an instinctive suspicion of charismatic speakers, whatever their sex. In contrast to Howells, who affirmed his own democratic ideals in the sermons of his fictional ministers, James made most of his ministers either humourless Puritan moralists like Babcock in *The American* and Brand in *The Europeans* or artful hypocrites like Hubert Lawrence.

James's politicians are either urbane aristocrats like Sir Rufus Chasemore ('A Modern Warning') and Lord Warburton (*The Portrait of a Lady*), who enjoy taking political views that do not threaten their positions, or they are pompous fools like Edward Antrobus MP and Lord Northmore, 'a great political figure' whose posthumously published letters reveal 'an abyss of inanity' ('The Abasement of the Northmores', XI, 127). Nick Dormer, in *The Tragic Muse*, speaks for James when he denounces campaign oratory as 'a cursed humbugging trick' which 'has nothing to do with the truth' but instead appeals 'to everything that for one's self one despises . . . to stupidity, to ignorance, to prejudice, to the love of names and phrases, the love of hollow idiotic words, of shutting the eyes tight and making a noise' (VII, 103). Nick Dormer wins election to Parliament but redeems himself by resigning his seat and renouncing public life to be a portrait painter.

One should remember these male figures when reading *The Bostonians* (1886), James's most sustained satire, which engages almost all its characters, male and female, in a prolonged struggle to control the career of a female public speaker for the cause of women's rights. Because all the public figures identified by name are women, if the novel is isolated from the rest of James's fiction it might appear that James singled out women speakers as the chief offenders against taste and reason. But the images associated with the veteran female reformers in *The Bostonians* – featureless statues and mask-like faces of 'lithographic smoothness' reflective of the glare of 'ugly lecture-lamps'[34] – these images signify the loss of identity and the affront to the senses that James identified with male as well as female public speakers, with MPs in Westminster as well as reformers in Boston.

But in *The Bostonians* as in *The Tragic Muse*, James made women the most ardent supporters of causes and cast a male character as the chief critic of oratory that captivates audiences and wins public office. In presenting Verena Tarrant, James locates his standard of judgement – not in the passionate admiration of Olive Chancellor, Verena's ardent friend and sponsor, but in the speculative scrutiny of Basil Ransom, Olive's cousin from Mississippi and the suitor of Verena, who at the end literally wrests Verena from Olive's control. James presents Verena's two public performances through the impressions of Ransom, who identifies Verena as an *improvisatrice,* 'naturally theatrical' (B, 44), a 'personality' as she would be called today, important not for her ideas but for her power to charm audiences by the beauty of her voice and her presence. After her second performance, he concludes that 'she might easily have a big career, like that of a distinguished actress or singer' (B, 271).

Ransom is not only the novel's primary register of Verena's spellbinding power over audiences; as the chief opponent of the cause she and Olive champion, he is the most uncompromising critic of her speeches, which he denounces as 'third-rate palaver', and 'perfected humbug' (B, 271). 'The stiffest of conservatives' (B, 51), he is, of course, a biased observer with potent reasons, apart from his political views, for finding Verena's speeches worthless, 'the veriest trash', 'neither worth answering nor worth considering' (B, 227). Her power to attract rich backers and fill the lecture halls of Boston with ticketholders exacerbates Ransom's sense of inadequacy in failing to build a lucrative law practice in New York. And he can better justify his relentless courtship, predicated on his determination to end Verena's public career, if he believes that career to be pernicious, destructive of social order and a violation of her true nature.

But James does not depend on Ransom's vitriolic epithets to expose the intellectual poverty of Verena's performance. He presents page-long passages from her two speeches so that readers may judge for themselves. Her first speech, delivered as in a trance, before an ill-dressed unfashionable gathering of enthusiasts at the home of Miss Birdseye, Boston's most venerable philanthropist, is correspondingly untutored and artless. Decrying the sorry state to which men have brought the world, Verena rambles to exclamatory intensity, then collapses into anticlimax and banality.

'Wars, always more wars, and always more and more. Blood, blood – the world is drenched with blood! To kill each other, with all sorts of expensive and perfected instruments, that is the most brilliant thing they have been able to invent. It seems to me that we might stop it, we might invent something better. The cruelty

– the cruelty; there is so much, so much! Why shouldn't tenderness come in?' (B, 52)

After two pages of this, Ransom's criticism seems surprisingly restrained. 'It was full of school-girl phrases, of patches of remembered eloquence, of childish lapses of logic' (B, 51).

When months later Ransom hears Verena address several hundred fashionable New Yorkers, he recalls her first appearance and appreciates her gain in conscious power and authority. 'This exhibition was much more complete, her manner much more assured; she seemed to speak and survey the whole place from a much greater height' (B, 223). (Elevation was James's favourite image of artistic power.)

Unlike Verena's unstructured outpouring at Miss Birdseye's, the second speech is like a written text, rehearsed and delivered from memory. Here Verena deploys the orator's traditional strategies:

the rhetorical challenge: 'Who dares to say "all" when we are not there?' (B, 226);

apostrophe: 'Good gentlemen all' (B, 226);

paraleipsis: 'I shall not touch upon the subject of men's being most easily influenced by considerations of what is most agreeable and profitable for *them*' (B, 226);

metaphor: 'We require simply freedom; we require the lid to be taken off the box in which we have been kept for centuries' (B, 226–7);

anticipation of opponent's response: 'You say it's a very comfortable, cozy, convenient box, with nice glass sides, so that we can see out, and that all that's wanted is to give another quiet turn to the key' (B, 227);

rebuttal: 'That is very easily answered. Good gentleman, you have never been in the box, and you haven't the least idea how it feels' (B, 227).

Verena's performance at Mrs Burrage's is the most visible measure of Olive's success in undertaking to 'train and polish' (B, 99) Verena's qualities. Who composed the speech is not indicated – one assumes that the two friends collaborated – but Verena's poise, authority and command of the orator's techniques reflect the 'educative process' (B, 107) including reading, conversation and

European travel, that Verena has undergone during her months as Olive's housemate and constant companion.[35]

The speech itself, however, has little more intellectual substance than Verena's first performance, at Miss Birdseye's. Her vocabulary has expanded to include such words as *sovereign, elixir, inestimable, recriminate* and *transfigure*, but her metaphors are merely substitutes for analysis. The speech owes its power to the fact that Verena is 'unspeakably attractive' (B, 227); in itself, it is, as Ransom perceives, 'vague, thin, rambling, a tissue of generalities' with the value 'of a pretty essay, committed to memory and delivered by a bright girl at an "academy" ' (B, 227). It is notable that at both performances Ransom diminishes Verena by comparing her to a schoolgirl.

That James rarely enters Verena's mind and presents her political views primarily through her speeches suggests that she does not think for herself but like an actress recites the scripts composed by others. But the common view of Verena as an empty vessel into which others pour their ideas misrepresents James's conception of her. Unlike Pansy Osmond, she is never compared to a blank page on which others write their texts. Far from exhibiting the 'blank passivity' that one critic ascribes to her,[36] she is given a 'quick sensibility' (B, 76), and a ready wit in repartee with men who lead her on. She counters Ransom, her most aggressive critic, 'with a high spirit of retort' (B, 276).

James also favours Verena by allowing her to speak unflawed standard English. Although her father began as an uneducated vendor of lead-pencils, although she lacks the 'home-culture' (B, 76) that Olive will provide, Verena, in Mrs Farrinder's words, 'has a fine command of language' (B, 55), the ability not only to emit 'streams' of eloquence (B, 63) as Mrs Tarrant believes, but to speak without solecisms. Unlike Dr Prance, who presumably has more education than any of the Tarrants, Verena never says 'I don't know as' – the substandard locution Howells made the chief linguistic mark of provincial or lower-class origins.

Both Ransom and Olive consider themselves qualified to judge and educate Verena, to decide what is best for her. But neither exhibits greater intellectual depth than she does. Their dominant impulse is to possess and control, where hers is to please. Unlike her, they are fixed in their point of view, immovable in their opposition to the position the other represents. But they convey ideas with the same rhetorical formulas and clichés that Ransom criticizes in Verena's speeches. His outburst to Verena exhibits the very qualities he condemns in post-Civil War culture:

> '. . . it's a feminine, a nervous, hysterical, chattering, canting age, an age of hollow phrases and false delicacy and exaggerated solicitudes and coddled sensibilities, which, if we don't soon look out, will usher in the reign of mediocrity, of the feeblest and flattest and the most pretentious that has ever been.' (B , 283)

The narrator dissociates himself from this harangue by patronizing Ransom, 'the poor fellow', and his 'narrow notions' (B, 283)

But the narrator's undercutting of Olive's hyperbolic reflections, by inserting ironic parenthetical asides into her feverish monologues, is more deadly. After recording Olive's longing to martyr herself for the cause of women's rights, 'asking no better fate than to die for it', the narrator coolly reflects: 'It was not clear to this interesting girl in what manner such a sacrifice (as this last) would be required of her . . .' (B, 30).

The narrator's irony makes it impossible to take seriously Olive's vision of 'the sacred cause', 'the just revolution' that would 'exact from the other, the brutal, blood-stained, ravening race, the last particle of expiation!' (B, 30). Like Olive, Ransom mentally expresses frustrated desire in images of violence, but his are truly chilling for they are directed at the person he loves and he has the power to perform the act. Thinking of Verena's public success in New York he reflects that 'if he should become her husband he should know a way to strike her dumb' (B, 271). Apparently, he does not consider that in silencing Verena he will destroy the power to captivate large audiences that enthralled him, and that once married to him she will no longer have the allure of the prize to be won.

None of James's characters has elicited more diverse responses from readers than Ransom; none has more clearly revealed competing ideologies informing criticism in the past several decades. Until the 1970s, most critics saw Ransom in positive terms, 'the knight in armor that shines brightly because he has intellectual integrity', a chivalric hero, champion of health and heterosexuality, who rescues Verena from life-denying bondage to a morbid woman.[37] In more recent readings, the one-time hero, stripped of his armor, emerges as cruel, predatory, and ruthless, a 'rigid personality' in whom 'inner tension' turns into a 'controlled aggression'.[38]

How James viewed Ransom can only be surmised. (He says nothing of Ransom's qualities in his Notebook entries.) The narrator of the novel holds himself superior to both Olive and Ransom (and to all the other characters), but he subjects Olive more than Ransom to that irony that invites readers to see a character as self-deluded, illogical and morally blind. By introducing almost all the characters – Olive, Mrs Luna, Dr Prance, Mrs Farrinder, Miss Birdseye, the Tarrants – as Ransom first sees them, James establishes him as the centre whose impressions, often corroborated by the narrator, the reader is encouraged to accept. The narrator's final words – that Verena's tears as she enters a union 'so far from brilliant' are destined not to be her last – should disabuse the reader of the notion that Verena, silenced in marriage, has exchanged the better for the worse fate. But James also makes it clear that Ransom in wresting Verena from her expectant audience at the Music Hall has not deprived society of any enlightenment. Society loses nothing of substance if Verena never speaks in public again.

In later letters James expressed indifference or hostility to the struggle for women's suffrage in England. But his hostility to feminist causes in *The Bostonians* is part of a greater mistrust of all political causes and the oratory that promotes them. *The Bostonians* indicates one source of his mistrust – his recognition of the power of speakers to mesmerize audiences by their charismatic personalities, sexual magnetism and seductive voices. Verena on the platform offends against genteel prejudice against women speaking in public, but much more important is her extraordinary personal success, matched by no other public character – male or female – that James portrayed. Olive and Verena cannot prevail against the will of Ransom in a patriarchal society, but together the two woman represent power that requires the most relentless man in James's fiction to suppress.

VI

Few writers have equalled James in reverence for order and hierarchy, expressed in the desire to see distinctions preserved in every part of civilized life. In his preface to *The Awkward Age*, he affirmed the eternal verity of literary 'kinds', 'the very life of literature', upon which 'truth and strength' depend. On the 'confusion of kinds' he blamed 'the inelegance of letters and the stultification of values' (IX, xvii). He saw in the lamentable condition of the English stage in the 1890s evidence of 'the great general change which has come over English morals – of the confusion of many things which were formerly kept distinct'.[39]

As he deplored the lapse of distinctions in Victorian English society, so in *The American Scene* he dwelt on the absence of order in 'our vast crude democracy of trade' where the ugliness of New England towns was traceable to 'the so complete abolition of *forms*', where immigrants quickly lost the 'manners' which had once defined them, where architecture effaced distinctions between the public and the private by sacrificing 'enclosing walls' for 'the indefinite extension of all spaces and the definite merging of all functions'.[40] In the same spirit that he criticized the 'masculinization' of English society, namely the infusion of women in the business world, he analysed the contrasting situation in society in the United States: 'a picture poor in the male presence', caused by 'the failure of the sexes to keep step socially', resulting in a 'queer deep split or chasm'.[41] Although he satirized Basil Ransom, who fulminates against the 'feminization' of American society, he satirized more sharply the dysfunctions of that society in which a father sells his daughter to a rich young woman seeking companionship, and a young man's proposal of marriage is conveyed by his mother to the woman whose friend he wishes to marry.

By 1890, lament for the loss of distinctions and forms is a recurrent theme in James's essays and letters. But not all 'confusions' were to be condemned; his fiction conveys attitudes more complex than simple disapproval. In particular, his treatment of gender roles subverts as well as reinforces the binary oppositions he maintained in his criticism. It is true that his male characters such as Hubert Lawrence and Roderick Hudson, whose traits are characterized by the word *feminine*, are morally inferior. But characters such as Roger Lawrence and Rowland Mallet, morally dubious in their control of another's life, nevertheless secure the narrator's approval by exhibiting the traditionally feminine qualities of gentleness, sensitivity and forbearance. The greater the genius of James's male writers in the artist tales, the more readily do they assume the roles of invalid, victim, or dependant – roles traditionally assigned to women. Although James always viewed women writers as inferior to men, in his Prefaces to the New York Edition of his fiction, he defines literary creation in metaphors of female activities – cooking, embroidery and the nurture of children

– as well as the masculine pursuits – hunting, mining, and exploring.

In the realist fiction of the first half of his career, James's female characters, especially comic figures such as Mrs Hudson (*Roderick Hudson*) and Aunt Penniman (*Washington Square*) exhibit habits of speech habitually ascribed to women: exaggeration, intensity, verbosity, loquacity, illogic. But in the late novels, notably *The Awkward Age*, *The Ambassadors*, *The Wings of the Dove* and *The Golden Bowl*, male and female characters of the same class speak the same language: they use the same syntax; they have the same vocabularies. On their lips words such as *wonderful, prodigious, beautiful* and *splendid* are no longer the stigmatized 'women's words' but private signs, ceaselessly modulating, to be understood only by the initiated.

James often compared the drama of his characters to the playing of a game, their conversations to contests with well-matched players who are sometimes opponents, sometimes partners. Men and women may work together to tease meaning out of a remark and to expand the implications of each other's words. As Ruth Yeazell has noted, the characters of James's late novels are 'verbal collaborators' who 'build on one another's formulations'.[42] When one character controls a conversation it is usually the woman, as Maria Gostrey guides Strether to a new understanding of what he sees and hears; as Kate Croy through her words draws Densher into the role she conceives for him.[43] In the end it is the male characters – Strether and Densher – who make the decisive choices, but beginning with *The Princess Casamassima*, in almost all James's novels the effect of women upon the main male character is more profound than his effect upon them.

James's love of symmetry often dictated that the acts of one sex be balanced by the acts of the other. But in many of his novels and novellas, the central female character is superior to the male characters in energy or intelligence or strength of purpose. If the woman's destiny ultimately depends on the decisions men make, men owe their power less to their own resources than to the laws and codes of Victorian patriarchal society. None of James's women escapes the bonds of this society or seeks to live outside it. But James grants to many of his women characters the powers of expression and insight that make them the equals of men – until they venture into the literary marketplace. There only male writers have the privilege of writing masterpieces that unite the highest powers of the masculine and feminine, masterpieces rejected by an unperceiving public which helps to destroy the artist as well. In the little band of choice spirits who can recognize the master, however, women have their place.

4
Language and Convention in Wharton's Hieroglyphic World

The fashionable New York society into which Edith Wharton was born in 1862 included no female novelist in its ranks. Indeed, her society relegated writers and artists to the margins of its world, if it granted them any place at all. In her autobiography, *A Backward Glance*, Wharton recalled that New York literary society, composed of men who 'foregathered at the Century Club',[1] maintained the most tenuous connection to the 'social aristocracy' to which her parents belonged. During her childhood and adolescence, she found intellectual companionship chiefly in the books in her father's library. After her marriage, when she began to publish poetry and fiction and won international recognition with her first volume of short stories, *The Greater Inclination* (1899), she found the spiritual kinship she sought, not in associations with women writers, but in friendships with men of her own class: among her literary mentors and friends were her editors at Scribner's, William Brownell and Edward Burlingame; later, Henry James; and above all, the New York lawyer, Walter Berry, the lifelong friend and critic who was, she said, 'an expansion, an interpretation, of one's self, the very meaning of one's soul' (BG, 115).

The only woman to whom she acknowledged a literary debt was the English novelist and critic Vernon Lee, the author of studies of Italian art and aesthetic philosophy.[2] Wharton publicly separated herself from the tradition of domestic fiction that she identified with women writers in America; she disparaged the work of female predecessors such as Mary Wilkins Freeman, Sarah Orne Jewett and Louisa May Alcott.[3]

In that Wharton found her literary companionship among men and sought her place in the ranks of the male novelists, she regarded literature as a man's vocation. The writers she celebrated in *The Writing of Fiction* were Balzac, Tolstoy, Thackeray, James and

86

Proust. But she did not conceive of the writers she revered as belonging to a masculine tradition inherently hostile to women. It is true, she was sensitive to the prejudice against women writers; she attacked the double standard that allowed critics to praise male writers such as Milton and Goethe for drawing metaphors and analogies from modern science while claiming that George Eliot 'sterilized her imagination' and 'deformed her style' by studying biology.[4] But she did not seek to create or validate a woman's tradition implicit in the idea of a masculine tradition to which women are alien. Unlike Virginia Woolf, she did not regard the language of English literature as the creation of men, its syntax ill-suited to the needs of the female writer.[5] She did not view the English language itself as an instrument of male domination or feel the need to create a new sentence or a new language. Paradoxically, the fashionable society which marginalized writers, denied her literary companionship and never acknowledged her importance as a writer, in at least one way made men and women equal. In upholding as part of its code of manners a standard of speech to which both men and women were taught to conform, her society made its language the possession and privilege of both its male and female members.

I

Edith Wharton traced her conception of 'good English' to the example and instruction of her parents, who insisted that their children speak the language with 'scrupulous perfection' (BG, 48–9). In *A Backward Glance*, she recalled the importance parents, tutors and governesses placed upon 'niceties of speech', an essential element in 'good breeding'. To speak 'bad' English was to be guilty of 'bad manners' – the 'supreme offence' (BG, 52). Important as any element of her early education, Wharton remembered, was 'a reverence for the English language as spoken according to the best usage' (BG, 48).

Wharton devotes several pages of her autobiography to the ways by which the adults – parents and older brothers – imparted their standard of the 'best usage' – natural idiomatic speech, neither pedantic and pompous nor lax and careless. From their example she learned to shun slovenly phrases such as 'a great ways', 'any place' (for 'anywhere') and 'back of' (for 'behind'), as well as

locutions of the pseudo-cultured such as *gotten* and *you would better*
(BG, 50–1). She was allowed to indulge in 'the humour and expressive side of American slang' so long as she remembered that
slang was not 'pure English' (BG, 50). Her mother's tart criticisms
seem to have cut deeper than her brothers' 'wholesome derision'
that deflated her childish self-importance. In her satire of uncouth
speakers in her fiction, Wharton perhaps transmitted the sting of
ridicule she herself felt in her mother's 'ironic smile' and her caustic
response, 'Where did you pick *that* up?' when told that a caller's
visit lasted 'quite a while' (BG, 49).

In her childhood, Wharton recalled, the 'best tradition of spoken
English' was first undermined by the 'new class of uneducated
rich', 'the big money-makers from the West' beginning to arrive in
New York in the 1880s. They strove to assume 'existing traditions'
but said '*a* barracks' and '*a* woods', and '*a* phenomena', and were
deaf to 'all the inflexions and shades of meaning of our rich speech'
(BG, 50–1). Awareness of the loss is registered by a character in *Old
New York* (1924), who remembers that his parents 'never let any of
us children use a vulgar expression without correcting us' and is
said to protest 'the hazy verbiage with which American primary
culture was already corrupting our speech'.[6]

After the First World War, the shades and inflections Wharton
had learned to revere as signs of civilized society seemed to her like
relics of a dead age. In her essay, 'The Great American Novel'
(1927), she declared that the epithet *American* had become synonymous with the bland uniformity represented in Sinclair Lewis's
Main Street – a 'dead level of prosperity and security' achieved by
conformists who prized telephones and cars and modern plumbing
more than sculpture and painting and did not even perceive themselves lost to the sources of European culture that had once formed
the 'common heritage' of English-speaking peoples. As a conse-
quence, language, like the telephones and the plumbing, had
become standardized, reduced to a 'mere instrument of utility'.[7]

In this essay, Wharton explicitly linked the preservation of 'the
best usage' to the existence of clearly defined social classes. A
society that preserved nuances and shades in language, which
knew that *a wood* might be defined by 'the innumerable shadings of
coppice, copse, spinney, covert, brake, holt, grove' (p. 650) was a
society that discriminated as precisely in defining social relations
and prescribing the manners appropriate to each. The impoverish-
ment of the language Wharton attributed to the disappearance in

America of 'traditional society, with its old-established distinctions of class, its pass-words, exclusions, delicate shades of language and behavior . . .' (p. 652).

Edith Wharton most fully represented the language and behaviour of 'traditional society' in portrayals of the New York 'social aristocracy' to which her parents belonged. The virtues and defects, as she remembered them, in the world of her childhood are most fully documented in *The Age of Innocence* (1920), in which Anglo-Dutch society in the 1870s reposes in the full ripeness that precedes decay. Vestiges of the old order appear on the periphery of turn-of-the-century fashionable New York in *The House of Mirth* (1904), in the glacial person of Lily Bart's aunt, Mrs Peniston. For Undine Spragg in *The Custom of the Country* (1913), the families that ruled New York society in the 1870s represent only meaningless conventions observed by ineffectual figures she soon leaves behind in her triumphal march of social conquest. In the four novellas of *Old New York*, set in successive decades of the nineteenth century, the fates of characters who deviate from convention reveal both the power of the old order and the forces presaging change. In the later novels, the 'delicate shades' of language, if not of behaviour, are preserved by such characters as Kate Clephane (*The Mother's Recompense*, 1925), Rose Sellars (*The Children*, 1928) and Halo Tarrant (*The Gods Arrive*, 1932) who leave New York to live abroad and seek in inherited traditions a bulwark against the disintegrating culture of promiscuous pleasure-seekers assembled at Europe's casinos and spas.

Characters of 'traditional society' observe conventions compromised by the defects of their virtues. Conformity to an ideal of 'best usage' produces speakers who unite grace and force and make every word count. Habitual observance of the polite forms saves characters from displaying their worst selves and wounding others. But politeness and self-restraint may degenerate into prudery and evasion. The refusal to speak certain words may lead one to deny the realities they signify. Repression of feeling may atrophy emotion. For Edith Wharton, the crippling vice of old New York society was the code which forbade talk of the unpleasant and the scandalous and elevated equivocation to a moral duty.

Societies that forbade bold speaking in women also held women more responsible than men for the very codes that constricted women more than men. The double standard that condemned in

women behaviour it condoned in men naturally restricted
women's speech as well as their actions. For both sexes, such words
as *mistress, sex, bastard* and *adulterer* were taboo in fashionable
drawing rooms; women were doubly constrained, however, when
the speaking of a word implied knowledge that convention forbade. But when women owed their sense of identity to their position in a society that demanded their conformity, when they
instilled in their daughters allegiance to the code they had inter-
nalized and when they ostracized women who violated it, then
women appeared to be agents, not victims, of the system.

Wharton had in her own mother compelling evidence of the
importance of women in sustaining the social order. Such works as
The Age of Innocence and *Old New York* portray women powerful in
their roles as social arbiters and guides. But Wharton's fiction re-
futes the conventional idea that women were more instrumental
than men in perpetuating the codes that sanctioned evasion and
denial. Despite the stifling force of convention – or perhaps because
of it – women, not men, in Wharton's fiction make the decisive
breaks with social codes. Not only do they voice truths men do not
acknowledge; they, not their husbands, defy coercive families and
end stultifying marriages to seek happiness and self-fulfilment,
often with artists on the margins of the fashionable world. Whether
Wharton's imagination naturally gave more energy to her female
characters than to the male, whether she believed that repressive
codes most powerfully impel to rebellion the persons they most
relentlessly repress, whether the sense of imprisonment she suffered in her own marriage moved her to write narratives of escape,
she repeatedly portrayed the woman who sacrifices home and
position and family to escape immolation on the altar of socially
prescribed duty. She appears as Lydia Tillotson in 'Souls Belated',
Christine Ansley in 'Joy in the House', Mrs Lidcote in 'Autre
Temps', Kate Clephane in *The Mother's Recompense* and Halo Tarrant in *The Gods Arrive*.

In what seems a reversal of traditional roles, male characters are
often passive registers of the effects of the code that drives female
characters to defiant action. The forces compelling evasion and
denial are most fully analysed by reflective observers such as Newland Archer and Ralph Marvell, whose minds generate the images
and metaphors through which Wharton transforms concepts into
visible structures of imprisonment. But those characters who most
vividly imagine states of entrapment seem least able to escape

them, as if mental representation satisfied the need, or crippled the will, to act.

The lineaments of the male critic who reinforces the system he analyses appear in several of Wharton's early stories. The aspiring poet Birkton, in 'That Good May Come,' writes verses, consistently rejected by magazine editors, that purport to expose unsanctioned emotions behind the 'obligatory virtues' and the 'superficial fitnesses of life'.[8] To buy his sister a confirmation dress, he then retails unsigned licentious gossip to the editor of a scandal sheet. In 'The Line of Least Resistance', Mr Minden's craven acceptance of his wife's infidelity is approved by a society that defends 'the expediency of calling the Furies the Eumenides' (I, 218). Thursdale, in 'The Dilettante', a refined predator reminiscent of James's John Marcher and the first of Wharton males eager to form women, so successfully subjects his May Bartram to 'the discipline of his reticences and evasions' that she acquires verbal skills of concealment 'almost equal to his own' (I, 412). Thus Wharton begins to challenge the common assumption that women are the chief promoters of euphemism and evasion.

All these male characters are ironic portraits in which futility, not intelligence, is the dominant note. In *The Custom of the Country*, Wharton created in Ralph Marvell her first male analyst of the social code whose weakness is a function of insight and refinement that make him a tragic, not a comic, figure. Secure in a nexus of New York's interlocking ruling families, he has the marks of the fashionable class: a dilettante's cultivation of literary interests approved by his society as 'gentlemanly'; loyalty to ancestral traditions, even those he sees as outmoded; distaste for the parvenus' architectural hybrids expressive of the 'social disintegration' that disfigures Fifth Avenue and affirms the 'intrinsic rightness' of his grandfather's house in Washington Square.[9]

In marrying Undine Spragg, Ralph would seem to divorce himself from his past and of course his choice of the crude daughter of a Midwestern 'big money-maker' rather than a 'nice girl' of his class preferred by his mother is a break with tradition. But he does not propose to enter Undine's world of displaced westerners in rented mansions and hotel suites; rather, he proposes to draw her into his world, to guide her according to his own standard, to '[open] new windows in her mind' (CC, 718) – windows onto his own inner world peopled by poetic images from Rossetti and Whitman.

The tragedy of his life is that the marriage he believes will free him from repressive conventions ends in his complete bondage to them. When Undine abandons him, he believes that the responsibility for refusing to speak of his broken marriage rests upon his mother and sister, in whose vocabulary 'the word "divorce" was wrapped in such a dark veil of innuendo as no ladylike hand would care to lift' (CC, 842). But Ralph's hand is inert as well. Only when he loses custody of his son by refusing to defend himself in court against his wife's charges does he acknowledge his complicity in surrender to 'all the old family catch-words, the full and elaborate vocabulary of evasion: "delicacy", "pride", "personal dignity" ' (CC, 910). Perhaps the readings in anthropology that prompt him to classify his family and Undine's as the Aborigines and the Invaders encourage in him a deterministic view of his own case: 'The conventions of his class . . . had mysteriously mastered him, deflecting his course like some hidden hereditary failing' (CC, 911). In retrospect, the suffering that eventually drives him to suicide seems factitious, 'conventionalized and sentimentalized by this inherited attitude' (CC, 911). The implicit Darwinism is made explicit by another male observer and social analyst, Ralph's brother-in-law, who pronounces Ralph 'a survival and destined, as such, to go down in any conflict with the rising forces' (CC, 807). The narrator of the novel neither corroborates nor undercuts the characters' deterministic analysis, leaving the reader to judge whether Ralph is more the victim or the agent of the situation he blames for his fate.[10]

Men's responsibility for the code that imprisons the most sensitive of its male critics is made clear in the portrayal of Newland Archer, whose reflections in *The Age of Innocence* contain Wharton's classic statement of the effects of evasion in fashionable New York society. Despite differences among its members, Archer reflects, 'in reality they all lived in a kind of hieroglyphic world, where the real thing was never said or done or even thought, but only represented by a set of arbitrary signs'.[11] At the beginning of the novel, in the first days of his engagement to May Welland, than whom 'there was no better match in New York' (AI, 1044), he rejoices in her complete conformity to the code, in her 'resolute determination to carry to its utmost limit that ritual of ignoring the "unpleasant" in which they had both been brought up' (AI, 1035). When he senses that she herself understands her presence at the opera as the 'arbitrary sign' that Archer perceives it, he appreciates that the 'atmosphere of faint implications and pale delicacies', forbidding speech, promotes the silent communication that unites them as no 'explanation' could do (AI, 1028).

Archer's allegiance to the code is both undermined and strengthened when his role as legal counsellor to May's cousin, Ellen, the Countess Olenska, subjects him to conflicting impulses that ultimately paralyse him. He can perceive the hypocrisy in the 'verbal generosities' of his society that would chivalrously defend Madame Olenska's right to release from a dissolute husband so long as she doesn't seek a divorce; he can condemn such chivalry as the 'humbugging disguise of the inexorable conventions that . . . bound people down to the old pattern' (AI, 1049). Yet, in discussing Ellen's situation with her, he would deny its 'ugly reality', consigning her words to a 'vocabulary . . . unfamiliar to him' that 'seemed to belong to fiction and the stage' (AI, 1102). At the same time, he takes refuge in 'all the stock phrases' (AI, 1105) of his own convention, which to Ellen seems no less remote from reality as she knows it. When she exclaims to him, 'I don't speak your language' (AI, 1120), he reacts with angry jealousy of her admirer and would-be protector, the dubious speculator, Julius Beaufort, who, Archer is sure, 'understood every turn of her dialect and spoke it fluently' (AI, 1125).

So long as Archer perceives Beaufort as a rival, jealousy intensifies his need to find his highest value in his betrothed and 'the old New York note' as she sounds it (AI, 1091). When he understands that Ellen cares nothing for Beaufort, his defences against jealous pain give way, after his marriage, to undisguised longing to unite himself to Ellen. Yet even as he contemplates leaving May, his impulse to 'keep on the surface, in the prudent old New York way', survives (AI, 1105). Remaining the 'prisoner of [a] hackneyed vocabulary' (AI, 1261), he is more shocked by Ellen's speaking the word *mistress* than by his own adulterous fantasies. When his will to act seems most concentrated in the intent to speak, he seems most paralysed by the conventions he can objectify and criticize but cannot escape. At the formal dinner that May insists they give, ostensibly to honour Ellen on the eve of her return to Europe, in reality to signal her expulsion from the tribe, Archer's keenest perception of this most potent expression of the family's united will traps him in the vision of himself as utterly powerless, 'a prisoner in the centre of an armed camp', emasculated by the 'inexorableness of his captors' (AI, 1282).

That Wharton voices through Archer her own perceptions of New York society does not make him an infallible observer in every instance. In fact, his thoughts illustrate the inconsistencies inherent in the conventions he rebellingly obeys. He can perceive the symbolic value of May Welland in a world of 'arbitrary signs'; he can recognize her as the ultimate hieroglyph, 'the centre of this elaborate system of mystification'; he can define the paradox of the virginal center: 'the more inscrutable for her very frankness and assurance' (AI, 1051). But he persists in believing her possessed of a 'faculty of unawareness' that will never change (AI, 1164), that he will always know her thoughts, that her words and silences conceal nothing that will ever surprise him. Only years after her death does he learn from his son the depth of her understanding.

Like Ralph Marvell, Archer readily embraces the role of educating female innocence. Yet he can believe that men have no part in making the 'factitious purity' that young men of the genteel class seek in their brides (AI, 1051). He sees May as a sign created solely by other women, 'so cunningly manufactured by a conspiracy of mothers and aunts and grandmothers and long-dead ancestresses' (AI, 1051). He tosses off the thought that a woman is 'the subject creature and versed in the arts of the enslaved' (AI, 1259), but he sees women as his inexorable captors. In thought, if not in action, he exemplifies the so-called 'masculine tradition' which casts women as the oppressive agents of convention from which men seek escape.[12] Absurdly, he sees May's father, a comic valetudinarian whose temperature rises at the hint of scandal, as the victim of the wife and daughter who make his comfort their perpetual concern. But he never reflects that although women may be the dominant figures in the hieroglyphic world of the drawing room, the whole structure rests upon systems created and controlled by men, upon legal and financial institutions, such as the law firm in which he is a junior partner. He does not seem to perceive that men such as Lawrence Lefferts and Sillerton Jackson are more avid and influential disseminators of gossip than women are. Nor does he ever reflect upon the assignment of living quarters in the house he shares before his marriage with his mother and unmarried sister: 'An upper floor was dedicated to Newland and the two women squeezed themselves into narrower quarters below' (AI, 1042).

At the end of *The Age of Innocence*, Archer's son, Dallas, appears briefly to represent a new generation of New Yorkers, strangers to 'even the rudiments of reserve' (AI, 1298), who speak casually of matters their parents never discussed. But the forces of evasion continue to rule Wharton's fashionable New York, most notably in *Twilight Sleep* (1927), her most ambitious study of postwar American society. Now, however, language is not the product of a code of manners but the spawn of technology and the new rhetoric of evasion is embodied in a female protagonist whose androgynous name, Pauline Manford, implies the woman's appropriation of the man's role.

The title of the novel refers to the state induced by the anesthetic given to dispel the pain of childbirth, but the 'twilight sleep' of dulled consciousness is sought by nearly all the characters, most relentlessly by Pauline Manford. An indefatigable clubwoman who incessantly meets, entertains, lectures and makes appointments, she seems the dynamo powering the social machine, but activities are her shield from the pain of self-knowledge and awareness of others' suffering. She goes beyond Archer's New York in not only forbidding talk of the unpleasant but denying that any cause to suffer exists. The illogical creed she recites to her daughter, Nona, is far removed from May Welland's stoic acceptance of pain. 'Being prepared to suffer is really the way to create suffering. And creating suffering is creating sin, because sin and suffering are really one. We ought to refuse ourselves to pain.'[13]

Through language and money, themselves systems of signs substituting for things or other signs, she makes her refusals. With cheques she pays for doctors, nurses, X-rays and rest cures for stricken family members and dependants, whose sufferings she can then ignore. With 'verbal defences' ('If I thought I could do the least good') she justifies refusals to visit friends in the hospital. She depends on the words of the spiritual healers she consults, as ' "addicts" do on their morphia' (TS, 179). She wonders if the healers' words lose their efficacy, 'like an uncorked drug' (TS, 309). New words excite her; new meanings attached to familiar words, such as *frustration*, *immediacy* and *rejuvenation*, suggestive of her spiritual emptiness, fascinate her as if they held 'some unsuspected and occult significance . . . like a phial containing a new remedy' (TS, 138).

In Pauline's sterile world (more dehumanizing than the hospitals she refuses to visit) male characters – shallow ectypes of Marvell and Archer – denounce the habits of evasion they themselves practise. Dexter Manford, displaced by his wife's frenetic schedule, perceives the hypocrisy of his circle, who 'dressed up their selfish cravings in some wordy altruism' (TS, 190). He longs to escape 'the perpetual evasion, moral, mental, physical, which he heard preached and saw practised, everywhere about him, except where money-making was concerned!' (TS, 56). But his only recourse is an affair with his stepson's sensual and amoral wife, who, he tells himself, he values as 'the one person in his group to whom its catchwords meant absolutely nothing' (TS, 190).

Another barren union prompts another male observer, Stanley Heuston, to inveigh against the 'perpetual evasion' on which he can blame his own failures. As if his rhetoric vindicated him, with unconscious irony he informs Nona Manford, who conceals her love for him out of regard for his wife, 'there are things one doesn't ever have a chance to face in this slippery sliding modern world, because they don't come out into the open. They just lurk and peep and mouth' (TS, 52). A 'disillusioned idler', he has abandoned the occupations pursued by Newland Archer – the law, philanthropy and municipal politics – and with them any authority as a social critic.

None of Pauline's circle, male or female, fails to participate in the evasion that vitiates their society. In the spiritual vacuum they have created, there emerges a new figure in Wharton's fiction, to appear again in *The Children* (1928) and the unfinished *The Buccaneers* (1938) – the girl on the verge of adulthood, sexually innocent but wise in awareness of the liaisons, broken marriages, divorces and alcoholic excesses of the adults. Pauline's daughter, Nona Manford, the most fully drawn of these figures, is the moral centre of *Twilight Sleep*. Reminiscent of James's Nanda Brookenham, she loves a man unworthy of her, suffers her mother's neglect and suppressed hostility, but struggles to know and do the 'decent thing' in a society ruled by self-interest. The character least given to self-deception, she renders the definitive judgement of her mother's life – 'a long uninterrupted struggle against the encroachment of every form of pain' (TS, 306). Wharton honours Nona as the only female character she associated with the heroic sacrifice of soldiers in the First World War. As Nona observes her father and the wife of her half-brother in covert pursuit of each other, she 'felt more and more like one of the trench-watchers pictured in the war-time papers. There she sat in the darkness of her narrow perch, her eyes glued to the observation-slit which looked out over seeming emptiness' (TS, 280).

In the battle of the sexes, men in this novel may seem the emasculated victims of a woman's blind energies. Nona identifies the agents of 'perpetual evasion' as female warriors like her mother: 'All those bright-complexioned white-haired mothers mailed in massage and optimism' (TS, 48). But men supply the armour even if some of them fall in the front line. All the 'spiritual advisers', purveyors of narcotic words to Pauline Manford, are male – a Russian mystic, a 'Hindu sage' called the Mahatma, and Alvah Loft, the 'Inspirational Healer'. Pauline is most energized by overseeing the operation of the country estate financed by her husband complete with a village 'patriarchally clustered' below the manor house (TS, 180). In this feudal realm, Nona becomes literally a sacrificial victim when Pauline's first husband, to avenge the betrayal of his son, seeks Dexter Manford but shoots and accidentally wounds Nona instead.

Characters such as Marvell, Archer and Heuston disprove the notion that men are more effective opponents of hypocrisy and evasion than women are, that women do more than men to maintain repressive codes, although several qualifications must be made. It is true that in Wharton's fiction society's disapproval of those who transgress its rules is more often publicly conveyed by women than by men. In *The Gods Arrive*, for instance, a succession of women – a Spanish marquesa, an American socialite and an English chaplain's wife – shun Halo Tarrant in her position as Vance Weston's mistress. Women more often than men use the polite formulas and platitudes to thwart or wound their antagonists. In their meeting in a restaurant, Judy Trenor in *The House of Mirth* effectively snubs Lily Bart by meaningless pleasantries, a signal to the rest of the Trenor party that Lily is to be ignored: 'Where Judy Trenor led, all the world would follow.'[14] 'Conversational rubbish' defeats Nora Frenway in 'Atrophy', when her attempt to see her lover before he dies is thwarted by his dowdy old-maid sister, by 'the stifling web of platitudes which her enemy's hand was weaving around her' (II, 508).

It is also true that weapons of evasion and silence achieve their most decisive, far-reaching results when they are used by women. Like James's Maggie Verver, May Archer preserves her marriage, secures her husband and displaces her rival by refusing to voice her grievances and by maintaining a surface harmony that allows no one to speak openly. May goes beyond Maggie, offering Archer no sign or symbol – no broken golden bowl – to reveal to him what she knows. But actually May hides less from Archer than he hides from her. Only because the power of the family works through May, who achieves her end while Archer feels himself trapped, does she seem more responsible than he for sustaining the 'inexorable conventions' of evasion and silence that bind them both.[15]

In the marriage markets of Wharton's fictional world where men control the sources of wealth, naturally women more often than men deploy the verbal arts of flattery, subterfuge, repartee and innuendo. In the verbal games of courtship, Wharton's most accomplished player is Lily Bart. In early encounters with Percy Gryce, Gus Trenor and Simon Rosedale, Lily skilfully elicits the responses she wants. But the financial power of the men she manipulates frees them from the need to rely on verbal weapons. Paradoxically, Lily's verbal expertise becomes a mark of her weakness.

Given the vulnerability of women whose status depends on the decisions of men, it is notable that such women in Wharton's fiction are more forthright at moments of crisis than men, are more willing to break taboos and speak the unspeakable. Ellen Olenska, not Archer, insists that they look 'not at visions, but at realities', and with a laugh deflates his romantic yearning for a world where words like *mistress* won't exist: 'Oh, my dear – where is that country? Have you ever been there?' (AI, 1245). When he groans that he is 'beyond' duty and loyalty to those who trust them, she punctures his masculine presumption of greater knowledge and experience: 'You've never been beyond and *I* have . . . and I know what it looks like there' (AI, 1246). He literally escapes the truth by leaving the carriage in which they are riding.

Martin Boyne in *The Children* likewise denies the home truths delivered to him by Rose Sellars, who finally identifies his unacknowledged feelings for a 15-year-old girl: 'You're in love with Judith Wheater and you're trying to persuade yourself that you're still in love with me.'[16] His response to this is to '[cover] his eyes, as if from some intolerable vision' (C, 234). When she begs him, 'Try to see the truth and face it with me', he dwells instead on the signs of age in her face, reflects on the pathos of her love for him, then fantasizes himself as her prey, her love as 'something grasping and predatory' from which he must escape (C, 234, 235).

Articulate women such as Ellen Olenska, Rose Sellars and Halo Tarrant are more incisive and forthright than the men they love, but in verbal confrontations with male characters they rarely, if ever, achieve the triumph that allows May in her last scene with Archer to '[hold] his gaze', 'her blue eyes wet with victory' (AI, 1288). The assertive need of men like Boyne, Selden and Archer to deny truths

damaging to their self-esteem deflects the wounding spears of female insight. The psychological need of such women as Halo Tarrant and Rose Sellars to exonerate the men they love compels them
to temper or retract their criticism and find themselves at fault.

Wharton's most eloquent female characters disprove the myth
that women, not men, perpetuate the 'full and elaborate vocabulary
of evasion'. But eloquence does not enable either sex to prevail over
the institutions or break the codes that sustain such myths. Indeed,
language itself in Wharton's definition becomes one of the institutions most potent in protecting the social order from challenges to
its authority.

II

To Edith Wharton, *language* meant more than fixed systems of
grammar and syntax. Language meant also the web of allusions,
references, idioms and intonations that united members of a group,
such as her parents' society described in *A Backward Glance*, 'a little
"set," with its private catch-words, observances and amusements'
(BG, 79). Like a secret language, the talk of such a group excludes
outsiders and creates bonds among the initiated, including those
who might otherwise be estranged. In 'The Other Two', Alice Waythorn's third husband feels akin to his wife's second husband because they 'had the same social habits, spoke the same language,
understood the same allusions' (I, 389). With Alice's first husband,
who says 'ain't', 'don't know as' and 'I presume', and wears a
'made-up tie attached with an elastic' (I, 389), Waythorn at first
feels no common ground. In *The Custom of the Country*, after Undine
has left Ralph Marvell, he finds momentary relief in talking with
his cousin, Clare Van Degen (the wife of Undine's lover), who 'had
his own range of allusions' and finds the 'right word' in their talk
of 'books, pictures, plays' (CC, 832). The Lansings' denationalized
circle in *The Glimpses of the Moon* is united by 'their private jargon',
their nicknames and 'tribal welcomes'.[17]

Wharton differs from Howells and James in defining as a language the speech habits of a particular group. Paradoxically, the
effect is not to create a pluralistic multilingual world but to emphasize the privileged status of one language over the others and to
isolate speakers from each other.[18] Characters who speak 'different
languages' generate in each other feelings of superiority or inade-

quacy, contempt, dislike, or fear. Characters of different social classes may form temporary liaisons (as do George Darrow and Sophy Viner in *The Reef*); ungrammatical characters, such as Rosedale and Elmer Moffatt, may buy a place in fashionable New York society; but Wharton's lovers do not cross class lines to make happy marriages as Howells's characters do.

Language in Wharton's fiction acquires such divisive power in part because her characters read even greater moral significance into manners than Howells's and James's characters do. To Wharton's privileged characters, the meanings of words are possessions, like family heirlooms, signs of social and moral worth. These characters, especially men unable to act decisively, cultivate their sense that the meaning words retain for them elevates them above those lacking their knowledge. Both Newland Archer and Martin Boyne ground moral judgments in distinctions between the language of genteel New York and what Archer calls the 'dialect' of the deracinated pleasure-seekers wandering about Europe. Talking with Judith Wheater's twice-divorced sybaritic father, Boyne 'had the sense of using an idiom for which the other had no equivalents. Superficially their vocabularies were the same; below the surface each lost its meaning for the other' (C, 118).

Language reflecting moral codes also separates the generations, creating estrangements usually registered by a character of the older generation. When Pauline Manford's first husband, Arthur Wyant, learns that his son Jim has no sense of honour requiring him to fight Dexter Manford, who has cuckolded Jim, Wyant exclaims: 'We don't speak the same language . . . I don't understand the new code' (TS, 315). (Trying to live by the old code he accidentally shoots Nona Manford instead of her father.) John Campton and his son, George, in *A Son at the Front*, have a 'private language' in which 'they' always means Campton's wife and her second husband. But on one occasion when Campton interprets 'we' and 'our' to refer to himself and his son, George corrects him: 'I meant "we" in the sense of my generation, of whatever nationality.'[19] More profoundly isolated, Kate Clephane in *The Mother's Recompense* stands forever outside the 'mysterious circle' of her daughter's generation and gropes for 'their passwords, holding the clue to their labyrinth'.[20]

Cataclysmic events such as the First World War create new languages to which not all people have access. Troy Belknap, the young protagonist of *The Marne*, venerates and longs to join the soldiers at the front who 'knew its vocabulary, its dangers and its dodges'.[21] Anticipating the observation of Hemingway's Frederick Henry in *A Farewell to Arms*, a journalist in *A Son at the Front* observes that 'meaning had evaporated' out of words like *honour* and *right*, 'as if the general smash-up had broken their stoppers. So many of them . . . we'd taken good care not to uncork for centuries' (SF, 187). Wharton's image here, as in *Twilight Sleep*, of words held, like elixir in phials, suggests a conception of language as both potent and evanescent, a precious substance easily dissipated. Into the vacuum new words come: the middle-aged painter, Campton, is struck by the ease with which civilians in Paris adapt themselves to 'the monstrous idea' of war, 'acquire its ways, speak its language . . . A new speech was growing up in this new world' (SF, 111).

Most pervasive in Wharton's fiction is the power of language to separate people of different social classes. Usually the separation is registered by a male character who reads in the difference proof of his own superiority. But Halo Spear in *Hudson River Bracketed* expresses the view of the privileged class when she objects to her mother's proposal to invite their poor relations, the Tracys, to lunch with the Spears' friends: 'What on earth should we find to say to each other? They talk another language and it can't be helped.'[22] Those like Halo Spear, social arbiters by birth and training, regard the outsider's language as an act of appropriation which devalues words by altering their meaning. Thus Ralph Marvell distinguishes the Invaders from the Aborigines: 'They spoke the same language as his, though on their lips it had often so different a meaning' (CC, 673). To outsiders, the insiders speak – not 'the same language' – but one filled with words incomprehensible to them. When the Tracys' Midwestern cousin, Vance Weston, first meets Halo Spear, he hears 'another language of which he caught only an occasional phrase' (HRB, 69). Even after months of living with Halo, he recognizes himself as the outsider when he observes that she and an acquaintance of her own class 'talked the same language and would always be at ease with each other'.[23]

Both male and female outsiders in Wharton's fiction recognize the barriers of language, but the class structure, more than other conditions separating characters, places women at a disadvantage. That those of different generations or different nationalities but of the same social class speak different languages does not necessarily handicap women more than men or subject women to more rigorous standards than men. But among the Invaders – outsiders who strive to cross the boundaries that exclude them from the privileges of the established order – the social codes of fashionable society and the assumptions they reinforce impose special burdens upon women. In Wharton's novels, both male and female characters of inferior social status betray their origins in the defects of their speech – in solecisms and expressions the genteel deem vulgar and uncouth. But in Wharton's fashionable New York, as in Howells's patrician Boston, where women are expected to conduct the rituals of calls, social correspondence and polite conversation, solecisms and vulgarities are judged a more serious defect in women's speech than in men's.

An early story, 'The Introducers', neatly contrasts the kinds of instruction a man and a woman must undergo to enter polite society. Belle Grantham, in her capacity as secretary to the rich outsider, Mrs Bixby, must constantly monitor her employer's speech, telling her what to say and what not to say, 'reminding [her] not to speak of her husband as *Mr Bixby*, not to send in her cards when people are at home, not to let the butler say "fine claret" in a sticky whisper in people's ears, not to speak of town as "the city", and not to let Mr Bixby tell what things cost' (I, 534). Frederick Tilney, the secretary of the rich man, Mr Magraw, has little to do 'except to tone him down a little' (I, 534).

What society disapproves in women's speech it permits, even enjoys, in men's. In *The House of Mirth*, the parvenu, Welly Bry, can freely exhibit 'his slang and his brag and his blunders', but his wife, inhibited by her sense of what polite society requires and values in women, strives in vain to be 'queenly' (HM, 196). A woman who behaved with Elmer Moffatt's 'loud easiness' in Old New York's society would not be encouraged, but Ralph Marvell's sister, entertaining Moffatt at dinner, 'seemed to enjoy provoking him to fresh excesses of slang and hyperbole' (CC, 789). So great is his power on Wall Street that talk of his exploits that 'poured from him with Homeric volume' (CC, 789) lifts him above the irony of the mock-heroic.

The importance of a linguistic standard in creating or revealing the advantages enjoyed by men in a class society is best seen in a comparison of Wharton's two protagonists who are outsiders: Undine Spragg in *The Custom of the Country* and Vance Weston in *Hudson River Bracketed*. Although the two novels are separated by 16 years, the protagonists are in a sense contemporaries in that the personality of the writer, Vance Weston and the main events of his life evolved from the unfinished novel, 'Literature', some seventy pages of typescript, which Wharton began writing in August 1913, shortly after finishing *The Custom of the Country*.[24]

Both Undine Spragg and Vance Weston grow up in a culturally barren Midwest filled with towns bearing such names as Prune-ville, Crampton and Hallelujah – caricatures of the towns Sinclair Lewis would create. Vance has a state university education, but his family, like Undine's, is uprooted, completely cut off from genteel eastern culture. Both protagonists come to New York filled with crude yearnings and undefined longings for self-fulfilment and success unattainable, even unimaginable, in Undine's Apex City or Vance's Euphoria.

Both protagonists become aware of class barriers when they are entertained by members of cultivated society, whose words, allusions and intonations are so unfamiliar to the outsiders that they seem to be hearing a foreign language. The effects on the male and female outsiders, however, are completely different. Vance Weston is stimulated and inspired by the conversations he hears at gatherings of the Spears and the Tarrants. Initially he feels that between him and them 'the gulf was untraversable' (HRB, 125), but their talk of 'unseen places, unheard-of people' is 'intoxicating in its manifold suggestions' (HRB, 420). He does not resent the superior knowledge of Halo Spear, who guides him to the great English poets and prose-writers – his realms of gold; he is inspired by everything in her conversation unfamiliar to him: 'Allusions to people and books, associations of ideas, images and metaphors, each giving an electric shock to his imagination' (HRB, 101).

What stimulates and enlightens Vance Weston simply baffles and unnerves Undine Spragg. At the dinner given by Ralph Marvell's sister, which introduces Undine to the old New York society, she is disconcerted by questions about new books and exhibitions she has never heard of; she is oppressed, not stirred, by the Marvell–Dagonet 'world of half-lights, half-tones, eliminations and abbreviations' (CC, 645). Vance Weston so readily enters the world of art and ideas Halo opens to him that 'every word she spoke was a clue to new discoveries' (HRB, 337). After her marriage to Ralph Marvell, Undine, who 'always scented ridicule in the unknown' (CC, 747), is merely irritated and bored by her husband's 'strange allusions' to myth and poetry; to his words she opposes 'a blank wall of incomprehension' (CC, 832).

As a male artist destined to write great novels, Vance Weston is creative and independent. He can easily imitate the 'tricks of language and technique' of other writers, but 'he always ended by feeling that it wasn't his natural way of representing things' (HRB, 335). Nor does he try to imitate the speech of the characters whose culture he envies. At times, his failure to master the 'art of social transitions' pains him, as when Halo Spear compliments his wife and he stands 'abashed and awkward', having 'no answer in his vocabulary to such amenities' (HRB, 340). But the lapse is unimportant. The artist's need is not to master the language of a particular social class but to discover the voice of the soul that he feels as a 'stranger inside of him, a stranger speaking a language he had never learned, or had forgotten' (HRB, 47).

The keynote of Undine's actions and aspirations is imitation. As a female player in the marriage markets of New York and Paris, she is 'passionately imitative', dependent on others to define her desires – 'I want what the others want' (CC, 688). She knows herself only through reflections of herself – in mirrors, in portraits painted of her, in the attitudes and opinions of others. The 'image of herself in other minds was her only notion of self-seeing' (CC, 886). To her, words are like clothes, to be copied or discarded. Her first act in the novel is to copy the wording of a dinner invitation in her note of acceptance.

Vance's 'intellectual hunger' is more powerful than any fear of social gaffes. He habitually begins conversations with strangers by asking questions, a disconcerting habit that Halo Spear nonetheless admires as his virtue of 'leaping straight at the gist of things' (HRB, 91). Undine decides early that *'it's better to watch than to ask questions'* (CC, 664). From the start, she is 'quick to learn the forms of worldly intercourse' (CC, 721), even as she is baffled by the substance. Imitation enables her 'to modulate and lower her voice and to replace "the *i*-dea!" and "I wouldn't wonder" by more polished locutions' (CC, 682). She learns to scorn her childhood friend, Indiana Frusk, who 'spoke of her husband as "Mr Rolliver" ' and 'twanged a piercing *r*' (CC, 848). During her marriage to the Marquis de Chelles, Undine acquires 'shades of conduct, turns of speech, tricks of attitude' (CC, 991) to which her rich American friends in Paris are strangers.

'Shades', 'tricks' and 'turns', however, are not the equivalents of the culture represented by Halo Spear and Ralph Marvell. Undine can impress American friends less highly developed than she is, but when tested by the standards of the French aristocratic society into which she marries – standards which, according to Wharton, produced 'the best school of talk and of ideas that the modern world has known'[25] – Undine is a failure. A compatriot who has also married into the French aristocracy evaluates Undine's performance at a reception: 'You don't work hard enough – you don't keep up . . . I watched you the other night at the Duchess's and half the time you hadn't an idea what they were talking about' (CC, 979). Undine herself is aware that beauty cannot substitute for conversation, that 'as soon as people began to talk they ceased to see her' (CC, 979). She makes a futile attempt to 'cultivate herself' by spending a morning at the Louvre and developing 'opinions' about what she sees – the one time in the novel when Undine seems merely pitiful in her ignorance. She is incapable of the kind of intellectual communion Vance and Halo enjoy, 'the absorbing, illuminating, inexhaustible exchange of confidences and ideas' (HRB, 410). Because Undine has no more literary and artistic interests to share with Raymond de Chelles than with Ralph Marvell, 'little by little their talk died down to monosyllables' (CC, 955).

Undine can imitate the forms of polite expression, but she cannot learn through imitation to appreciate 'language spoken according to the best usage', to prefer Ralph Marvell's 'quiet, deprecatory' way of speaking to the 'domineering yet caressing address' (CC, 636) of the vulgarly successful portrait painter, Claud Walsingham Popple. Ralph's quotations from English poetry impress her less than Popple's phrases taken from romantic fiction and 'the lighter type of memoirs' (CC, 747) that provide her with sentimental clichés to think her own thoughts: for example, she will exert 'a purifying influence' on the painter who has roused her to 'her higher self' (CC, 747). Ultimately, however, the words that move her most powerfully are the words of her first husband, Elmer Moffatt, words she receives 'like so many hammer-strokes demolishing the unrealities that imprisoned her' (CC, 975). Her true, natural idiom remains that of Moffatt, who regards Paris as 'a thunderingly good place' that 'beats everything' (CC, 894, 895). Always dependent on another person to reflect her to herself, she returns at the end to Moffatt, who alone can give words to desires signified by nothing in the language she has learned to imitate. 'Here was some one who spoke her language, who knew her meanings, who understood instinctively all the deep-seated wants for which her acquired vocabulary had no terms' (CC, 975).

Rather than imitating formulas and acquiring 'tricks of speech', Vance Weston from the beginning is fascinated by words, revealing a power of discrimination that Undine never develops. Even before he leaves Euphoria, he finds 'a strange attraction' in listening to the town's one speaker who meets Wharton's standard – a displaced Virginian named Harrison Delaney, whose words, Vance notes, were 'always good English words, rich and expressive, with hardly a concession to the local vernacular, or the passing epidemics of slang' (HRB, 15). For Vance the most potent words, instead of demolishing unrealities, generate powerful emotions and images. The name of the Hudson River 'stirred [him] more than the sight of the outspread waters' (HRB, 39). The word *Poetry* 'always made wings rustle in him when he read it' (HRB, 63). Words are not objects or signs of status to be acquired; words are springs that 'loosen' his 'formless yearnings'. One word begets a poem, as if 'the word had been a seed plunged into the heated atmosphere of his imagination' (HRB, 47).

To compare Undine's appropriation of language with Vance's fusing of words and feeling to create thought is to perceive the spiritual emptiness of a character in whom the faculty of imitation takes the place of any capacity for intellectual or moral growth. In technical ways as well, Wharton draws attention to Undine's linguistic deficiencies to place her female character in a less favourable light than her male character. In recording Undine's thoughts she uses quotation marks to distance her narrator from Undine's words and what they signify: a 'buggy-ride', a 'dinner party', her hope that Ralph Marvell will 'escort' her home, her pleasure in seeing at the theatre all the people she wanted to 'go with' (CC 658, 646, 687). Vance's formulations of the creative process and the emotions they evoke are often callow and overblown but his words never bear the stigma of quotation marks.

Undine is made comic by phonetic rendering of words she mispronounces. At the Fairfords' dinner she speaks of seeing Sarah Bernhardt in 'Leg'long' and 'Fade' (CC, 646). Halo criticizes Vance for reading his manuscripts too fast and slurring his words, but he is never seen mispronouncing words. Wharton does not present him as a polished speaker, but she lets him make his clumsiest speeches to the novel's most grotesque character, a rich patron of the arts, Mrs Pulsifer, whose absurd outpourings – 'I do so want to preserve my complete serenity, my utter detachment' (HRB, 284) – are a more embarrassing breach of decorum than Vance's assurance when he visits her: 'I do like wandering about this house first-rate' (HRB, 321). Even Halo, his guide and mentor, whose 'short-sighted eyes' suggest a limited perspective, even she is discredited when she informs him that he shouldn't use *urge* as a noun in his poem and that *dawn* and *lorn* 'do *not* rhyme in English poetry' (HRB, 105). In contrast, Undine utters her crude locutions ('I don't care if I do', 'I really couldn't say') in the presence of Marvell's sister, Mrs Fairford, a mistress of 'gradations of tone' (CC, 645) and the most accomplished of all the characters in the art of conversation.

Undine eventually learns to imitate 'the speech of the conquered race', but neither Vance nor Undine ever acquires the language of the Spears' and Marvells' world in the sense of sharing, or even understanding, the feelings, traditions and values that lie behind their words. What Raymond de Chelles says to Undine when she proposes to sell his family's tapestries might be said by Ralph Marvell: 'You come among us speaking our language and not knowing what we mean; wanting the things we want and not knowing why we want them . . . and we're fools enough to imagine that because you copy our ways and pick up our slang you understand anything about the things that make life decent and honourable for us!' (CC, 982). At the end of the scene they face each other, 'the depths of their mutual incomprehension at last bared to each other's angry eyes' (CC, 982–3).

The effects of the class barrier separating Halo and Vance are most dramatically represented in *The Gods Arrive*, during the first months of their life together in Europe, when Halo vainly tries to explain to Vance her distress at being excluded from social occasions to which he is invited. Here the character's failure of comprehension is registered by the woman, whose cry to her lover that prejudice would not disturb her 'if I felt you knew how to protect me' (GA, 53) simply mystifies him. Aware of his ignorance of the code that has governed her relations with men of her own class, she feels powerless to make him comprehend her equivocal situation. 'To discuss things with him was like arguing with some one who did not use the same speech' (GA, 55). Her perception that he is struggling vainly to understand her, that 'he felt the distance between them and was wondering how to bridge it over' (GA, 54) only reinforces her sense of 'the impenetrable wall' (GA, 53) between them. 'He seemed remote, out of hearing, behind the barrier that divided them' (GA, 55).

In contrast to Marvell and Chelles, who see Undine as their moral and intellectual inferior, Halo must find something more admirable in her lover's point of view than in her own knowledge of 'the conventional rules of life'; she must credit him with an 'inflexible honesty' (GA, 56) that brings him 'disconcertingly close to realities' (GA, 54). Her judgement of him may reflect both her emotional dependence on him and her need to see him as in some way superior to her, thus worth the sacrifice of her marriage and her position in the society whose code she has violated. But Vance, too, in his encounters with Halo's coldly impeccable husband, Lewis Tarrant, feels himself the stronger through his very ignorance of the 'accepted formulas' by which Tarrant and his kind disguise their thoughts and feelings. Even as Vance feels caught 'in the old verbal entanglements' that are Tarrant's defence, he perceives that his opponent is crippled by them. 'This studied attitude of composure which gave him a superficial advantage over an untutored antagonist was really only another bondage. When a man had disciplined himself out of all impulsiveness he stood powerless on the brink of the deeper feelings' (GA, 145). At even greater disadvantage than the rejected husband with his power to refuse a divorce is his wife, Halo, whose eloquence in her confrontation with Tarrant only exposes her powerlessness when her words fail to move him.

Of all Wharton's characters, the most enviable is the male artist, like Vance Weston, freed by his status as an impoverished outsider from the conditions of the fashionable world that sap the energies and make dilettantes of would-be artists such as Lewis Tarrant and Ralph Marvell. That Vance Weston cannot acquire 'the conventional attitude and the accepted phrase' (GA, 145) matters little when his mind opens to 'the brooding spirit of understanding in the pages of all the great creative writers . . . impossible to define, but clear to the initiated as the sign exchanged between members of some secret brotherhood' (GA, 183). Like all Wharton's male characters, he profits from the double standard which leaves the woman far more vulnerable than the man to social ostracism and legal retribution that may follow violation of the social codes. The poverty that oppresses him in *Hudson River Bracketed* is not enviable, but his novels – artistic if not commercial successes – are a passport to the fashionable world whenever he wants to enter it. And for the male artist, unhindered by his sex, poverty can serve as the obstacle which it seems necessary that Wharton's artist surmount to gain entrance to the 'secret brotherhood' of writers.

III

Like Howells's social analyst, Bromfield Corey, Wharton's Charles Bowen in *The Custom of the Country* locates the ruling principle of American society in the exclusion of women from the man's world of business and the professions. In Bowen's view, Undine is not to be blamed for her extravagance and her callous indifference to Ralph Marvell's business worries. She, like her husband, is a victim, a 'monstrously perfect product' (CC, 759), of a system in which the typical American man (unlike Ralph) considers his obligations to his wife fulfilled when he lavishes money on her to spend. The woman, according to Bowen's Veblenist analysis, when denied the man's opportunities to achieve identity and autonomy, contrives her life out of the material results of his labour – 'the money and the motor and the clothes' (CC, 758).

Bowen's determinism does not entirely account for Undine. Other married women of the fashionable world, such as May Archer and Laura Fairford, are not callous egoists. Floss Delaney, Undine's soulless mate, in *The Gods Arrive* does not become less heartless when her energies are engaged in the business world, where she outmanoeuvres men to clinch big deals in real estate. But the similarity in the language describing Undine's marital conquests and her father's financial dealings indicates her possession of faculties like his – boldness, persistence and when necessary a 'lucid force of resistance' (CC, 816) – that, in her life, can find outlet only in seeking pleasure and status. As the resemblance of daughter to father suggests, 'Wall Street' and 'Fifth Avenue', Wharton's favourite metonyms for the male sphere of finance and the female sphere of society, are inextricably bound. In *The House of Mirth*, Rosedale's masterful deployment of his wealth reverberates in both spheres, 'placing Wall Street under obligations which only Fifth Avenue could repay' (HM, 251). To Undine, the 'meaningless syllables' in Moffatt's account of his financial dealings signify success, for 'every Wall Street term had its equivalent in the language of Fifth Avenue' (CC, 976). But the structure of the epigrams, balancing the two terms in opposition, represents the disjunction implicit in the connection.

The deleterious effects upon each other of male and female spheres that can be neither joined nor separated is a recurrent theme in Wharton's fiction. The isolation of women by what Bowen calls 'the custom of the country' contributes to the decline of Lily

Bart, the failure of John and Bessy Amherst's marriage in *The Fruit of the Tree*, the estrangement of May and Newland Archer, as well as the collapse of the marriages in *The Custom of the Country*. (Justine Brent in *The Fruit of the Tree*, Wharton's only female character who works with her husband, is a nurse, a profession traditionally identified with women.)

In *French Ways and Their Meaning* (1919), Wharton develops Bowen's comparison of American and European societies in her sharpest attack on the system which cripples American women, 'cut off from men's society in all but the most formal and intermittent ways' (FWM, 116). The effect upon American society was to reduce the opportunities for men and women to meet on common ground and to extend their influence over each other – an essential condition of a civilized society (FWM, 112). One measure of such a society, best exemplified by the French Salon, was the stimulus of conversation among its members, men and women, attuned to each other's minds and producing together the modern world's 'best school of talk and ideas'. Because American women 'are each other's only audience', Wharton contended, they are stunted in their social development, 'like children in a baby school' (FWM, 102).

As Alan Price has noted, Wharton's unmodulated criticism of American women in *French Ways and Their Meaning* may reflect the postwar fatigue of the novelist after years of passionate service in the Allied cause.[26] But in her novels, early and late, Wharton attributes to women deficiencies exposed, if not caused, by the American system. One evidence of the unhealthy separation of the sexes is the frequency with which Wharton's female characters are said to pick up the jargon of a man's vocation without understanding his work. The woman's vain attempt to relate to a man's world may be noted by the narrator or by a character, but always the imitator is cast in a negative light. Halo Tarrant's distaste for the young women living with their artist lovers in Paris extends to 'their artistic and literary jargon, picked up from the brilliant young men whose lives they shared' (GA, 91). The narrator of *The Custom of the Country* associates feminine beauty and mindlessness in describing Undine's tour of the Paris galleries with Moffatt: 'She even acquired as much of the jargon as a pretty woman needs to produce the impression of being well-informed' (CC, 993). (French society, Undine discovers, requires more than 'the jargon'.) The painter, John Campton, in *A Son at the Front*, hides a superior smile at his first wife's praise of the 'rhythm' and *'tempo'* of his painting, knowing that 'the jargon of art was merely one of her many languages' (SF, 41). A rare instance of a male character imitating a woman's language is Roger Talkett, who parrots his wife's clichés, unwittingly satirizing both his wife and himself: 'Resistance to the herd-instinct (to borrow one of my wife's expressions) is really innate in me' (SF, 321).

Campton's reference to his wife's 'many languages' implies that women have no language of their own and are naturally imitative, like chameleons, who take on the tone and idiom of the voices surrounding them. But a fact of profound importance in Wharton's fiction suggests another cause, in the novelist's refusal to allow her female characters even so much cultural authority as women in James's and Howells's fiction command. With few exceptions, Wharton's female characters are excluded not only from business and the professions but from intelligent appreciation of the arts. Not only are they not painters or writers; they exhibit little knowledge of the cultural heritage to which scores of the male characters have ready access. Women in Wharton's fiction do not feel themselves deprived of culture; they do not share the yearning of George Eliot's Maggie Tulliver and Dorothea Brooke for education that society denies them. Women in her fiction leave imprisoning marriages to live with men they love (usually artists) but never to develop talents of their own. Rather, with the exception of Halo Spear, Wharton simply gave her own creative powers and her knowledge of literature and painting and architecture to her male, not her female, characters.

The disparity is evident in the 22 first-person narratives in the two-volume *Collected Stories*. Not only do 19 of these stories have male narrators; keys to the treasure stores of literary image and metaphor belong only to the male narrators, most of them bachelors of the ruling class, highly placed lawyers, diplomats and scientists with means and leisure to read, travel, collect rare works of art and listen to each other's stories. Typical of the select group is the painter-narrator of 'The Portrait' who draws his analogies from the Old Testament, meteorology, music, exploration, hunting, billiards and banking. The mental world of the art critic who narrates the story of 'The Daunt Diana' contains facts about medieval religion, the Kohinoor diamonds, Tanagras and the Latmian kiss received by Endymion. Halo Spear, the only female character to command a similar range of reference, in conversations with Vance Weston quotes eight lines of *Faust* in German, refers to the myth of the Sphinx, defines the architectural style, 'Hudson River Bracketed', and identifies the First Temple of Delphi. Otherwise, intelligent sophisticated women such as Ellen Olenska, Rose Sellars and Anna Leath reveal their culture in their social poise, their dress and the decoration of their rooms, not in references to poetry or novels or paintings.

Female characters such as Undine, whose reading is noted, usually read the sentimental romances that Wharton scorned and unthinkingly absorb their clichés into their speech. In *A Son at the Front*, a female friend who tells Campton that the war 'will be the making' of his son moves the painter to respond: 'You always get your phrases out of books' (SF, 84). When female characters are familiar with works of high culture their knowledge is often trivialized or mocked. Lily Bart's awareness of the Furies comes from a translation of the *Eumenides* 'she had once picked up, in a house where she was staying' (HM, 156). The narrator of *Hudson River Bracketed* and *The Gods Arrive* treats Vance Weston's artistic ambitions seriously but satirizes his sister, Mae, 'the cultured daughter' (GA, 15), whose request to study art in Chicago is casually dismissed by her father. A favourite target of Wharton's satire is the ladies' club lecturer, such as Mrs Amyot in 'The Pelican', who, the male narrator notes, mistranslates Greek, misquotes Emerson's 'Rhodora', and is further compromised by having an aunt named Irene Astarte Pratt, author of a poem in blank verse on 'The Fall of Man' (I, 88). In 'Xingu', Wharton sinks the 'celebrated Osric Dane', author of the reminiscently Jamesian *Wings of Death*, through her association with the ladies of the Lunch Club, 'indomitable huntresses of erudition' who 'pursue Culture in bands as though it were dangerous to meet alone' (II, 209). In 'The Verdict', the capacity to tell true art from false, exhibited only by the male characters, is like a secret knowledge denied to all the artists' wives and female sitters.

Wharton spoke and read French, German and Italian, but except for Halo Spear only her male characters display her knowledge of foreign languages. Ralph Marvell has her 'command of foreign tongues' (CC, 724) but Undine remains 'hampered by her lack of languages' (CC, 724). The gender difference extends even to a commonplace parvenu couple named Shallum: he 'conversed with a colourless fluency in the principal European tongues'; his wife commands 'but a few verbs, all of which, on her lips, became irregular' (CC, 725). Of the three characters in 'Confession', only the male narrator speaks foreign languages with ease. The woman he marries speaks 'a carefully acquired if laborious French', her companion only an unintelligible 'local vernacular' (II, 808).

Although Wharton criticized the American system which isolated men and women in their separate spheres, she herself voiced conventional assumptions on which the system was based. Like James in *The Bostonians*, she satirized women who cross gender lines to assume the traditionally masculine role of public speaker. Pauline Manford has the assurance, poise, presence and power to move assemblages of hundreds of women, but the narrator undercuts her by ridiculing her audience: women 'united by a common faith in the infinite extent of human benevolence and the incalculable resources of American hygiene' (TS, 112).

The novelist who created Fulvia Vivaldi, Halo Spear, Ellen Olenska and Justine Brent obviously did not think women unintelligent, but she could lapse into the conventional idea that charm and intellect could not coexist in a woman. In a letter to Walter Maynard, she called H. G. Wells's novel, *The New Machiavelli*, 'magnificent', but added, 'I don't believe that nice girl . . . really wrote *good* articles on Political Economy. She couldn't have been so nice if she had!'[27] Wharton singled out the character Lucrezia in E. W. Phillips's play about Francesca da Rimini as 'the most life-like and forcible character in the drama – the only man in it, one might say'.[28]

Wharton exempts her important female characters, such as Halo Spear, Lily Bart, May Welland and Ellen Olenska from the defects traditionally associated with women's speech, but many of her female characters abound in hyperbole, intensity and capitalized abstracts. One woman speaks in 'agonized italics' ('The Friends', I, 208); another 'with a tearful prodigality of italics' ('Souls Belated', I, 111). The appropriately named Mrs Talkett in *A Son at the Front*, whose 'imperatives were always in italics', exclaims and complains in a 'plaintive staccato' (SF, 87). In the same novel, which has no attractive female character, an 'elderly virgin', infected by the war fever, 'moved and spoke in explosives, as if the wires that agitated her got tangled and then were too suddenly jerked loose' (SF, 83). The female nurse who attends Troy Belknap in *The Marne* is emotional; the male doctor is calm, strong, self-contained. In 'The Letters', the protagonist's friend, who fancies herself a confidante in a romantic melodrama, does not merely speak but successively 'gloated', 'panted', 'breathed', 'wailed', 'moaned', 'gasped' and 'cried out'.

With Wharton as with Howells, it is difficult to tell whether the deficiencies of female characters reflected in their speech are to be traced to defects of the social system, to individual weakness, or to traits inherent in their sex. But, as with Howells, Wharton's use of the modifier *feminine* defines certain habits and qualities as typical of women in general. Mrs Waythorn, in 'The Other Two', asks her husband 'vague feminine questions about the routine of the office' (I, 385). Until Penelope Bent, in 'The Friends', suffers a broken engagement and loss of her job, she is 'little given to feminine falterings and incoherencies' (I, 201). Westall in 'The Reckoning' 'combined a man's dislike of uncomfortable questions with an almost feminine skill in eluding them' (I, 423). His wife thinks it 'horrid' – she 'found herself slipping back into the old feminine vocabulary' – to allow her daughter to listen to her husband's lectures on 'The New Ethics' (I, 421). Wharton, in a letter to Morton Fullerton, declares that she will 'throw tact, discretion and all other feminine qualities to the winds'.[29]

In his introduction to the two-volume *Collected Stories*, Wharton's biographer, R. W. B. Lewis, noted her 'masculine wit' and her 'masculine vein of satiric humor', asserting that 'everyone who knew her has commented on a certain masculinity in her make-up; in her devotion to the orderly, in the vigorous play of her mind, and in her energetic sense of the satirical' (I, xxi). Wharton in her writing did not explicitly define satire as masculine and she gave to one female protagonist, Lily Bart, a measure of her own 'energetic sense of the satirical'. But Lily is the exception. Satire in Wharton, usually in the form of the epigram, is far more typical of the male than the female characters, particularly of the male narrators of the short stories. A favourite target of their epigrammatic wit is the speech of female characters. A typical satirist is the narrator of 'The Verdict', who observes of a certain Midwestern woman that she is not only ignorant about art; the word, as she speaks it, 'multiplied its *rs* as though they were reflected in an endless vista of mirrors' (I, 655). The narrator of 'Miss Mary Pask' patronizes the elderly cousin he visits, 'one of the sweet conscientious women who go on using the language of devotion about people whom they live happily without seeing' (II, 374).

Most of Wharton's male protagonists, including Campton, Boyne and Archer, make disparaging generalizations about the female sex. Anti-feminism is most baldly displayed by the male narrators of the stories, whose satire, often gratuitously cruel, reflects a misogyny suggestive of unacknowledged fear or jealousy of female vitality. The narrator of 'The Portrait', recalling talk about a painter at a social gathering, praises his own analogies as 'not unapt', but when a woman threatens to dominate the conversation with an eloquent analysis of the topic he dismisses her contribution as a 'flushed harangue' (I, 176). The insistence with which the narrator of 'The Pelican' belabours the deficiencies of Mrs Amyot and her store of 'stock adjectives' – 'a whole wardrobe of slop-shop epithets irrelevant in cut and size' (I, 91) – seems his attempted defence against her power to impel him to aid her against his better judgement. The narrator of 'The Rembrandt', a museum curator, overtly acknowledges the power of a woman's weakness to confound him. When Mrs Fontage insists upon the authenticity of her 'Rembrandt', the 'screen of verbiage' she erects disarms him: 'My words slipped from me like broken weapons' (I, 29).

The satire in these stories, which reveals more about the male narrators than the women they mock, may be seen as a method of exposing the feelings underlying male attitudes. But Wharton herself found in women's speech an inviting target of her satire, as though, like the male narrators, she wished to distance herself from female weakness (without participating in male fears). Her Commonplace Book, dated circa 1901,[30] which is filled with the kinds of epigrams that appear in the fiction, includes an outline for a story, 'The Alternative', about a (male) magazine editor 'persecuted by a pretty girl who writes obvious stories full of every old cliché'; and a 'Literary conversation' in which one woman says to another: 'I read such a good book the other day. I don't remember who wrote it – No, I can't think what it was called; but it was *so* clever – do read it if you come across it.' Ten epigrams under the heading 'The Vortex' include the following:

'His capacious silence seemed large enough to hold all the volubility of all the women in the world.'

'Words to her were mere domestic utensils, the pots and pans of her moral kitchen.'

'Her words were few but her ideas being fewer, she had never felt the restrictions of her vocabulary'.

'Her mind seems so thin. I suppose she suffers from mal-assimilation of ideas.'

Wharton's female characters do not have a monopoly on verbosity, solecism, clichés, vulgarity. Halo Spear's father fulminates in the newspapers against 'what he called crying evils' (HRB, 187); Roger Talkett speaks in capital letters of the Barbarian, the Hero, the Artist, the Elect, in a voice 'flat, toneless and yet eager' (SF, 320). The failed sculptor in 'The Potboiler' releases his grievances in a self-pitying 'torrent of denunciatory eloquence' (I, 672). A few male characters are as cruelly fixed as the female by the narrator's epigrams: a man at an artist's studio in *Twilight Sleep* has 'a voice like melted butter, a few drops of which seemed to trickle down his lips and be licked back at intervals behind a thickly ringed hand' (TS, 90). Male public speakers given to bombast are satirized for 'rolling periods' and 'oratorical accents' (Harvey Mayhew dilating on war atrocities in *A Son at the Front*, 202–3); for 'erudite allusions and apt quotations' culled from Bartlett (Elmer Moffatt, CC, 986); for 'windy eloquence and sanctimonious perfidies' (Grandfather Scrimser, HRB, 19). Only male characters are stigmatized by speech that creates a racial stereotype: for example, the novelist, Gratz Blemer, who 'spoke with a slight German accent, oiled by Jewish gutturals' (HRB, 417); an insinuating picture-dealer in 'The Potboiler' whose 'pronunciation grew increasingly Semitic in moments of excitement' (I, 666); Rosedale, whose tone 'had the familiarity of a touch' (HM, 15).

With the exception of Rosedale and Moffatt, men whose speech is satirized are fixed minor characters whose status as comic types is clear. Wharton's intention is less clear in representations of the language of possession and control used by most of the important male characters when they think and speak of women. The male viewpoint is rarely expressed so crudely as in *The Reef*, when George Darrow is said to assume that women 'had been evolved' to the end of 'ministering to the more complex masculine nature'.[31] But this is essentially the attitude of most of the men, from the most refined, such as Selden, Archer and Marvell, to the least cultivated, such as Rosedale and Moffatt. To the male invaders and aborigines alike, women exist to be used, moulded, rescued and gazed at; their functions are to nourish, sustain, comfort, gratify the ego and elevate the status of men. Female characters rarely objectify men in similes or metaphors but male characters habitually perceive women in the centuries-old figures, as vessels, pictures, statues, trees, flowers, books, figureheads, musical instruments to be played upon and fields to be sown.

What did Wharton think of men's habit of objectifying women? The Duke of Tintagel in *The Buccaneers*, who thinks it safe to marry an American girl because 'I shall be able to form her', is both comic and sinister – a true grotesque, in his obsession with regulating clocks.[32] The pathology of his response to his wife's sexual refusals is obvious: he 'felt a nervous impulse to possess himself of the clock on the mantelshelf and take it to pieces . . .' (B, 328). But another Englishman, Guy Thwarte, represented as the ideal friend and lover who 'understood not only all [Nan] said, but everything she could not say' (B, 350), likewise sees her as an object, although one to be animated, not dismantled, 'the finest instrument he had ever had in his hand; an instrument from which, when the time came, he might draw unearthly music' (B, 273).

More disturbing is the narrator's apparent acceptance of the taxonomic similes of the painter Campton, the most misogynous of Wharton's protagonists. The practice of his art may account for his comparing Mrs Talkett, when he paints her portrait, to an 'instrument on which he played with careless mastery' (SF, 227). But without disapproval the narrator later presents the specular economist at his most cold-blooded, doing to Mrs Talkett what the Prufrockian male fears that women will do to him: he 'sat staring at her as if the weight of his gaze might pin her down, keep her from fluttering away and breaking up into luminous splinters' (SF, 339). Knowing that his son is in love with 'the poor little ephemeral creature', he sees her as he wishes her to be: self-destructive. More subtle than Basil Ransom, who imagines striking Verena dumb and watching her writhe like a dying insect, Campton sees Mrs Talkett trapping herself on her own passion, 'wriggling on it like a butterfly impaled' (SF, 339).

Occasionally a female character protests comparison to a symbolic object. 'How horrid of you', exclaims Judith Wheater when Boyne greets her, 'You look like a pansy this morning' (C, 119). But so deeply instilled is the culture's ideology that women view themselves and other women as objects or as sources of support to male characters. Whether or not Wharton intended Nona Manford to play on words when Nona says of her half-brother, Jim, that 'getting married has given him an object' (TS, 49), she like the other characters sees Jim's wife, Lita, as an object, her face 'like a delicate porcelain vase' (TS, 333). Lita herself encourages the process of objectification by presenting herself as mentally and emotionally inert.

Beautiful women like Lily Bart and Undine Marvell willingly allow male portrait painters to turn them into representations. Women of cultivated literary tastes, such as Halo Spear and Mary Anerton ('The Muse's Tragedy') seek fulfilment in the role of muse and inspiration to a male artist, who considers his obligation to her discharged in treating her mind as 'the perfect tuned instrument' on which he plays (I, 74) or the fertile soil in which the seed of his genius flowers (HRB, 359). To the end of *The House of Mirth*, Lily Bart is impelled by her need to create in a man, Selden, a moral guide whose approval validates her sense of moral worth, just as Susy Lansing, in *The Glimpses of the Moon*, must continue to measure herself by her husband's presumably superior standard, as if aware that 'from the moment that she had become his property he had built up in himself a conception of her answering to some deep-seated need of veneration' (GM, 64).

In this passage, the 'need of veneration' is the man's, but his need is inseparable from the woman's need, as deep-seated as his, to answer his conception, to be worthy of his veneration. Granted, male characters who attempt to form women by imparting to them their own tastes and interests always fail – as Ralph Marvell fails with Undine Spragg, John Amherst with Bessy Westmore, Newland Archer with May Welland, Tintagel with Nan St George. But in countless ways the thoughts, words and actions of all Wharton's characters, male and female, are shaped by the roles their society assigns to men and women, concepts of gender too powerful for individual characters of either sex to escape.

Nor did the creator of these characters completely resist the ideology that encloses them. Like James and Howells, Wharton perpetuates assumptions and attitudes that reinforce the inequities her own characters eloquently protest. No character of James or Howells cries out so passionately against women's lot as Wharton's characters do, from Lily Bart, who exclaims to Selden, 'what a miserable thing it is to be a woman' (HM, 7), to Kate Clephane, who fears the power of 'lawyers, judges, trustees, guardians . . . all the natural enemies of woman' (MR, 10) and sees her plight as typical: 'One had to manoeuvre and wait, but when didn't a woman have to manoeuvre and wait?' (MR, 6). Like James's and Howells's female characters, however, women in Wharton's fiction are always portrayed in relation to men, as if their importance as fictional characters had to be validated by the presence of male characters. Her favourite narrative pattern, like James's, is the triangular relation of two women drawn to the same man, the dynamic which propels the plot in *The House of Mirth, The Fruit of the Tree, The Reef, Ethan Frome, The Age of Innocence, The Children, The Mother's Recompense, Summer, The Old Maid, Bunner Sisters,* and *The Gods Arrive.* Inevitably the triangle, which forces the women to become rivals, taints their ties of friendship and kinship with sexual jealousy and fear.

Sexual rivalry calls forth the least attractive traits of some characters (for example, Lily Bart, Rose Sellars), traps others in desperate self-destructive acts (for example, Justine Brent, Mattie Silver), and transforms several into ruthless manipulators (for example, Bertha Dorset, Zenobia Frome). The rivalries which expose women at their most vulnerable or most malevolent, as Susan Goodman shows, reflect the power of society's expectations and customs to determine the conduct of both women and men.[33] But Wharton's placement of men at the centre of women's lives reflects also her own belief, most directly stated in *French Ways and Their Meaning,* that women cannot achieve 'true womanhood' without the influence of men, that women cannot develop without 'the stimulus, and the discipline that comes of contact with the stronger masculine individuality' (FWM, 102–3). Although the 'two sexes complete each other', women have more than men to gain from their association if, as Wharton contends, the man 'is the stronger and the closer to reality' and thus imparts to a woman 'A much larger view of the world' than other women could give her (FWM, 103–19).

Many characters in Wharton's fiction belie her assertions in *French Ways and Their Meaning.* Male figures at the apex of the triangle, such as Selden, George Darrow, Marvell, Archer, Ethan Frome and Martin Boyne do not prove men 'stronger' or 'in closer contact with reality' (FWM, 119). Most of the female characters with whom these men are involved see more clearly and speak more candidly than the men. At the same time, Wharton attaches the conventional negative meanings to the word *feminine,* satirizes the speech of women's characters far more often than the men's, and enforces the division she inveighs against, refusing to almost all her female characters the professional knowledge and artistic power she granted her male characters. She could imagine women surpassing men in courage and insight, but unlike the women writers she disparaged, such as Alcott, Jewett and Freeman, she did not portray women achieving professional success or achieving happiness apart from relations with men. And yet, the picture of

Wharton's insufficient male characters creating rivalries between women often more vigorous than they, and enjoying privileges she denied her most intelligent and cultivated female characters, is itself a powerful indictment of a system which constrained even its most eloquent critics.

5

Singers, Writers and Storytellers in Cather's America

The early years of Willa Cather's professional life were more typical of a male than a female writer. Like Howells, she published short stories and essays while still in her teens; by the age of 20 she too was a regular contributor to the leading newspaper of a Western state. During the winter of 1893–94, when she was a junior at the University of Nebraska in Lincoln, she became the regular drama critic for the *Nebraska State Journal* and began publishing there a weekly column, 'The Passing Show', which she continued for seven years. At 21, the age when Henry James published his first critical essay, in the *North American Review*, she was establishing her reputation as one of the foremost western drama critics, 'in production and distinction the equal of metropolitan critics'.[1]

Like the young Henry James, Cather asserted her authority and articulated her aesthetic principles in reviews notable for satiric exposure of inferior work by the famous and obscure alike. If she felt inhibited in judging the work of well-known men, if she knew the kind of anxiety Virginia Woolf described in recalling the writing of her first review (of *The Son of Royal Langbrith*), this is not apparent in Cather's critical onslaughts. The 23-year-old reviewer who called Thomas Hardy's *Hearts Insurgent* (revised as *Jude the Obscure*) 'that crowning piece of arrant madness and drivelling idiocy' (KA, 358) can hardly be imagined confessing herself haunted by the Angel in the House who whispered to Virginia Woolf:

> My dear, you are a young woman, you are writing about a book that has been written by a man. Be sympathetic; be tender; flatter; deceive; use all the arts and wiles of our sex. Never let anybody guess that you have a mind of your own. Above all, be pure.[2]

So relentless was the young Cather that she became notorious as a 'roaster' of plays (KA, 258). Viewing words as weapons, criticism as a battle against weakness and sham, she herself became known as 'the meatax young girl'. According to Will Owen Jones, managing editor of the *Journal*, 'she wrote dramatic criticisms of such biting frankness that she became famous among actors from coast to coast . . . ' (KA, 16, 17).

Virginia Woolf declared that eventually she won her battle against the Angel in the House: 'I killed her in the end.'³ Willa Cather might seem to have escaped the need of the battle altogether, but in fact, in her early years, she was more completely than Woolf the prisoner of Victorian ideology in that she was apparently unaware of its power over her. In achieving professional success as an aggressive critic, Cather took an unconventional path, but she was often indistinguishable from the most conventional defender of separate spheres and gender-based difference. As Sharon O'Brien has demonstrated, Cather rejected for herself the role of passive observer that her culture assigned to women, yet unquestioningly affirmed its assumption that women were inferior to men in intelligence and artistic power. Unable to repudiate the culture's 'polarization of the sexes', O'Brien observes, Cather 'could reject the female role she found limiting only by continuing to repudiate her sex'.⁴

Cather's repudiation is most sweeping in her early criticism of women writers. Like Edith Wharton, she viewed literature as a masculine profession, scorned women's domestic fiction, and regarded 'sentimentality' as an artistic weakness endemic to women's writing. But she went far beyond Wharton in declaring limits to women's intellectual capacity and in doubting even the existence of literary genius in women. Like those critics who warned women against bold language and then criticized their utterance as weak and trivial, Cather advised women poets to confine themselves to 'highly subjective' lyrics about love or religious faith – the only kind of poetry by women 'worth reading', then criticized female poets and novelists for their 'sex consciousness' that limited them to a single subject (KA, 409). She declared a woman capable of greatness only when she could command the man's world of action to write 'a story of adventure, a stout sea tale, a manly battle yarn' (KA, 409).

Edith Wharton protested the refusal of critics to allow a woman writer such as George Eliot the advantage of knowing philosophy and science. Cather declared 'learning and a wide knowledge of things' injurious to women writers. 'It seems . . . to cripple their naturalness, burden their fancy and cloud their imagination with pedantic metaphors and vague illusions' (KA, 348). Elizabeth Barrett Browning's ten years' study of Greek 'to perfect her style' resulted only in lifeless imitations of classical tragedy, Cather asserted. Browning achieved her 'only great poem', 'Sonnets from the Portuguese', by respecting 'the artistic limitations of her sex' and confining herself to women's proper subject – 'the power of loving'.[5] (Cather never expressed fears that she herself might be crippled and burdened by her study of Greek.)

The young critic who sneered at the authors of *The Woman's Bible* and patronized women writers as 'the ladies' made the familiar complaints about women's writing. In Ouida's *Under Two Flags* she found 'the rudiments of a great style' spoiled because 'adjectives and sentimentality ran away with her, as they do with most women's pens' (WP, I, 275–6). At times, Cather herself fell into the clichés of the sentimental literature she condemned. Her pronouncement, 'a woman has only one gift . . . the power of loving' (WP, I, 146), might have been spoken by Augustin Daly's heroine Laura, whose words in the melodrama *Under the Gaslight* – 'Remember, love is all a woman has to give' – Dreiser made famous in *Sister Carrie*.[6]

Cather celebrated another Victorian ideal in praising writing by men that was *manly*, the supreme masculine virtue that Cather linked with such words as *noble, strong* and *tender* in reviews of Kipling, Eugene Field and Robert Louis Stevenson.[7] Predictably she made the traditional association of *feminine* with the weak, slight, trivial. Women are destined to write inferior novels, she said, because 'the feminine mind has a hankering for hobbies and missions' (KA, 406). The phrase 'feminine mind' in itself implies limitations attributed to all women.

Cather's favourite images of the artist, as military hero and divine creator, identified literary genius with masculine power and authority. She pronounced Frances Hodgson Burnett doomed to fail in her attempt to write a novel in the eighteenth-century style by imitating such 'mighty warriors of the pen' as Smollett and Fielding (KA, 373). The idea of artist as divine creator did comprehend powers of love and sympathetic identification, as Sharon O'Brien notes,[8] but in celebrating the 'priesthood of art' (KA, 153) Cather identified literary transformation with the sacrament celebrated only by men. Only George Sand and George Eliot she considered 'real creators' among women writers, and 'they were anything but women' (KA, 409). Mary Anderson's retirement from the stage moved Cather to ask whether 'any woman ever really had the art instinct, the art necessity? Is it not with them a substitute, a trans- ferred enthusiasm, an escape valve for what has sought or is seek- ing another channel?' (KA, 158).

An actress's decision had prompted Cather to generalize that 'for a woman [marriage] is plainly the proper consummation – and the happy one' (KA, 158). But in the performances of actresses and opera singers, especially Wagnerian sopranos, Cather saw embo- died the creative power and authority she believed denied to women writers. On the stage, a woman's sex empowered rather than diminished her. Cleopatra is not obscured by Antony. The soprano's is the dominant, privileged voice, as Cather observed wryly: 'All the operatic virtues are supposed to express themselves only in the soprano register' (WP, II, 758). The art of the actress and singer transcends her physicality but is inseparable from it. Men wrote the plays and operas Cather saw, but their words lived for audiences only as the performers sang and spoke them.

Cather lambasted the performances of many actresses but in sev- eral she saw realized the power of the greatest male artist without sacrifice of female identity. Above all, Sarah Bernhardt, 'dread goddess of mortal speech', united attributes traditionally identified as masculine and feminine. According to Cather, she expressed 'tremendous emotion' by her 'perfect technique' (KA, 120). Her art, compounded of 'passion and power' (KA, 116), was the product of 'the most rigorous training' informed by the 'perfect under- standing and sympathy' (KA, 120) she brought to every role. Like male writers she commanded the power of warriors and conque- rors: her art, 'like the Roman army . . . subdues a world, a world that is proud to be conquered when it is by Rome' (KA, 120).

Likewise, the great opera singers Cather heard at the turn of the century could be conquerors without ceasing to be women. Nordi- ca (Lillian Norton), 'the splendid Amazon warrior', who trium- phed at Bayreuth, 'full armed and girded for the fray', also embodied 'all that is best in American womanhood' (WP, II, 644, 646). Ernestine Schumann-Heink, the mother of nine children, was unsurpassed in the 'rigorous labor of her profession' (WP, II, 758). On occasion, Cather betrayed her society's sense that the woman artist was an anomaly, to be marvelled at in a culture where the male performance was the norm. For Cather, the Venezuelan pianist and soprano, Teresa Carreño, a 'consummate artist', with 'the face of a conqueror', displayed 'broad comprehensive mastery' at the piano that 'made you wonder if this could be a woman' (WP, I, 398). Cather did not wonder if male pianists such as Pochmann or Lhevinne could be men. But had she reviewed Carreño the soprano rather than the pianist the performer's sex would have been taken for granted.

Naturally in her reviews of operas, Cather described the voices of the singers. What is remarkable is her fascination with the voices of actresses, which preoccupied her more than their stage presence or their interpretation of their roles. Bernhardt's greatest gift was 'the most perfect voice that ever spoke through a human throat' (KA, 120). Clara Morris was remarkable by 'the wonderful power' of her voice (KA, 262). Only rarely did Cather comment on the voices of male actors. She admired the 'agility' and the 'charming audacity' of Salvini (KA, 122), the culture and intelligence of Richard Mansfield, but she said nothing about their voices.

Cather's early reviews of writers and performers suggest the central importance of the 'gender divide' that separates the male and female characters of her fiction. Written texts – histories, diaries, memoirs, manuscripts – are the products of men, as are forms of public discourse, such as sermons and lectures. The woman's instrument is the voice, not the pen; her female characters express themselves in words sung or spoken, not written. They are singers, actresses and oral storytellers, not writers. The actress on the stage may be 'an author who writes a book every night' (KA, 215), but Cather derided the *Ladies' Home Journal* for seeking 'articles from actresses, prima donnas, and eminent divines' (KA, 188). Of course, Cather did not confine her fictional characters by their sex to certain categories. A male singer, Sebastian Clement, is a central character in *Lucy Gayheart*. Tellers of stories and legends include the woodsmen Antoine Frichette and Pierre Charron in *Shadows on the Rock* and a score of priests, scouts and traders in *Death Comes for the Archbishop*. But the division in *My Ántonia*, in which Jim Burden writes the manuscript incorporating Ántonia's stories and the Widow Steavens's account to Jim of Ántonia's darkest year, exemplifies a pervasive pattern in Cather's fiction.

To a lesser degree, both James and Howells in their fiction make a similar identification of men with writing and women with vocal performance. In Howells's fiction men write sermons, speeches, novels and essays; his most accomplished storyteller is Penelope Lapham, whose mastery of the comic monologist's art provides entertainment for her family and Tom Corey. James's female character who displays the artistry and wins the critical acclaim accorded his male novelists is the actress Miriam Rooth. But only Cather's fiction sustains the oral tradition by reproducing the tales told by her narrators to make stories within stories. Howells gives no text of Penelope's performances and neither James nor Howells portrays the process by which narrators transform events into stories passed from one generation to another, as the figures of Jim's and Ántonia's childhood become part of the family mythology, to live in the imagination of her children. No character of James or Howells has the role of Ántonia, 'an oral historian of the lives of the obscure'.[9]

In Cather's fiction, women are the chief preservers of the family's stories and traditions and rituals. Women as singers rise highest on the scale of creative power. A great voice was to Cather the ultimate blessing – 'the one gift that all creatures would possess if they could'.[10] The great female voice was the gift in its supreme form – not only 'a dramatic incarnation of femininity and creativity', as O'Brien says,[11] but in the novels the ultimate expression of divine power revealed in mortal art. The words by which Cather repeatedly described the great prima donnas of the opera stage – *confident, regal, majestic, valiant, magnificent, passionate, fearless, indomitable* – suggest the kind of transcendent power she invested in the female singers of her fiction. Most of her female characters are excluded from the male worlds of literature and scholarship, but women have energy, vitality and powers of endurance and feeling that the male writers and teachers cannot sustain. The contrast informs her fiction at every stage but is most dramatically represented in her third novel, *The Song of the Lark* (1915), in the portrayal from childhood to maturity of a great opera singer, Thea Kronborg, whose development, more fully than that of any other character in Cather's fiction, illuminates the gender divisions created by the interplay of music and language, the verbal and the non-verbal.

II

Before she wrote *The Song of the Lark*, Cather had published four stories of female singers. None questions the greatness of the

singer's artistry but all depict negative sides of the artist's experience: the exploitation of child prodigies ending in the collapse of
the girl ('The Prodigies'); the final death-haunted days of a singer
who had lived in her love for a composer beloved of many women
('A Death in the Desert'); the loneliness of a singer whose maid and
companion deserts her to marry ('Nanette: An Aside'); the disillu-
sionment of an aging singer who discovers that the man she has
fantasized as her admirer is in love with her maid ('A Singer's
Romance'). *The Song of the Lark* portrays the singer's progress from
the discovery of her gift in childhood, through the difficult years of
poverty and overwork, to conclude with her repeated success on
the opera stage, where she sings the roles of the great Wagnerian
heroines – Elsa, Elizabeth, Sieglinde – that parallel her own heroic
quest and triumph. Thea Kronborg is the only protagonist of
Cather's who achieves complete artistic fulfilment, who is neither
disillusioned nor betrayed. Except for a youthful rendition on the
piano of a ballad too long and technical to please the church-going
audience of Moonstone, Colorado, Thea never fails in a performance, whether she is auditioning for a prospective teacher, or
fulfilling her first professional engagements in Chicago, or making
her operatic debut in Munich, or filling in at the last minute at the
Metropolitan Opera in the role of Sieglinde. Musical genius, fortu-
nate circumstance and valiant character combine to produce artistic success of the purest kind, unclouded by failure or compromise.
Her singing to Harsanyi of Orpheus's lament from Gluck's opera,
by which her voice is discovered, identifies her not with the loss of
the beloved but with the god's power to charm all creatures by his
music.[12]

Apart from any gender distinctions a writer might make, a novel
about a musician naturally separates the verbal from the non-
verbal. In Chicago, at Thea's first symphony concert, for instance, a
performance of Dvorak's Symphony in E Minor, 'From the New
World', fills her mind with visual images of her childhood world,
enabling her on her return to the desert country to hear for the first
time 'a new song . . . which had never been sung in the world
before' – a song that 'had nothing to do with words' but is ap-
prehended 'like the light of the desert at noon, or the smell of the
sagebrush after rain; intangible but powerful' (SL, 220).

Destined to express the essence of her country's 'new song',
Thea's singing voice likewise for her listeners evokes images of the
natural and non-verbal. To Wunsch, her first teacher, hers is a

'nature-voice' 'apart from language, like the sound of the wind in the trees, or the murmur of water' (SL, 77). To Harsanyi, her teacher in Chicago, who begins Thea's education as a singer, her voice is a creature to be enclosed, and tamed, 'like a wild bird that had flown into his studio on Middleton Street from goodness knew how far!' (SL, 187).

The primacy of Thea's 'nature voice' 'apart from language' is emphasized by her own reluctance or inability to speak. As a small child, she 'never spoke at all, except in monosyllables'; at school, 'still inept in speech', although highly intelligent, she rarely expressed the ideas clearly formed in her mind (SL, 16). By temperament she is reticent, little given to self-revelations, even with friends; 'she was not naturally communicative' (SL, 179). At times, as with Harsanyi, when, unable to express her feelings, she confesses, 'There is no use in my talking' (SL, 211), her reserve reflects a sense of social awkwardness reminiscent of Cather's feeling of constraint in the Charles Street drawing room of Annie Fields. More important is Thea's sense that words are inadequate to convey her feelings, that to verbalize her dreams and desires is to violate them. Repeatedly she resists the efforts of others to draw her out. She protests to Wunsch: 'You are just trying to make me say things. It spoils things to ask questions' (SL, 78). With her patron Fred Ottenburg she refuses to dilate on her joy in self-sufficiency: 'it always makes me unhappy to talk about it' (SL, 318). In her longest speech in the novel, at the height of her powers, she explains to Dr Archie, her childhood friend and protector: 'What one strives for is so far away, so deep, so beautiful . . . that there's nothing one can say about it' (SL, 460).

Reticence, youthful ineptness, the artist's recognition of the inexpressible – these are not traditionally gendered traits. But Cather associates the non-verbal with the feminine by making her protagonist a singer acutely aware of her female body as a source of knowledge and artistic power. In Panther Canyon, where her artist self is born, her understanding of the Ancient People – 'not expressible in words' (SL, 303) – is formed in her body as she imagines herself in the bodies of the women who had climbed the water trail centuries ago. 'She found herself trying to walk as they must have walked, with a feeling in her feet and knees and loins which she had never known before, which must have come up to her out of the accustomed dust of that rocky trail. She could feel the weight of an Indian baby hanging to her back as she climbed' (SL, 302).

She will not become a mother in the novel, but the passage implies that her birth as an artist is inseparable from her birth as a woman. As Hermione Lee has noted, her ripening sexuality is registered by women, not men;[13] by Thea herself on the train from Chicago as she thinks of death, then feels the warmth of her breast and 'the full, powerful pulsation' within (SL, 217); by her mother, who notes the milk-whiteness of her daughter's skin and her round firm breasts as Thea lies in bed (SL, 224). Thea's sexual union with Ottenburg is only hinted at – erotic love is not the main source of her artistic power – but once her female sexuality is established it is implicit for the reader in every reference to the expressive power of Thea's body, which on the opera stage becomes 'absolutely the instrument of her idea' (SL, 478). Nature, the female body, sound, music, and the abstract idea incarnate in the singer are all fused in the image of the river. In Panther Canyon, by the stream, symbolizing 'the continuity of life', Thea has her defining, universalizing vision of art: 'an effort to make a sheath, a mould in which to imprison for a moment the shining, elusive element which is life itself' (SL, 304). Like the pots the ancient women made to carry their water, the singer's throat is a vessel, from which the voice issues, 'a river of silver sound' (SL, 412) to be held by the memory of those who hear it. When Thea sings one of the Rhine daughters in *Das Reingold*, she creates the voice of the river: 'she simply *was* the idea of the Rhine music' (SL, 396).

Cather's emphasis on the non-verbal, however, should not be allowed to obscure the importance of words in Thea's development as an artist. In childhood, she reads novels and poetry and learns the words of songs that others teach her. Although in conversation she is often inarticulate, not given to ready speech, she is remarkably sensitive to the meanings of words, as shown when she not only quickly memorizes the words of a poem by Heine but makes a fine distinction between meanings of *remind*: to bring to mind and to put one in mind of (SL, 77). As a Wagnerian singer she dedicates herself to the opera in which, Cather believed, words and music are most completely fused. When Thea's friend Dr Archie is to hear Thea sing Elsa in *Lohengrin*, Ottenburg tells him to study the libretto first: 'If you know the text you'll get a great deal' (SL, 397). In her introduction to Gertrude Hall's *Wagnerian Romances*, Cather applied her definition of opera – 'a hybrid art, partly literary to begin with' – particularly to Wagner, whose music 'is throughout concerned with words and with things that can be presented in language'.[14] All the elements of a Wagner opera – characters and their passions, places, landscapes, cities, rivers – symbolized by the leitmotif are, 'in the hands of the right person, readily translatable into words'. Gertrude Hall's translations of Wagner's text were exemplary in that 'the words here are not divorced from the action but vividly accompanied by the action (in narrative) as Wagner meant them to be'.[15]

Thea is a transcendent figure whose triumphant performances as Elsa and Sieglinde completely fulfil Cather's definition of singing as 'idealized speech' and the ideal singer who 'preserve[s] the proportion and harmony between words and action' (KA, 217). Thea writes no texts, however, nor does she read any writings by women. The books she reads in childhood are by men – Byron, Tolstoy, memoirs by a minister and by a Polar explorer. Men have composed the words of the operas she sings and the poetry she recites. Her 'nature voice' is revealed when she recites a poem by Heine taught her by her first teacher, Herr Wunsch.

To Harsanyi, Thea's first teacher in Chicago, Thea herself is a being to be created, a blank page to be inscribed. 'She came to me like a fine young savage', he tells his wife, 'a book with nothing written in it' (SL, 203). Harsanyi's comparison might be dismissed as a commonplace – yet one more instance of a man presuming to 'write the woman' according to his idea of her.[16] But Cather seems to endorse the image of woman as book – not only by presenting Harsanyi in the most positive light as the ideal artist and teacher, but also by emphasizing the importance of men in the creation of Thea's professional career. Thea herself regards men as important to her primarily as teachers: 'In the natural course of things she would never have loved a man from whom she could not learn a great deal' (SL, 378). She is portrayed only with her male teachers – Wunsch, Harsanyi, and Madison Bowers. Cather dropped from the manuscript the chapters in which Thea studies in Germany with Lilli Lehmann. Thea merely speaks of 'my going to Lehmann' (SL, 376) and never mentions her again. Unlike James's Miriam Rooth, whom Thea resembles in her determination, early social crudity and belated marriage, Cather's artist heroine is never seen as the pupil of a great woman artist, like Madame Carré, and the inheritor of the tradition she represents. The absence of Lilli Lehmann, 'that powerful repository of tradition',[17] contributes to the sense of Thea as autonomous, born of the New World, outside of Old World traditions. The absence of a female teacher or critic also restricts to male characters occasions for discourses on music and the singer's art. A succession of men – Wunsch, Ottenburg, Harsanyi, and Thea's accompanist, Landry – name elements, such as desire, passion, colour and personality, that together compose the character and voice of the ideal artist that Thea represents. Of the men, only Harsanyi the pianist is fulfilled in his art as Thea is in hers. The lives of all the other male characters who aid and guide Thea are in some way constricted – by early death (Ray Kennedy); by poverty and drink (Wunsch); by ruinous marriage (Archie and Ottenburg); by meanness of spirit (Bowers). But each is essential in moving Thea to a new stage of her journey. Only male characters – Harsanyi and Ottenburg have the knowledge and critical vocabulary to certify the greatness of Thea's art, to define it for other characters, to provide the glowing reviews, as it were, that notify the world of the artist's success.

But Cather does not give the male characters the last word. The novel ends not with the male critics who analyse Thea's art but with her aunt, Tillie Kronborg, whose lifelong admiration and love of her niece redeem her foolishness and harmless vanity. Her rapturous stories of Thea's success in London and New York, although a source of amusement to others, nonetheless link the people of Moonstone to the great world outside where Thea has won fame. The words of Thea's aunt are life-giving, renewing the spirit of the listener as

> the many naked little sandbars which lie between Venice and the mainland, in the seemingly stagnant water of the lagoons, are made habitable and wholesome only because, every night, a foot and a half of tide creeps in from the sea and winds its fresh brine up through all that network of shining waterways. (SL, 490)

Given the prominence of Thea throughout the novel and the elevation of Tillie Kronborg at the end one might conclude that Cather wished to exalt female singing and storytelling over male discourse. Certainly Thea is a far more radiant figure than any of the male characters, who seem rather shadowy or colourless beside her. But Cather's conception of language is too complex, too multilayered, to permit a view that favours one sex over the other.

Although the growth of musical genius is Cather's subject, the novel simultaneously portrays Thea's development as a social being formed by particular conditions, those of the small Colorado

desert town, whose inhabitants reflect their culture in their habits
of speech. Thus the novel gives Thea two voices, which Wunsch
identifies when Thea is still a child: her everyday speaking voice
and the 'nature voice' in which she will ultimately sing the words
of Wagner's operas. When Thea recites poetry 'the character of her
voice changed altogether; it was no longer the voice which spoke
the speech of Moonstone. It was a soft, rich contralto, and she read
quietly; the feeling was in the voice itself, not indicated by emphasis or change of pitch' (SL, 77). Later, Harsanyi, after hearing
Thea sing, is startled when she speaks, having forgotten 'how hard
and full of burrs her speaking voice was' (SL, 188).

The beauty of Thea's singing voice is not marred by the defects of
her speaking voice. But Cather was as sensitive as any novelist of
manners to the power of speech, indicative of one's class and
training, to advance or retard one's way in the world. Thus she
makes Thea aware of the value of cultivated speech and conscious
of her own deficiency. With the Harsanyis, whose speech would
meet Wharton's standard of the 'best usage', Thea feels herself
crude and untutored, confessing to her teacher, 'I'm not like you
and Mrs Harsanyi. I come of rough people. I'm rough' (SL, 211).
Later, when she shares a table in a railroad dining car with a family
from the East, her understanding of what she lacks, articulated in
the flat conventional phrases of 'Moonstone speech', is most fully
expressed:

> They spoke in that quick, sure staccato, which Thea, like Ray
> Kennedy, pretended to scorn and secretly admired. People who
> could use words in that confident way, and who spoke them
> elegantly, had a great advantage in life, she reflected. There were
> so many words which she could not pronounce in speech as she
> had to do in singing. Language was like clothes; it could be a help
> to one, or it could give one away. But the most important thing
> was that one should not pretend to be what one was not. (SL, 219)

Cather develops the centuries-old analogy of language and clothes
to highlight their importance and the social identity they create.
During Thea's early years of struggle and privation, her social
awkwardness and crudities of speech are matched by ill-fitting or
inappropriate clothes: the country 'fascinator' and 'clumsy plush
cape' lined with 'farmer's satin' she wears to the Harsanyis' (SL,
179), the outgrown white organdie dress of childhood from which

she seems 'struggling to be free' (SL, 243), the cheap purple suit and hat she wears in Chicago, 'like the attire of a shopgirl who tries to follow the fashions' (SL, 255). The connection between language and clothes is reinforced by Ottenburg, who compares Thea's 'perfectly good Moonstone' formulas (for example, the 'keepsakes that I value so highly') to 'ready-made clothes that hang in the windows, made to fit everybody and fit nobody, a phrase that can be used on all occasions' (SL, 378). He assures her that in Germany she will acquire 'a new speech full of shades and color like your voice; alive, like your mind. It will be almost like being born again' (SL, 378). The transformation of Thea from an impoverished socially insecure music student to an authoritative woman who commands every scene on and off stage begins even before her opera debut in Germany. Shortly before her departure, Dr Archie notes 'her greater positiveness, her whole augmented self' (SL, 371) of which her 'worldly clothes' are part.

In one sense, however, artists never escape their origins and early influences. Again functioning as the author's surrogate to define Thea, Ottenburg tells Dr Archie, 'Her scale of values will always be the Moonstone scale' (SL, 369), by which he means that she will never repudiate her past or reject her intrinsic self. What Thea must resist and escape are the ignorance and intolerance that oppress all Cather's sensitive and ambitious characters confined in small Midwestern towns.[18] Outsiders such as Wunsch and Ottenburg, who associate small-town life with the mean and ugly, imply that 'the speech of Moonstone' and 'pure Moonstone' are things to be rejected. But for Cather this is true only if 'Moonstone' is made synonymous with the self-righteousness of Thea's 'natural enemies' such as her priggish sister Anna and the town's moral censor, Mrs Livery Johnson.

The narrator represents the positive values of 'pure Moonstone' by contrasting natural speech, rooted in a character's experience, with conventional formulas and professional jargon. The difference is illustrated by the conversation of Ray Kennedy, the self-educated railroad man who dreams of marrying Thea but dies in an accident, leaving her all his savings, $600, to study in Chicago. When he attempts an 'educated' style, using 'newspaper phrases, consciously learned in his efforts at self-instruction' (SL, 50), his language is stiff and forced. When he speaks 'naturally' of places and people he knows, he 'could talk well' and was 'always worth listening to' (SL, 50).

Cather does not make the conventional versus the natural into a male–female dichotomy, but in *The Song of the Lark* formulaic speech is primarily a male attribute. Thea's father, a minister in a small Swedish church, betrays his commonplace mind and lack of imagination, when in his pulpit 'he wielded . . . a somewhat pompous English vocabulary he had learned out of books at college. . . . The poor man had no natural, spontaneous human speech . . . he habitually expressed himself in a book-learned language, wholly remote from anything personal, native, or homely' (SL, 15–16). Likewise, Dr Archie, although much more intelligent and enlightened than Thea's father, at times resorts to professional language to assert his authority and protect his self-esteem. But he is stiff and unnatural not because he wishes to seem learned or cannot speak otherwise, but because he is a romantic who 'had not the courage to be an honest thinker. He could comfort himself by evasions and compromises' (SL, 85).

It is a measure of the power of traditions that define women as the subordinate sex that Mrs Kronborg, portrayed as far more intelligent, wise and humane than her husband, should feel 'profound respect' for his 'erudition and eloquence' and sit 'under his preaching with deep humility' (SL, 11). By his standard, which she herself accepts, her speech would be judged inferior: 'Mrs Kronborg spoke Swedish to her own sisters and to her sister-in-law Tillie, and colloquial English to her neighbors' (SL, 16). But hers is the 'natural spontaneous human speech' which is never dissipated in meaningless talk, as Thea perceives: 'Her mother knew a great many things of which she never talked, and all the church people were forever chattering about things of which they knew nothing' (SL, 225).

For Cather, speech is an index to character: the divorce of words and realities in the speech of Kronborg and Dr Archie reveals deficiencies in the men themselves. Thea rightly perceives her mother's forthright speech and reticence as signs of her moral worth. But the novel insists upon the aesthetic and moral values of both the vernacular and standard English; without the voices of Ottenburg and Harsanyi, the novel would be incomplete. The male characters articulate ideas that Thea herself cannot express and they help to create the circumstances in which her artist's self is born. But when Ottenburg mocks Thea's Moonstone expressions ('You are delicious when you fall into your vernacular', SL, 378) and assures her she will learn a new (and better) language abroad, he assumes the conventional masculine role as critic of vernacular speech traditionally identified with women[19] – a role that puts him at odds with the narrator and author of the novel. As Susan Rosowski has shown, the novel is filled with expressions belonging to the 'colloquial English' identified with Mrs Kronborg.[20] Cather in her long letter to Dorothy Canfield about *The Song of the Lark* stated that she wrote the novel in the language of Moonstone, at first using quotation marks which she later removed. More than any other, this novel proves Cather's belief, expressed in her preface to Sarah Orne Jewett's stories, that the language of a community – its 'pithy bits of local speech, of native idiom' indicative of its 'attitude toward the world and its way of accepting life' – language that is rooted in the people's experience – 'makes the finest language any writer can have'.[21] The 'native idiom' is not given to one sex exclusively, but in *The Song of the Lark* women speak it, the most prominent male character scorns it, and the author validates it by making it the language of the novel.

III

Although – or because – the world of journalism and letters is almost entirely dominated by men in Cather's fiction, those narratives portraying writers and scholars expose most starkly the conflicts between men and women that touch most of Cather's characters. Whether male characters are frustrated would-be writers or recognized masters of literary art, the women in their lives are portrayed as victims of men's careers, or as exploited subordinates in the modern business world dominated by men, or as destructive presences threatening to male creative power.

During her six years on the staff of S. S. McClure (1906–12), Cather published stories, essays and poems in his magazine. From 1908 she served as its managing editor, and shortly after her resignation she wrote McClure's autobiography. In her fiction, however, the approved function of women in offices is to take dictation from men and prepare the copy of male contributors. In 'Ardessa' (1918), Cather's one story set in an editorial office, the title character, a rigidly genteel woman who initially enjoys a privileged position as the editor's private secretary and 'social mentor', tries to assume an editor's prerogatives during his prolonged absences. She writes letters 'in her most polished and elegant style',[22] encourages would-be contributors to gather in her office for advice, and refuses to perform mundane tasks she considers beneath her until the editor replaces her with a young copyist, Becky Teitelbaum, so eager for work that she gladly allows herself to be exploited. To the editor, women are machines to be worked hard and cast aside when they wear out. Dictating letters to Becky, 'who raced ahead with him . . . was like riding a good modern bicycle after pumping along on an old hard tire' (UV, 112). Cather remains critically aloof from both the predatory rider and the 'old tire', Ardessa, who becomes absurd in her presumptions.

Both the male writer and the young female copyist who transcribes his words are figures of pathos in 'Her Boss' (1919), a story foreshadowing *The Professor's House* in its portrayal of a middle-aged man oppressed and seeking escape from a household dominated by a socially ambitious wife and two daughters. Like Tolstoy's Ivan Ilytch, Cather's protagonist, Paul Wanning, learns that he is mortally ill, and suffers the refusal of his cold conventional family even to acknowledge his condition. He finds acceptance and understanding only with an old Negro servant, and the copyist Annie Wooley, to whom he dictates the reminiscences of his youth. With her he seems to realize long-buried literary ambitions dormant through years of married life – 'it was like living his life over again' (UV, 132). In service to his need, she is victimized when his psychological dependence on her creates gossip among his law partners, who after his death connive at the family's decision to deprive Annie of the bequest to her in Wanning's will.

The ironies which govern the reader's response to 'Ardessa' and 'Her Boss' are clear in intention. More ambiguous are the ironies in 'The Willing Muse' (1907), notable for Cather's only portrayal of a female professional writer. This James-inspired tale of the marriage of two novelists reverses traditional roles: the young wife, Bertha Torrance, initially prepared to be the 'willing muse' of her husband's art, becomes the prolific writer of popular historical novels, while her husband, seemingly paralysed by her 'phenomenal productiveness',[23] assumes the traditional wifely roles – reading her proofs, writing her letters, and protecting her from interruptions, until he can bear no more and disappears. Like Ray Limbert of 'The Next Time', the husband, Kenneth Gray, writes books of the highest literary quality – a concentrated psychological study illustrating Cather's ideal of 'the novel démeublé', followed by 'an exquisite prose idyl', *The Wood of Ronsard* (CSF, 114). But instead of trying to emulate the successful woman writer, he marries her, becoming the sacred fount from which she draws her imaginative energy: 'she had absorbed from Kenneth like a water plant' (CSF, 117). Like the Brissendens in *The Sacred Fount*, he ages as his wife seems to grow younger – 'taller, straighter . . . positively childlike in her freshness and candor' (CSF, 120).

The male narrator, a college friend of Gray's, who observes the effects of this vampirish marriage, diminishes the literary importance of Bertha Torrance, referring to her 'making' of novels 'each cleverer and more damnable than the last' (CSF, 123). In his view, her 'fatal facility' is almost diabolic, the incessant click of her typewriter in her husband's ears like an instrument of torture. The story clearly exposes male fears of female creativity, but the reader must determine whether Cather shares her narrator's view of the marriage or whether she intended an ironic exposure of him. His demonizing of Gray's wife suggests more than simple concern for his friend, but otherwise there is no suggestion of spiritual blindness such as dictates an ironic view of Wharton's narrator in 'The Eyes' or James's narrator in 'The Aspern Papers'. Rather, the male narrator in 'The Willing Muse' seems a device enabling Cather to distance herself from both the popular writer of inferior novels and the failed aesthete.

Bertha Torrance has no successors in Cather's fiction, but despite his failure, Kenneth Gray foreshadows the successful male scholars and writers of Cather's later fiction: notably Gaston Cleric in *My Ántonia* and Godfrey St Peter, the protagonist of *The Professor's House*. Like Gray, who is a student of the French Renaissance, St Peter has made the study of the past his life's work, expending his creative energies in writing a monumental eight-volume history of Spanish adventurers in North America. Cleric, head of the Latin Department at the University of Nebraska where Jim Burden becomes his devoted student, is not the author of books, but his lectures have the imaginative power of poetry. Unlike Kronborg and Archie, who 'often dodged behind a professional manner' (SL, 13), Cleric 'had no platitudes, no stock of professorial anecdotes'.[24] To the responsive listener such as Jim Burden, his words are instinct with newly created life: 'He could bring the drama of antique life before one out of the shadows – white figures against blue backgrounds' (MA, 295).

The masculinist nature of scholarship is evident not only in the scholars' choice of subjects (explorers, conquerors, male poets), but in the virtual exclusion of women from the scholarly world. Their absence is highlighted by the importance Cather attached to the characters' study of Greek and Latin, especially the poetry of Virgil. For Cather herself, no academic subject was of greater importance than the classics. At the University of Nebraska she studied Latin for two years and Greek for three years, appeared in a student production of *Elektra* in Greek, and after graduation she taught Latin for a term in the Central High School in Pittsburgh. In her fiction, however, Cather followed the tradition that for centuries had excluded women from the study of classical languages and had preserved knowledge of Greek and Latin as a privilege reserved for men. Cather recreates her study of the classics at the university only in Jim Burden's account of Cleric's inspired teaching. Thus Cather reinforces the status of Latin as the 'father-speech', in Walter Ong's terms, an acquired language 'learned by males from other males'.[25]

A few of Cather's intelligent female characters study Latin in high school. Peggy, the narrator of 'The Joy of Nelly Deane', recalls a 'delightfully easy passage' from Caesar in which merchants brought to Gaul 'those things which effeminate the mind' (CSF, 60) – even here sexual bias obtrudes. Vickie Templeton, in 'Old Mrs Harris', 'stumblingly' translates the verses of the *Dies Irae* hymn in *Faust* when her friend, Mrs Rosen, confesses her ignorance of Latin. But Thea Kronborg, in *The Song of the Lark*, must ask her piano teacher, Herr Wunsch, to translate a passage from Ovid. Euclide Auclair, in *Shadows on the Rock*, reads Latin with his 12-year-old daughter, Cécile, but the Reverend Mother disapproves, reminding him that 'he had a girl to bring up, and not a son whom he was educating for the priesthood'.[26] The one time Cécile is shown reading Plutarch with her father, she is unable to concentrate and makes so many mistakes that her father takes the book and reads to her instead.

Female characters, such as Alexandra Bergson, Thea Kronborg and Ántonia Shimerda, embody mythic qualities celebrated in classical epic and pastoral, as Susan Rosowski, Donald Sutherland and others have shown.[27] But only Cather's male characters consciously identify themselves with classical authors and with figures of classical literature. Only for the male characters is the reading of the classics a transforming experience, an intellectual awakening.

Classical literature is not only a source of inspiration for male characters; it also creates a bond between men – almost always a bond between a young man and his teacher and mentor. This bond, often the deepest attachment Cather's male protagonist feels, excludes women, as if Latin and Greek were secret languages that women cannot know. If a woman becomes a rival for the affection of the male teacher or pupil, she is cast aside, as are Lena Lingard in *My Ántonia* and Lillian St Peter in *The Professor's House*. The bond between male characters survives although – or perhaps because – it is always physically broken by death. The pupil or the teacher – whoever is the source of inspiration to the other – inevitably dies, leaving the survivor to enshrine the lost one in his memory. No woman is a partner in such a relationship with another of her own sex. The tradition that excludes women not only safeguards male friendship from rival claims but elevates to the plane of art and scholarship an attachment that might otherwise appear suspect.

The bond of shared knowledge is not fully developed until the mature novels, *My Ántonia* and *The Professor's House*, but the pattern appears in an early story, 'Jack-a-Boy', a sentimental tale, first published in 1901, important mainly for what it foreshadows. The central character is a middle-aged professor of Greek, who at the beginning of the story is devoting his solitary and bloodless existence to writing a book on Greek prosody. He is awakened to the spirit of the poetry he dissects by the appearance of a stranger in his neighbourhood, a six-year-old boy of unearthly charm and beauty, who attaches himself to the professor and begs to hear tales of Achilles and Odysseus and the Trojan War. To the professor, the child seems less a mortal boy than the divine embodiment of the scholar's passion for the classical world. In the professor's words, the child 'was of that antique world, and he would have lived in it always, like Keats . . . the Greek spirit was his' (CSF, 321). The professor dreams of teaching the boy to read Greek, but when the child lies dying of scarlet fever, his fatal illness confirms for the professor the reality of the divine spirit inhabiting the child's body. The elements of the pattern, to be fully realized in the symbolic realism of the novels, are here: the appearance of the gifted stranger, the spiritual awakening, the attachment of pupil and teacher bound by their love of the classics, the early death of the one who calls the other to life. Even the woman's awareness of exclusion appears. The narrator, identified as 'Miss Harris', confesses herself injured when she sees the child going with the professor to hang May baskets: 'I did not try to conceal my jealousy. I felt rather lonely and ill-used' (CSF, 317).

In Cather's later fiction, characters usually find their comparisons and their sources of inspiration in Latin, rather than Greek, literature, particularly in the poetry of Virgil. The protagonist of another early story, 'The Namesake' (1907), foreshadows the later characters, such as Jim Burden and Tom Outland, when he narrates to a group of male friends the climactic experience of his life: the revelation that followed his discovery in his ancestral house in Pittsburgh of a worn copy of the *Aeneid*, 'dog-eared and rubbed and interlined' (CSF, 145) by his uncle, Lyon Hartwell, who died in the Civil War at the age of 15. The young soldier's sketch of the Federal flag on the flyleaf endows the book for his namesake with a kind of talismanic power that resurrects the boy and his past and unites him and the narrator: 'I seemed, somehow, at last to have known him . . . I could see him, there in the shine of the morning, his book idly on his knee, his flashing eyes looking straight before him' (CSF, 145–6). For him, as for Cather's later students of Virgil, the poem that creates his consciousness of the ancient world at the same time roots him in his own past. 'For the first time I felt the pull of race and blood and kindred, and felt beating within me things that had not begun with me' (CSF, 146).

These might also be the words of Jim Burden, the narrator of Cather's fourth novel, *My Ántonia*, whose reading of Virgil's *Georgics* under Cleric's inspiring tutelage invests the persons of his own life with a reality they never had before. 'Mental excitement was apt to send me with a rush back to my own naked land and the figures scattered upon it . . . They stood out strengthened and simplified now, like the image of the plough against the sun' (MA, 296–7). Jim is thus preparing himself to write Ántonia's story and to realize Cather's mission, expressed when he dwells upon the lines interpreted by Cleric: 'for I shall be the first, if I live, to bring the Muse into my country' (MA, 299).

Inseparable from Jim's 'mental awakening' (MA, 292), which he owes to Cleric, is his friendship with his teacher, whose influence seems enhanced by the illness that marks him for early death. Before Jim meets Cleric, he has studied alone, learning long passages of the *Aeneid* by heart. But no illumination attended those solitary hours. Only when Cleric visits him in his rooms at the university and talks of Italy does 'the drama of antique life' (MA, 295) become reality for Jim. Together they touch the generative power of Virgil's poetry through the interchange of another master and pupil, as Cleric recites to Jim 'the discourse between Dante and

Virgil, his "sweet teacher" ' (MA, 296). When Cleric quotes from the *Purgatorio* the lines of the poet Statius in veneration of the *Aeneid*, 'mother to me and nurse to me in poetry' (MA, 296), the words by analogy identify Cleric, Jim's 'sweet teacher', with the maternal role hitherto assumed by Ántonia.

Of all Cather's novels, *My Ántonia* most directly connects men's study of the classics to their withdrawal from women. When his grandparents' disapproval compels Jim to give up seeing the hired girls at the Firemen's Hall dances, he studies Latin, 'not in our High-School course' (MA, 259), to meet college entrance requirements. When Jim allows his relations with Lena Lingard to consume his time and energies, Cleric stands like a guide at the crossroads, instructing Jim in his choice. But Jim's response to the *Georgics* has already detached him from Lena. The 'revelation . . . inestimably precious' (MA, 306) to which Virgil leads him – that without girls like Lena 'there would be no poetry' (MA, 306) – transforms the sexually desirable woman into an aesthetic image that inspires male poets. Reading Virgil with Cleric removes the reaping hook from the figure that once threatened and enticed Jim in his erotic dream of Lena but now 'floated before me on the page like a picture' (MA, 306). Deeply felt response to Latin poetry removes women as a threat to the friendship between men and at the same time legitimates that friendship, making it a bond of spirit and intellect, immune to criticism.

Seven years later, in *The Professor's House*, Cather again portrayed the friendship of two men whose bond is sealed at the beginning by recitation of lines from Virgil. But the relation of Professor St Peter and his student, Tom Outland, is far more complex, ambiguous and far-reaching in its effects than is the relation between Cleric and Jim Burden. The ghostly presence of Outland, who dies in the First World War, years before the events of Book I take place, pervades the entire novel and affects not only St Peter but his colleague Professor Crane, Crane's wife, and all the members of the St Peter family.

Like the other students, Jim meets Cleric in the customary way, when he registers at the university. Outland, in contrast, simply walks into St Peter's garden one day, unannounced, unforeseen, like a deity in an epic. To St Peter, in retrospect, 'his strange coming, his strange story', seem 'all fantastic'.[28] At their first meeting, Outland, when asked to demonstrate his proficiency in Latin, recites 50 lines of the *Aeneid*, as if giving the sacred password to prove his worth. He invites his listener to identify him with Aeneas by beginning at the Opening of Book II, when Aeneas, a stranger at the court of Dido, is bidden to speak and launches into his tale of trial and suffering: *Infandum, regina, jubes renovare dolorem* (PH, 113).

St Peter has the eminence that Cleric will never have, but unlike Cleric, he becomes psychologically and spiritually dependent upon his student. Outland not only conducts St Peter on his two trips through the Southwest and Old Mexico; to the professor, he brings 'a kind of second youth' (PH, 258), a source of vitality and knowledge to which St Peter feels that he owes the power and eloquence of the last four volumes of his monumental work on the Spanish adventurers.

Deliberate hints of deviance like those in 'Paul's Case' do not appear in *The Professor's House*. But the exclusiveness of the intellectual bond between the men is clear. When Lillian St Peter's hostility to Outland, which St Peter attributes to jealousy, forces him and Outland to meet outside the house, 'in the alcove behind the professor's lecture room at the university' (PH, 173), their relationship takes on a furtive character.

After Outland's death, St Peter speaks of him as if he were the only person to give life any value. Without Tom Outland, he tells his wife, all his years of teaching would have been 'largely wasted' (PH, 62). To violate the memory of the friendship would make it 'commonplace like everything else' (PH, 62).

In contrast to St Peter, who remembers his friendship with Tom as the vital experience of his life, Outland, like Thea Kronborg, is most profoundly moved when alone amidst the ruins of the ancient Indian civilization. The difference between the female and the male experience is the difference between knowledge through physical sensation and knowledge through observation and analysis; between the courtesy of the guest and the reverent pride of the owner. Thea sees herself as a visitor who should disturb nothing of the 'dead city' (SL, 297) and take nothing away. Tom and his companion, Roddy Blake, build a cabin on top of the mesa and hire men to restore a road. They appropriate the place by words as well, referring to 'our city' and 'our mesa', and by giving names: 'Cliff City', 'Eagle's Nest', 'Mother Eve', 'the wide valley we called Cow Canyon' (PH, 213).

Unlike Thea, who makes no written records, Tom keeps a daybook in which he describes the articles excavated from the houses and rubbish piles and stored on shelves in the cabin. His story of finding the Blue Mesa is ostensibly a spoken narrative addressed to a listener, but it expresses the writer's yearning search for the right words: 'I wish I could tell you what I saw there, just *as* I saw it, on that first morning, through a veil of lightly falling snow' (PH, 201). Aware, like Conrad's Marlow, of the inadequacy of words to convey experience, Tom concludes a poetic description of 'the little stone city', reminiscent of the 'little town' on Keats's Grecian Urn, with the simple confession: 'I can't describe it. It was more like sculpture than anything else' (PH, 202).

Thea's culminating vision of the nature of art comes unbidden, a sudden insight that 'flashed' through her mind (SL, 304). In contrast, Tom's climactic vision occurring during his first night alone on the Mesa – 'the first night that all of me was there' – recalls the process of literary composition that St Peter discovered in writing his history. As the historian remembers 'the whole plan of his narrative . . . coming clearer and clearer all the time', while he felt 'his relation with his work . . . becoming every day more simple, natural, and happy', so Tom recalls his first apprehension of the mesa 'as a whole':

> It all came together in my understanding, as a series of experiments do when you begin to see where they are leading. Something had happened in me that made it possible for me to coordinate and simplify; and that process, going on in my mind, brought with it great happiness. It was possession (PH, 250–1).

His knowledge of Latin, 'inherited as land is, an external possession',[29] not only gives him the words to define the 'religious emotion' that he feels, but helps to create that emotion. 'I had read of filial piety in the Latin poets, and I knew that was what I felt for this place. It had formerly been mixed up with other motives; but now that they were gone, I had my happiness unalloyed' (PH, 251).

A puzzling feature of Tom's story is that he owes the solitude which gives him unalloyed happiness, the 'high tide' of his life, to his unfeeling rejection of his 'fides Achates', Rodney Blake, who in Outland's absence sold the Indian relics to help Outland continue his education. In virtually driving Rodney Blake off the mesa, Outland violates the classic ideal of friendship celebrated in the poem he devotedly memorizes. Indeed, he breaks a link in a chain of friendships forged when he begins the study of Latin with the Belgian priest, Father Duchene. It is Rodney who insists that Tom translate for him the hundred lines of Caesar that Tom promises the priest to read every day. Tom Outland's failure ever to find Rodney again is part of the price he realizes must be paid by 'anyone who requites faith and friendship as I did' (PH, 253).

According to Mary Ruth Ryder, in *Willa Cather and Classical Myth*, Tom in another way fails to embody Virgil's ideal of filial piety, in assigning no value to maternal love, in failing to acknowledge that 'Vergilian *pietas* constitutes love of *mother*, as well as love of God and country' (author's emphasis).[30] In naming the murdered woman 'Mother Eve', Tom and Rodney accept the Biblical image of woman as tempter, the source of man's fall. Neither protests when Father Duchene imagines Mother Eve an 'unfaithful wife' murdered by her husband when he discovered her in 'improper company' (PH, 223).

But whether or not Cather saw Tom Outland as a failed or imperfect Aeneas, her fiction attests to the surpassing importance of male bonds in the lives of her male characters. Whatever the outcome of their friendships, male characters who are identified with classical poets and their heroes discover in their attachments to other men the determining forces in their lives. Although Gaston Cleric appears only briefly in *My Ántonia*, his effect on the course of Jim's life is greater than anyone else's. In Cather's next novel, *One of Ours*, the ship *Anchises* carries the protagonist, Claude Wheeler, away from the isolation of his failed marriage to fulfilment in male friendship and to the discovery that in ideals lie 'the real sources of power among men'.[31] Marriage places St Peter in a house of women – his wife, his two daughters, and Augusta, the sewing woman. But it is his bonds with men – the Thierault boys, then Tom Outland – that nourish his heart and imagination. His daughter Kathleen has attended the university, but St Peter seems to teach only male students. After the end of one of his lectures, his wife and son-in-law enter as 'the young men filed out of the room' (PH, 69). Afterwards, Lillian St Peter refers slightingly to 'those fat-faced boys' (PH, 70) he has been addressing. Tom Outland is engaged to the professor's elder daughter, Rosamond, when he goes to war, but that fact has none of the reality of his male friendships – with St Peter, Father Duchene and Rodney Blake.

It is unlikely that Willa Cather wished readers to see anything deviant in the friendships of the male protagonists of her novels. In fact, she devised strategies to protect them. By making Latin, not Greek, the sacred language binding men she avoided the suggestion of homosexual love that might have attached to characters who read the *Symposium* instead of the *Aeneid*. By making women in *The Professor's House* either ostentatious materialists or their jealous victims she would justify St Peter's attachment to Tom Outland. In both *The Professor's House* and *My Ántonia*, she presents male friendships retrospectively, through the memories of the survivor. The death of the other, claimed by war or sickness, casts over the friendship the romantic aura of lost youth and sacrifice. As readers of the Latin poets, both Jim Burden and St Peter dwell elegiacally upon time that consumes the best days first. Thus they invest the beloved dead with the august beauty of the poetry which in life bound them in time-honoured tradition.

Cather does not suggest that the male friendships cherished by Jim Burden and St Peter deprive them of experiences promising greater fulfilment. But the ending of both novels suggests that such friendships are in some sense incomplete, if not sterile. Jim Burden's decision to follow Gaston Cleric to Harvard determines the course of his adult life, but it is Ántonia, the 'rich mine of life' (MA, 398), who inspires him to perform his most creative act, the writing of his manuscript which memorializes all the figures of his youth, including Gaston Cleric.

In *The Professor's House* a woman is literally the salvation of the male protagonist. When St Peter, feeling himself mortally oppressed by a life from which all joy has gone, allows himself to lie in his gas-filled attic study until he is unable to open the window blown shut in a storm, he is found by the sewing woman Augusta, who revives him and restores him to acceptance of a diminished life. Her name connotes the calm endurance and wisdom of a woman who has ministered to many families in times of suffering and death. In conjunction with the Virgilian references, her name also identifies her with the age made immortal by its poets (whose writings she would be unable to read). She literally fulfils the role of nurse, Statius's metaphor for the Aeneid, 'nurse to me in poetry', but in the world of Cather's novels, as in the classical world she evokes, nurses are not poets. The unbridgeable distance between the Roman emperor and the humble sewing woman is a measure of the gulf between the lives of men and women in Cather's modern world – a gulf that women, by the power of maternal love, can best hope to bridge.

IV

My Ántonia and 'Tom Outland's Story' raise an issue addressed by many critics of Cather's fiction – her frequent use of male narrators. In addition to the two novels, nine of her short stories are narrated by male characters, some functioning merely as observers, others as protagonists. Howells, James and Wharton also created first-person narrators of the other sex, and Cather's six female narrators outnumber Wharton's two to one. Yet only the Cather criticism is filled with speculation and surmise about the choice of narrator. Cather, it is true, was the only writer of the four to make a character of the other sex the narrator of a long novel. Moreover, before the onset of feminist criticism, reviewers and critics – most of them men – more readily questioned the authenticity of male narrators created by women than female narrators created by men. (Who has criticized James's female narrators as unrealistic depictions of women?) Finally, in the past twenty years preoccupation with Cather's 'sexual orientation' has made her male narrators more promising subjects of speculation than the scores of male narrators created by Edith Wharton.

Cather's use of a male narrator was questioned early in her career by her most important literary friend and mentor, Sarah Orne Jewett, who had herself been warned against the practice by William Dean Howells. After reading Jewett's story 'Hallowell's Pretty Sister', Howells, then editor of the *Atlantic Monthly*, wrote to the author in friendly admonition: 'it appears to me impossible that you should do successfully what you've undertaken in it; assume a young man's character in the supposed narrator . . . when it comes to casting the whole autobiographical being in a character of the alien sex, the line is drawn distinctly.'[32] Thirty-two years later, Jewett, in an often-quoted letter to Willa Cather, praised the portrayal of wife and husband in Cather's story 'On the Gull's Road', but continued: 'The lover is as well done as he could be when a woman writes in the man's character – it must always, I believe, be something of a masquerade.'[33]

Cather's letters to Jewett in the Houghton Library contain no reference to Jewett's criticism of 'On the Gull's Road'. But we know that for Cather the idea of 'masquerade' was congenial. Her fascination with performance and impersonation is evident in her first novel, *Alexander's Bridge*, first published in *McClure's Magazine* as 'Alexander's Masquerade', which represents the dual identity of the actress Hilda Burgoyne, on and off stage, and the double life of the protagonist, an engineer, bound to his wife in Boston, attached to his mistress in London.

Cather herself in adolescence assumed the masquerade of boys' clothes; in later years, as Bernice Slote observed, 'she could be a consummate actress in language and print' (UV, xiii). According to Mildred Bennett, Cather aided in the writing of Ellen Terry's auto-biography.[34] As the managing editor of *McClure's*, Cather easily assumed the perspective of the writers whose work she edited, and she created the personality of the magazine in her professional correspondence. Her last service for McClure was to capture his voice and his idiom in the autobiography she wrote for him

Cather cited this experience in justifying to Will Owen Jones, editor of the *Nebraska State Journal*, her choice of Jim Burden as the narrator of *My Ántonia*. In a long letter to her old associate and friend (20 May 1919), she attributed her confidence in writing the novel as Jim Burden's story to her success in recreating the charac-ter of McClure in his autobiography, which his wife and his partner John S. Phillips had praised as a completely successful repre-sentation. Initially feeling herself confined within McClure's per-sonality, she had come to find the assumption of another's identity so stimulating that she had wished to repeat the performance by assuming the identity of a different kind of man.[35] In terms reminis-cent of Jewett's observation to her that 'one must know the world *so well* before one can know the parish',[36] she explained in her letter to Jones why, in the introduction to *My Ántonia*, she had stressed the narrator's wide knowledge of the world beyond the Nebraska of his childhood. In the importance she placed on this knowledge she followed Edith Wharton, who so often found in the male nar-rator of high professional and social standing what she believed a story required – reflection by a mind 'so situated and so constituted as to take the widest possible view of it'.[37] Likewise, the majority of Cather's male narrators are professional men – journalists ('Behind the Singer Tower' and 'The Willing Muse'), an artist ('The Name-sake'), a diplomat ('On the Gull's Road'), a geologist ('The Affair at Grove Station'), and Jim Burden, a lawyer for a railroad.

The confidence Cather expressed in her power to write 'in a man's character' seems justified by the number of readers of *My Ántonia* who praised the novel for its realism. According to an anonymous review in the *New York Sun*, 'her method left the reader with the conviction of absolute authenticity'. H. L. Mencken, who would rank the second half of *One of Ours* with a 'serial in the *Ladies' Home Journal'*, found in both the characters and background of *My Ántonia* 'an extraordinary reality', indicative of her unerring sense of form and style.[38] Ferris Greenslet, Cather's editor at Houghton Mifflin, wrote to her after receiving the first two chapters of *My Ántonia*: 'It begins admirably – with the utmost confidence-inspiring grip on reality.'[39]

There were dissenting opinions. Recalling Jewett's criticism of 'On the Gull's Road', Cather's biographer E. K. Brown questioned whether Jim Burden was necessary to the success of the novel. 'What is excellent in *My Ántonia* does not depend on a masculine narrator. It inheres in the material itself and in the appreciation of it, which might have been just as sensitive, just as various, if Willa Cather had presented this story omnisciently . . . as she had presented Alexandra Bergson's.'[40] Brown did not question Jim's masculinity, but an early critic, Grant Overton, thought Jim Burden unconvincing as a man, 'his sexlessness' betrayed by 'details' (not specified) that 'no boy would have observed and that a man would not recall. The intonation in some scenes is not in the least masculine.'[41] (Bernice Slote noted one lapse in the male view, when Jim describes the wardrobe in his room in Lincoln that 'held all my clothes, even my hats and shoes', KA, 239n.) In more recent criticism Jim often appears, not as sexless, but as feminized in a complex gender transposition that gives him, according to Patrick Shaw, 'the masculine role in society' to shield his 'feminine sensibility' while Ántonia, celebrated as Earth Mother, exhibits 'the conventional male traits in a feminine disguise'. Together, Jim and Ántonia become 'dual halves of Cather's psyche'.[42]

As this reading suggests, contemporary critics have been more concerned to divine the reasons for Cather's use of male narrators than to prove them realistic or unrealistic as men. Like Cather herself, her critics have seen the male narrator as a way to transcend limitations that tradition has imposed on women. Hermione Lee observes that men have a natural claim on literary genres such as the epic and the pastoral, which inform *My Ántonia*.[43] Sharon O'Brien distinguishes between male narrators whose gender, she believes, is 'not contradicted by the text' and those who are 'masks of lesbian feelings', allowing Cather to 'explore a woman's passion for another woman' without appearing to represent 'unnatural' love.[44] Sandra Gilbert and Susan Gubar, who associate Cather's assumption of male dress with her creation of male narrators, also describe these narrators as masks, which enable the author not merely to disguise feelings but to assume the authority and 'linguist potency' identified with male authorship.[45] Similarly, Anne Robinson Taylor sees the transposition of gender as a 'literary masquerade' which liberates the author from prescribed gender roles and allows her or him to achieve wholeness through identification with the other sex.[46]

The creation of male narrators may have been liberating for Cather, but she was not moved to liberate her female narrators from the attitudes and responses that conventional society expected of women. It is true that Cather, unlike Edith Wharton, did not make her female narrators inferior to the male narrators in class or linguistic culture. Jim Burden, Nellie Birdseye (*My Mortal Enemy*) and Marjorie ('Uncle Valentine') are equally privileged as exponents of Cather's literary art. The male narrators, however, are more given to pronouncements and judgements than are the female narrators. The tone of the men's narratives is authoritative and decisive. Characteristically, the male narrator feels himself intellectually or socially superior to those he is observing. His self-assurance may be reflected in pity ('A Wagner Matinee') or in the epigrammatic wit and wordplay with which the narrator of 'The Willing Muse' pronounces on his unworldly friend: 'There must be either very much or very little in a man when he refuses to make the most of his vogue and sell out on a rising market' (CSF, 116).

Except for the narrator of 'The Diamond Mine', a sophisticated woman of wealth and worldly knowledge, the female narrators seldom pronounce judgement, often profess uncertainty, and disclaim knowledge. No male narrator begins as does the female narrator of 'Jack-a-Boy': 'I am quite unable to say just why we were all so fond of him, or how he came to mean so much in our lives' (CSF, 311). Of her Aunt Charlotte, the narrator of 'Uncle Valentine' confesses: 'I find that I did not know her very well then', that 'I began really to know her' only after her death (UV, 8). She never states what becomes apparent to the reader, that Charlotte's love of the young composer was the great passion of her life.

Indicative of their assurance and sense of their authority and importance, male narrators, more than the female, make themselves and their feelings the subject of their narratives. The narrator of 'On the Gull's Road' is more preoccupied with his response to the mortally stricken woman he meets on shipboard than he is with her suffering. His sentiments seem rather factitious beside those of the female narrator of 'The Joy of Nelly Deane', whose love of her schoolmate suffuses the story and expresses itself as a tribute to the girl whose beauty and vitality charmed a whole town. Even Carrie, the narrator of 'The Diamond Mine', who unsparingly judges the exploitative relatives and lovers of the singer Cressida Garnett, even she never upstages the protagonist, but within the story and in narrating it she puts herself wholly at the service of her friend.

In keeping with their roles as observers subordinate to others, the female narrators rarely quote themselves when they engage in conversations, unlike the male narrators, who give themselves prominent speaking parts. The female narrator of 'Uncle Valentine', four times longer than 'On the Gull's Road', contributes fewer words to the dialogue than the male narrator of the shorter tale. Two of the male narrators ('The Namesake' and 'Behind the Singer Tower'), but none of the female narrators, address a group of friends, thus turning their narratives into public performances that test the speakers' power to justify assuming control of the conversation.

The differences evident in the short stories are fully illustrated by the male and female narrators of Cather's longest first-person narratives: Jim Burden in *My Ántonia* and Nellie Birdseye in *My Mortal Enemy*. Each novel places at its centre a woman who more fully than anyone else captures the imagination of the narrator without determining the course of the narrator's life. Jim is effectively separated from Ántonia when he enters high school and she becomes a hired girl. For 20 years, during which she marries and bears ten children, he does not see her at all. Nellie Birdseye observes Myra Henshawe at three different stages in their lives, separated by months or years: their first meeting when Nellie is 15; her visit to New York several months later; and ten years later, her chance encounter with the Henshawes, now poverty-stricken, living out Myra's last days in a jerry-built apartment-hotel in a city on the West Coast.

Despite the feminine traits imputed to Jim Burden, he exhibits all the authoritative confidence and self-absorption that distinguish the male narrators from the female narrators. Although four years younger than Ántonia, Jim always has the advantage of his grandparents' established place in Black Hawk and the privileges of education accorded to males of his social standing. At their first meeting, he becomes Ántonia's instructor when he begins to teach her English words. Throughout the novel, he is constantly judging her by *his* standards, criticizing her behaviour, even shunning her when she fails to conform to his conventional ideal of gentility.

The retiring nature that typifies the female narrators is reinforced in Nellie Birdseye by the circumstances of her first sight of Myra Henshawe, a commanding woman in her forties. As Nellie enters the room where Myra Henshawe awaits her, Nellie is immediately aware of herself as an object of scrutiny, perceiving that the visitor 'saw my reflection in a mirror' before they speak.[47] Jim sees Ántonia's eyes as warm reflecting surfaces, 'full of light, like the sun shining on brown pools in the wood.' Nellie feels appropriated by Myra Henshawe's 'deep-set, flashing grey eyes [that] seemed to be taking me in altogether – estimating me' (MME, 12). From the beginning Myra dominates the relationship. At their first meeting Nellie feels herself the one to be judged: 'I had begun to think she was going to like me' (MME, 13). Unlike Jim Burden, who repeatedly engages in conversation with other characters, Nellie is a silent observer who does not speak at all in the first two episodes. In the last part, she makes an occasional remark but she remains essentially the audience of Myra Henshawe's one-woman performance.

The differences between the assertive male narrator secure in his judgements and the reticent female narrator is, of course, a measure of the differences between Ántonia and Myra Henshawe, and the different methods by which Cather reveals them. The picture of Ántonia builds gradually, scene by scene, as Jim and Ántonia mature together. The novel represents a process of memory in which Jim's insights and reflections are always in the foreground. Nellie Birdseye's narrative records a series of revelations from which the portrait of Myra Henshawe slowly emerges. First knowing of Myra through the romantic stories of her elopement told by Nellie's mother and aunt, the narrator perceives more fully at each encounter the mundane or sordid realities behind the romantic legend. As Susan Rosowski has observed, at the beginning of each of the three sections Nellie has illusions about the Henshawes, which the ensuing scenes dispel.[48] But she does not speculate then or later on the meaning of the words and actions that disturb her, although because she is narrating from an adult's perspective she might be expected to comment on the significance of what she observed.

Nellie's name 'Birdseye' has prompted some critics to see her as an unreliable narrator whose vision remains limited by naiveté and romantic yearning which she never outgrows. For Marilyn Callander, Nellie remains 'frozen in a kind of Snow White/Sleeping

Beauty self-absorption', longing to continue 'in a state of adolescent sleep'.[49] Janis Stout credits Nellie with some insight in the last part of the novella but she finds Nellie even at the end a 'fallible center' whose vision is 'clouded' by her need to see the Henshawes as romantic figures.[50] But, as several critics have noted, Nellie, looking back on her younger self, indicates by her ironic comment her awareness of her innocent naiveté. According to Hermione Lee, 'a dry voice of experience undermines whatever idealization there may have been'.[51]

At the same time, the narrator seeks to capture the experience of her younger self, to convey the sense of wonder and excitement that gripped the observer who naturally sees more than she can understand or analyse. A 15-year-old girl seeing a couple for the first time in their New York apartment could not be expected to know exactly what lies behind situations: a gift of topaz sleeve-buttons, a quarrel over a key ring. Nellie observes Myra Henshawe advise an actor in his love affair, minister to a dying poet, send the most expensive Christmas holly tree to Helena Modjeska, and entertain artists and singers on New Year's Eve; she can sense the pulse of emotion in these acts but cannot then, and does not later, generalize them as expressions of a woman, without genius herself, who craves association with it and can satisfy her longing to create beauty and exercise power only through generosity often indistinguishable from manipulation.

Compared to Jim Burden, always ready to sum up characters and interpret actions, Nellie seems a shadowy figure: 'colorless, devoid of personality, lacking in self-definition', according to one critic;[52] 'the least obtrusive of [Cather's] narrators and window-characters', according to another.[53] That she, and other female narrators, are less authoritative, more self-effacing, than male narrators, may make them seem 'weaker.' But reticence and self-effacement may be an artistic strength. A narrator who does not force interpretations on the reader allows for a more subtle representation of character, in which words, gestures, actions become signs to be read by the discerning reader and the narrator together. Such a narrator may seem more sensitive to shades of behaviour and complexities of character than the analyst always prompt with his conclusions.

The absence of analysis and interpretation, then, need not evidence limited perception, but may be the means by which Cather achieved effects defined in her essay 'The Novel Démeublé': 'the inexplicable presence of the thing not named, of the overtone divined by the ear but not heard by it, the verbal mood, the emotional aura of the fact or the thing or the deed . . . '[54] A perfect illustration of the 'inexplicable presence' occurs in *My Mortal Enemy*, when Nellie reflects on the power of her memory of the 'Casta Diva' aria sung at the New Year's Eve party to recall the 'hidden richness' (MME, 61) of Myra Henshawe's nature: 'a compelling, passionate, overmastering something for which I had no name . . .' (MME, 60). How appropriate that 'the overtone divined by the ear', 'the verbal mood', should be evoked by the memory of music, by words the narrator sings to herself. How much would be lost were the narrator to fix a name to the 'overmastering something.'

Nellie as the adult narrator remains true to the limited understanding of her adolescent self in refusing to interpret scenes, but even a single word can convey an attitude, govern a reader's response, and capture the essence of a character. One of countless examples occurs as Nellie recalls the Henshawes at the climax of the novella's most memorable scene, as they listen to a young Polish woman sing the *Casta Diva* aria. 'I remember Oswald, standing like a statue behind Madame Modjeska's chair, and Myra, crouching low beside the singer, her head in both hands . . .' (MME, 60). How much of Myra's fierce primal energy, potentially explosive, is contained in the word *crouching* (repeated a few lines later), with its manifold suggestions of a humble worshipper, a cringing servant, and an animal tensed to spring. How different the effect had Myra *knelt* beside the singer.

The novel démeublé does not require a female narrator, but the reticence, the refusal to judge and define, essential to evoking 'the presence of the thing not named' – these are traditionally considered feminine rather than masculine traits. The contrasting methods of *My Ántonia* and *My Mortal Enemy* are also consistent with Cather's identification of men, but not women, with self-conscious literary composition. (In the revised introduction to *My Ántonia* Cather removed the passage in which the female narrator proposes that both she and Jim Burden 'set down on paper' their memories of Ántonia. But even in the original introduction she confesses to making only 'a few straggling notes', admits that 'My own story was never written', and presents the novel as 'Jim's manuscript, substantially as he brought it to me', MA, xii, xiv.)

Jim Burden is not a professional writer, but his narrative, which he claims 'hasn't any form' (MA, xiv), is a written text expressive of his awareness of himself as a character within a story and also the composer of that story. A 'self-reflexive narrator', as Blanche Gelfant terms him,[55] he draws on a novelist's vocabulary in composing the past as narrative. His departure for Harvard concludes one division of his story: 'My Lincoln chapter closed abruptly' (MA, 332). In retrospect, he most values Ántonia for her power to transform his memories of scenes into pictures 'like the old woodcuts of one's first primer' (MA, 397). He might be describing himself when he says of Frances Harling's interest in the country people: 'She carried them all in her mind as if they were characters in a book or a play' (MA, 171). He presents Mrs Steavens's moving account of Ántonia's suffering after her desertion by Larry Donovan as an archetypal tale within a frame, a story to be heard. The ambiguity of the title, 'The Pioneer Woman's Story', which could refer to Ántonia's experience or to the Widow Steavens's narration of it, increases the distance between the self-conscious writer-narrator and the other characters. Whether Cather intended it or not, the Widow Steavens's narrative – an unselfconscious unstudied expression of grief and love – makes Jim's professions of feeling for Ántonia seem fabricated, a literary construct that affords what Ann Romines terms 'the private satisfactions of ordering and control, as accomplished by an artist'.[56]

My Mortal Enemy is not cast as a written text or a narrative told to an audience. Like all the other female narrators, Nellie Birdseye is an autonomous narrator who does not see herself as the chief actor or the composer of the story she tells. Her shifting feelings about Myra Henshawe are of the essence, but she presents them as important not in themselves but as they reveal the variable capricious nature of the woman who dominates the novel. Jim Burden in the original introduction to *My Ántonia* tells the female narrator that if he is to write about Ántonia, 'I should have to do it in a direct way, and say a great deal about myself' (MA, xiii) – which indeed he does. In contrast, Nellie Birdseye says practically nothing about herself and her own affairs.

Because Jim Burden produces a manuscript he may seem to exercise more authorial power than Nellie Birdseye. But Nellie, no less than Jim, shapes meaning in selecting and arranging the contents of the narrative. In Deborah Carlin's words, 'Nellie, like a critic, reconstructs the text of Myra's life into a narrative in order to make some sense of it'.[57] In fact, the existence of Myra's life story seems more dependent on the narration of Nellie Birdseye than the existence of Ántonia's story seems dependent on Jim Burden's manuscript. Jim memorializes Ántonia but he does not call her into being. Myra Henshawe, one feels, would not exist if Nellie were not there to transform the figure of a romantic legend into the real woman.

Jim Burden seems to appropriate Ántonia, but her inexhaustible vitality precludes a narrator's possession of her. In ignorance of Ántonia's life struggle, Jim may transform her into an icon as several critics have contended (Jim thus reversing the process of de-mythicizing that Nellie represents), but Ántonia cannot be confined by another's mental processes. Many readers, I believe, would agree with Susan Rosowski that Ántonia 'breaks through [Jim Burden's] narrative, and thus through his attempts to possess her by writing about her'.[58] Nellie Birdseye at their first meeting feels that Myra's eyes are 'taking me in altogether', but as narrator Nellie always holds Myra in her gaze. By effacing herself, by subordinating herself to Myra, Nellie makes herself the reality-giving presence, she becomes the source of Myra Henshawe's reality. The female narrator who refuses to formulate her subject and offers only tentative readings of her ambiguous words actually assumes a kind of novelistic power that none of the male narrators commands.

This is not to imply that within *My Mortal Enemy* Nellie is manipulative or domineering. No character could be less so. Her refusal to name the 'something' in Myra's nature that she so strongly feels reflects her respect for the integrity of the other person, as does the absence of any attempt on Nellie's part to answer the questions her narrative raises. What was Oswald's relation to the giver of the topaz sleeve-buttons? What door was opened by the key over which the Henshawes quarrelled? Were Myra Henshawe's jealous suspicions groundless? Was Nellie right to feel in Oswald Henshawe's attitude 'indestructible constancy' (MME, 120)? We may assume that Nellie herself does not know the answers. But because she does not speculate, because she does not impose her concerns between herself and Myra Henshawe, she binds that character to her more tightly than if, like Jim Burden, she had converted the story of another person into the story of herself.

It is, of course, possible for a male narrator to be self-effacing, but Cather did not see her important male characters in this way. Whether they are narrators or 'window characters' like Niel Herbert or protagonists of third-person narratives, they are ego-centred, preoccupied with their own affairs and impressions. Some of Cather's female characters, it is true, such as Thea Kronborg, Myra Henshawe and Sapphira Colbert, are no less self-absorbed, but they are not narrators whose ostensible purpose is to portray another person. The effect of the self-concerned narrator such as Jim Burden suggests Virginia Woolf's image of the shadow across the page cast by the self-confident male voice: 'a straight dark bar, a shadow shaped something like the letter "I" ' – an intrusive presence that obstructs one's view of the world around it.[59] Unlike the male narrators fixed on the shadow of their own feelings, Cather's female narrators distil themselves in their subject and so preserve the integrity of the character that their unshadowed vision creates.

Cather's last female narrator, who appears at the end of her last completed novel, *Sapphira and the Slave Girl*, is a unique figure, as is the novel itself. The only narrative of her family's history, set in western Virginia, the place of her birth, near Winchester, the novel, unlike *My Ántonia*, centres on events before the Civil War, years before the author was born. Through the stories of the antebellum South told by her grandparents and their servants she entered her 'visitable past', in Henry James's phrase, but until the Epilogue, the novel, narrated in the third person, masks its source in the author's memory. Occasionally, as Merrill Skaggs notes,[60] the impersonal narrator indicates that a story is being told (for example, what brought the Colberts to the Back Creek 'is a long story – too long for a breakfast-table story').[61] Otherwise this narrator assumes the authority of the historian who speaks with equal certainty of past events such as the appalling history of the aged Jezebel's voyage from Africa to America in a slave ship, and the main action occurring in time present, 1856: the struggle for mastery that ensues in the Colbert family when the invalid Sapphira, jealous of her husband's attachment to her mulatto slave Nancy, encourages her rakish nephew to prey upon the helpless girl until Sapphira's daughter, Rachel Blake, effects Nancy's escape on the Underground Railroad.

The second half of the Epilogue, set in 1881, introduces a first-person narrator who recalls herself at the age of five, on the day she witnessed Nancy's return from Canada and her reunion with her mother Till, after a separation of 25 years. The source of the preceding third-person narrative is then made clear as the narrator recalls herself sitting in the kitchen sewing patchwork and listening as her grandmother and Nancy and Till talked of the past. When Nancy asked what happened to the Colberts in their last days, the narrator recalls: 'that story I could almost have told her myself, I had heard about them so often' (SSG, 291). The chief storyteller remembered by the narrator is the aged black woman Till, Sapphira's maid and the repository of the family history, which she recounts in the final pages of the novel. The narrator recalls visiting Till's cabin, where 'I heard the old stories and saw Till's keepsakes and treasures' (SSG, 291). It is in the repeated tellings that names become living persons and stories acquire the mysterious power of legend. Visits with Till to the Colbert graveyard elicit from her 'stories about the Master and Mistress [that] were never mere repetitions but grew more and more into a complete picture of those two persons' (SSG, 292).

The first-person narrator is not named but readers rightly identify her as Willa Cather. In her letters, Cather made clear that the novel was a re-creation of her own family's history, that she is the child who heard the 'old stories' and remembered the reunion of Nancy and Till. To Dorothy Canfield Fisher she wrote of her pleasure in hearing once again the voices of the Negro servants and recalling their two languages, one spoken among themselves, the other with white people. From the conversations of her grandmother, Till and Nancy, she stated, she owed her most intimate knowledge of her family's life before the Civil War. She identified her great aunt Sidney Cather Gore as the model for the postmistress in the novel, Mrs Bywaters, and referred to her grandmother Rachel Boak's taking Nancy across the Potomac River – the saving act of Rachel Blake.[62] A month later she wrote to Viola Roseboro that she could scarcely distinguish her own invention from the stories told by family and neighbours and that everything in the Epilogue was strictly true. In this letter she repeated the words she had written in the novel, that she had heard about Nancy 'ever since I could remember anything' (SSG, 281).[63]

A number of critics have agreed with Willa Cather's judgement of the Epilogue that Elizabeth Sergeant recorded in her Memoir: 'she had, she felt, made an artistic error in bringing herself into the story.'[64] Henry Seidel Canby's review, which Cather found just and discriminating, locates a weakness in the novel in 'the lack of unity resulting from the retrospection of the last pages'.[65] Eugénie Hamner, who has most fully analysed the relation of the Epilogue to the main narrative, makes a similar criticism.[66] But if one thinks of the Epilogue as a conclusion to the whole body of Cather's writing, it has its appropriateness. Having begun her career as a critic whose literary idols were men, she concluded it with a novel based on stories told by women whom she memorialized in its pages. As Sharon O'Brien notes, the Epilogue, in which Cather 'proclaim[ed] herself the inheritor of a tradition of female narrative', is her 'most direct acknowledgment of her writer's debt to the women storytellers of her childhood'.[67]

In identifying oral storytelling with women, *Sapphira and the Slave Girl* seems consistent with the gendered separation of the spoken from the written word. But in identifying herself within the novel as its author, Cather placed within her fiction one female character who creates with both the needle and the pen, who unites through her presence the powers of storyteller, novelist and historian.

6
Illusions of Change in Utopian Fiction

In his 'Editor's Study' of June 1888, Howells devoted two columns to a favourable review of Edward Bellamy's *Looking Backward*. The champion of realism then justified his attention to a work of 'pure romance', as he called Bellamy's utopian novel: 'The reversions or counter-currents in the general tendency of a time are very curious, and are worthy of tolerant study. They are always to be found; perhaps they form the exception that establishes the rule; at least they distinguish it.'[1]

The succession of utopian novels that followed *Looking Backward* might be better termed a flood than a counter-current: between 1888 and 1900 more than 160 utopian narratives were published.[2] Most of these works have long since sunk into oblivion but they rose from powerful impulses to which countless Americans responded. Most compelling was the reformist desire to expose corruption and inequity in the social order. Writers feeling powerless to effect reform on earth could abolish poverty, create equality, and transform human nature in fictions of the ideal state. Their novels depicted journeys to remote places – to the planet Mars, to islands found on no map, to mythic realms reached through uncharted passages. The adventures of utopian travellers allowed writers and readers to enjoy vicariously the perils and rewards of discovery that lured explorers to Africa and the polar regions in the nineteenth century. In creating what had never existed, writers also, consciously or not, often affirmed the values and traditions of the very society the utopian traveller was pleased to escape.

Contradictions in utopian fiction are revealed if we consider what happens to language in the ideal states. Few writers of utopian novels, it is true, singled out language as an institution in need of reform. Few even introduced language as a subject for discussion. But language, indicative of a writer's attitudes and assumptions, is a vital sign of the culture he or she portrays. Particularly is this true of utopian fiction, which frees writers from the constraints of

159

realism and allows them to represent the imagined worlds in whatever way they wish.

Language is a particularly telling sign of the relative power and status of men and women. In utopian fiction, as in all fiction, language may reflect and perpetuate traditional gender roles or it may reflect and reinforce changes in the relationship of the sexes. This function of language is especially important in the many utopian novels depicting societies that free women from economic dependence on men and make men and women political equals. Are these changes embodied in language? Has the utopian society created a new language? Has it modified American English, dropping certain words, adding new words, changing the meanings of others? Or has the language undergone no change at all? Do authors or characters even manifest awareness of the power of language as an instrument of social repression and social regeneration?

These questions are answered differently in works by the four most influential writers of utopian fiction in America: Bellamy, Howells, Elizabeth Stuart Phelps and Charlotte Perkins Gilman. *Looking Backward (1888)*, the most famous and widely read American utopian novel, inspired more than twenty narratives with Bellamy's characters or variations of his title[3] and led to the formation of Nationalist or Bellamy clubs in 140 cities in the United States.[4] Howells's utopian novels, *A Traveler from Altruria* (1894) and *Through the Eye of the Needle* (1907), contain his most sustained analysis of class-based capitalist society in nineteenth-century America. Phelps's novels, *The Gates Ajar* (1868), *Beyond the Gates* (1883) and *The Gates Between* (1887), remain the best-known fiction to envisage heaven as a utopian realm where all earthly injustices are rectified. Gilman's *Herland* (1915), described by one critic as 'the first truly feminist work in the American Utopian tradition',[5] has generated more critical analysis than any other utopian novel by an American woman.

The utopian novels of the four writers have certain elements in common. Like most works in the genre, they are first-person narratives which absolve the author of responsibility for the fantastic events recorded. With the exception of Mr Twelvemough, who narrates *A Traveler from Altruria*, and Mary Cabot, the narrator of *The Gates Ajar*, all the narrators are outsiders who journey to an alien world. All four writers observe the conventions of the traditional courtship plot that unites the sexes in marriage. Bellamy's Julian West will marry Edith Leete; the Altrurian, Aristides Homos, marries the American, Eveleth Strange. The narrator of *Herland*, Vandyck Jennings, marries Ellador of Herland and takes her to America in the sequel, *With Her in Ourland*. Phelps's narrator, Dr Thorne, courts, marries, is estranged from and reconciled with his wife in *The Gates Between*. The happiness of the narrator of *Beyond the Gates* is not complete until she is united with the man she loved on earth but did not marry. In the utopias of all four writers, women are said to enjoy rights, privileges and opportunities denied them in Victorian America. How much the status of women has actually changed in their novels is best revealed in the connections between language and gender that each writer makes.

I

For almost twenty years before writing *Looking Backward* Bellamy supported women's causes, as Sylvia Bowman has shown in her biography of the novelist. Throughout the 1870s and 1880s, in articles and editorials in the *Springfield Union*, he championed economic independence for both women and men as the foundation of an equitable society. He supported women's suffrage, which portended, he believed, 'a great and profound revolution in the status of the sex'. He advocated the admission of women to medical and law schools, defended their practice of trades and professions traditionally restricted to men, and attacked the social codes to which economic dependence bound women, fostering in them passivity, conservatism and unthinking obedience to political and religious authority.[6]

Given Bellamy's answers to the question he called the 'Proteus of the age',[7] one might expect language in *Looking Backward* to reflect the reforms that secure women's economic independence in the year 2000. But nothing in the language of the novel suggests that women have escaped the restrictions of the inferior status Bellamy had earlier protested. In his utopian world, male speakers dominate the narrative; women exist on the margins, their presence effaced, their voices almost silenced by the tireless voice of Dr Leete, who assists the narrator, Julian West, from his sleep of 113 years and explains the perfections of the new order in speeches that fill almost every chapter.

Dr Leete's beautiful daughter, Edith, described by West as an angel of compassion, is the conventional Victorian heroine, governed by the wishes of her father and the man she will marry. At their first meeting, Julian West recalls, she 'took little part in the conversation', but 'the magnetism of her beauty drew my glance to her face'.[8] In her few conversations with Julian, she speaks only of activities traditionally identified with women – shopping, reading novels, and listening to music in the home. Her mother's part in the conversations is even more limited. When Julian directs to her a question about housework, she is allowed a few sentences before Dr Leete takes over and discourses for half a dozen paragraphs on the advantages enjoyed by women in the new order. His lectures to Julian on the evils of capitalism and the virtues of nationalization take place after the women have retired for the evening.

According to Bellamy's sequel, *Equality* (1897), each nation in the twenty-first century has its own language, but a 'general language' is spoken by all.[9] Neither novel indicates whether the language of characters is national or general; it is universal in that the discourse of all is cast in the same style, praised by one reviewer as 'masculine, frank, and straightforward'.[10] Language in the two centuries differs only in that certain words, such as *menial, crime, corruption* and *demagoguery* have only 'an historical significance' in the year 2000 (LB, 60). In the first novel, all the gender bias of nineteenth-century conventional English remains intact. Both Dr Leete and Julian West use the generic *he* and *man* without any sense of excluding half the population of the country; their speeches abound in such phrases as 'the lives of all men', 'the labor of man' and 'the brotherhood of man'. The minister, Mr Barton, whose sermon is piped into the Leetes' house by telephone, equates 'the solidarity of humanity' with 'the brotherhood of all men', attributes thought and observation to 'men's minds', and purveys the familiar binaries, 'the grace of womanhood, the dignity of manhood' (LB, 279); 'tender women' and men 'strong to bear' (LB, 280).

The momentous change that frees women from economic dependence on men is not reflected in the characters' speech. Women as well as men work in the industrial army, but Dr Leete refers only to 'a young man', 'every man', and 'all men' in explaining how workers choose their trades. When Julian asks on what basis every worker (male and female) gets the same share of the wealth, Dr Leete replies, 'The basis of his claim is the fact that he is a man' (LB, 93). At the nation's schools, where male and female students are said to receive the same education, Julian sees 'stalwart young men' and 'fresh, vigorous maidens' (LB, 223). But Dr Leete tells him that the purpose of the 'higher education' available to 'all persons' is to give to 'every man' what was once called 'the education of a gentleman' (LB, 217).

Such is the power of the masculine pronoun, one would scarcely know that women still existed in Boston were it not for the presence of Mrs Leete and Edith. Not until Chapter 25, three chapters before the end, does Julian think to inquire about the position of women and is told by Dr Leete that women are 'an allied force', not an 'integral part of the army of men' (LB, 258). Economic equals of men but political inferiors, women do not vote for President of the nation but only select the female general who heads an 'exclusively feminine regime' (LB, 258). Far from freeing unmarried women from the stigma of the label 'old maid', the reformed society officially degrades them by forbidding them to hold high office in the industrial army on the grounds that only wives and mothers 'fully represent their sex' (LB, 261) and thus are fit to govern other women.

Men who do not marry also lose caste in the new order, in which women are no longer economic dependants and marriage is institutionalized as the ideal state, to be desired equally by men and women. Men who remain unmarried no longer enjoy the advantages connoted by the word *bachelor*; they are now 'celibates' of inferior qualities who failed to win a woman's love (LB, 269). (Julian does not ask whether a woman might marry an inferior specimen for the privilege of holding office in the industrial army.) In effect, political power is vested in an elite corps of married men. Matrimony and patriarchy thus continue to reinforce each other more potently than ever.

Women may serve in the judiciary and the cabinet of the President, Dr Leete tells Julian, but their presence poses no 'danger to the nation' because recognition of 'the distinct individuality of the sexes' precludes 'unnatural rivalry' between them (LB, 259). 'We have given [women] a world of their own, with its emulations, ambitions, and careers', Dr Leete continues, 'and I assure you they are very happy in it' (259). He might be speaking of children safe behind the bars of a playpen. His repeated references to men as *we*, women as *they* enforce the polarization of the sexes. The language of all the characters, like the system itself, supports the observation of Sylvia Strauss that politics in Bellamy's utopia is a 'male preserve', the 'religion of solidarity' a form of 'distinctively male bonding that excludes women'.[11]

Reviewers of *Looking Backward* in the mainstream periodicals such
as The *Atlantic*, The *Nation* and *Harper's Magazine* did not discuss
the position of women in Bellamy's utopia. Other critics, however,
notably feminists who joined Bellamy clubs and wrote for the
monthly magazine, the *Nationalist*, applauded the principle of
women's economic independence but criticized *Looking Backward*
for segregating women and relegating them to activities (never
specified) that men deemed suitable for women. The first volume
of the *Nationalist* included Mary H. Ford's 'A Feminine Iconoclast',
an imaginary conversation between women protesting the pater-
nalism of Bellamy's utopia, where men determine the 'proper distinction between the sexes' and restrict women accordingly.[12] Abby
Morton Diaz, a founding member of the Nationalist Club of Boston
and a writer of essays and children's stories, likewise argued that
women should join with men in conducting the world's affairs, that
'Co-operation is the Divine order', not the separation of the sexes.[13]
Mary Livermore, another member of the Boston club, a nationally
known lecturer, editor, temperance leader, and Vice-President of
the American Woman Suffrage Association, among her many offices, spoke and wrote tirelessly in defence of women in all the
professions and of their success as doctors, lawyers, ministers, and
college presidents.[14]

A year after its founding in December 1888, the Nationalist Club
of Boston numbered more than a hundred members, of whom 26
were women.[15] Among them were the temperance and suffrage
leader Frances Willard; Lucy Stone, a leader in the American
Woman Suffrage Association and editor of its newspaper, the
Woman's Journal; the sculptor Anne Whitney; Vida Scudder, later
professor of English at Wellesley College; Helen Campbell, author
of *The Problem of the Poor*, *Prisoners of Poverty* and *Women Wage-
Earners*; Maud Howe Elliott, a novelist and journalist; and her
mother, Julia Ward Howe. Names such as these disprove the idea
that women need men to give them a 'world of their own'.

In *Equality*, Bellamy reversed himself on positions his critics
found most objectionable. Early in the book he introduces the
speech of Edith Leete which informs Julian West that women are no
longer excluded from the occupations initially reserved for men.
Women in the reformed utopia are now 'machinists, farmers, en-
gineers, carpenters, iron workers, builders, engine drivers' (E, 43).
Instead of positing innate differences between men and women,
Dr Leete insists that 'entire physical equality' (E, 150) of the sexes

is possible, that differences in strength and athletic prowess are due entirely to conditions, not to any 'natural disabilities' of the female sex (E, 149).

Most striking are Dr Leete's long disquisitions on the effects of economic inequality upon women in the nineteenth century – a subject meriting only a few paragraphs in *Looking Backward*. Anticipating Charlotte Perkins Gilman's analysis in *Women and Economics*, Bellamy's spokesman identifies women as victims of a 'slave code', subjected by their economic dependence to a 'triple yoke' (E, 135) – the class rule of the rich, the rule of the men who supported them, and the dictate of conventions to which society demanded their 'slavish conformity . . . in all [their] thinking, speaking, and acting' (E, 136). The married woman, subject to a 'code of sexual economics', surrendered to her husband her mind and body in return for her livelihood. 'On condition of obtaining a lien on his property, she became a part of it' (E, 141).

Dr Leete does not refer to sexist language as such but he identifies realities it reflects and reinforces in noting the 'utter hypocrisy' produced by 'the pretended chivalric deference to women' conjoined with 'their practical suppression' (E, 129). His comparison of women to oppressed factory workers exposes a less obvious instance of deceptive language. Observing with genteel circumlocution that nineteenth-century capitalism was 'most fitly described by a word . . . reserved to designate a particular phase of self-selling practiced by women' (E, 101), he uncovers bias that not only degraded women but masked exploitation of the factory workers, shielding their employers from the opprobrium implicit in the word *prostitution*.

Dr Leete's pronouns in *Equality* also suggest that he has undergone some consciousness-raising since his appearance in *Looking Backward*. In discourses to Julian West he struggles from the hold of the generic *he*, sometimes with imperfect success: he tells Julian, for instance, that 'every one . . . has his own house and piece of land if he or she desires them, and always his or her own income to use at pleasure' (E, 27). He credits both 'cultured men and women' with championing the workers' cause, notes the state's guarantee to compensate everyone for 'his or her labor' (E, 368), and often refers to persons, citizens, individuals and human beings, instead of simply to men.

But *Equality* shows that old habits may be more compelling than new ideas, that assumptions survive the theory that discredits them. Dr Leete acknowledges that 'women are half the human race' (E, 400) but continues to refer to 'the rights of man', 'the inalienable equality of all men', 'modern man', and 'the universal brotherhood of man'. He declares that the new system which transformed captive women into 'absolute free agents in the disposition of themselves' has made 'every one absolute lord of himself' (E, 400). When describing the operations of the new government he may speak of *she* as well as *he*; when generalizing about human nature, *man* alone suffices: for example 'If a man's mainspring is not wound up when he is born, it never can be wound up afterward' (E, 390). *Man* signifies humanity; women are a class, a subgroup, like the farmers, 'the two classes', according to Dr Leete, that most benefited from the Revolution (E, 304). He champions women's economic equality – not primarily because it gave women freedom to be artists and scientists and doctors – but because it destroyed the 'virus of moral and mental slavery', carried by 'their veins' into 'the blood of the race' (E, 137) and thus gave 'free mothers to the race' (E, 138).

In other ways *Equality* subverts the principles it champions. Male speakers again predominate although the book opens with Edith Leete in control of the conversation, posing innocent questions that compel Julian West to acknowledge the inequities of his nineteenth-century society. But when Dr Leete appears at the beginning of the second chapter, she yields her place to him at once, protesting when he humorously accuses her of 'the design of supplanting her father in his position of historical instructor' (E, 14). Julian declares her a 'merciless cross-examiner' (E, 11) and a 'mistress of the Socratic method' (E, 14), but her assumed ignorance becomes genuine incomprehension when Julian attempts to explain to her and her mother the meaning of such words as *rent*, *profit*, *interest* and *dividend*. Noting 'the blank expression of their countenances', Dr Leete interposes with analogies and illustrations to 'make the matter a little clearer to them' (E, 94, 95). The infallible Dr Leete never even pretends ignorance, the state assumed to be natural to women.

Julian meets several pillars of the establishment who support the patriarchal structure of the language. Mr Chapin, the superintendent at the bank, explains the system that grants to 'everyone' (men and women) 'the same balance to his credit' (E, 30). The minister, Mr Barton, like Dr Leete, perceives the sexual oppression in the hypocrisies of nineteenth-century language but not the bias in his own words. He observes that the phrase, 'the religious sex', by

which Julian describes the women of his day, was merely a euphemism for 'the docile sex', obedient to male authority (E, 263).
But he seems unaware that the religion women sustained was and
still remains the creation of men conceived in their image. Seemingly unaware of any irony, he tells Julian, 'Man must be revealed to
man as brother before God could be revealed to him as father' (E,
268).

In the new order, Dr Leete tells Julian, women, like men, keep
their names when they marry; children take the last names of both
parents (E, 139). But women's names are less important than men's
names. Edith and her mother are identified only by the name of
Dr Leete. Dr Leete introduces Julian to Mr Chapin and Mr Barton,
but the female superintendent of the cloth factory who tells Julian
about fashions in the year 2000 remains unnamed.

The principle of equality is most nearly realized in the class of
students whose recitations in political economy transfix Julian
West, if not the reader. A male teacher summons by name seven
boys and six girls to discourse on such topics as 'over-production',
'the necessity of waste pipes', and 'the cost of the profit system'.
The girls recite their lessons as perfectly as the boys, but equality
here is merely the conformity of robots. What the teacher calls 'our
discussion' (E, 195) is the delivery of a catechism by students who
all sound exactly like Dr Leete. The one student, a girl, Marion (the
name of Bellamy's daughter), who attempts a modest break from
the straitjacket of orthodoxy by venturing a little humour, is re-
buked by the teacher for lacking 'a spirit of sympathy' (E, 169).

The new order can cast the minds of its children in identical
moulds but it does not banish from Julian's mind the age-old
interests and impulses accompanying nineteenth-century man's
'chivalric deference to women'. Although Julian is the flower of
courtesy with Edith (even when preoccupied with the novelty of
her unisex costume) he automatically sees woman's beauty as
man's justification for aggression. When he glimpses a charming
young woman operating an electric plough in a field, economic
equality is far from his mind. He thinks of Europa abducted by Jove
in the shape of a white bull and muses complacently, 'If her proto-
type was as charming as this young woman, Jupiter certainly was
excusable for running away with her' (E, 300).

Was Bellamy aware of the implications of this passage? There is
no evidence in either novel that he saw any divergence between
what he espoused and what he represented. He appears to take

Dr Leete and Julian West as they take themselves – as the infallible master and the disciple eager to be instructed and redeemed, in what John L. Thomas terms the 'psychological drama of conversion' that transforms both the individual person and the social order.[16]

II

Among those who met in Boston in December 1888 to organize the first Nationalist club was William Dean Howells, then at the height of his influence as a novelist and critic. A year later he attended the first Nationalist anniversary celebration in Tremont Temple, after which he wrote enthusiastically of Bellamy's speech there and 'the spread of the doctrine, and amongst the most intelligent class'.[17] He doubted that 'Bellamy's dream' would accomplish 'the salvation of the world', but he gave his father a subscription to Bellamy's magazine, *New Nation*, 'full of good reading and true doctrine'.[18] Reflecting the fading of Nationalism as a political force, Howells's last published statement about Bellamy, in the August 1898 issue of the *Atlantic*, was a general tribute to the utopian novelist's 'nobility of the heart', his humane democratic spirit, and the power of his romantic imagination, which Howells judged second only to Hawthorne's.[19]

The utopia Howells created in *A Traveler from Altruria* and *Through the Eye of the Needle* resembles Bellamy's ideal society in several ways. Although Altruria and Victorian America are coexistent in time, not space, Altruria, like Bellamy's utopia, originated in the corporate structures of nineteenth-century capitalism and evolved without bloodshed when the power and wealth concentrated in the great trusts and monopolies passed from the control of the plutocracy to the stewardship of the people. In both utopias, economic equality has banished class distinctions based on unequal distribution of wealth. All citizens, women and men, are guaranteed an equal share of the country's resources in return for service, to the best of their ability, in organizations governed by officials they themselves elect. No one profits at the expense of another, and personal fulfilment is not conceivable apart from the common good.

A novelist of manners, not a political economist, Howells, unlike Bellamy, was more concerned to expose inequities in American society than to detail the operation of utopian institutions. Instead of transporting an American to Altruria in his first novel, he brings an Altrurian, Aristides Homos, to a New England hotel, where his presence and his pointed questions reveal the class prejudices and social barriers that separate the genteel summer visitors from the hotel staff and the impoverished farmers and labourers of the region. Americans who remain unenlightened are more potent instruments of criticism than are characters like Julian West, who readily acknowledge all the evils of the old order. The blind complacency of the upper class is a more powerful indictment of their society than is the criticism of the Altrurian visitor.

The situation in *A Traveler from Altruria* produces the kind of irony absent in Bellamy's utopian novels, irony that constantly turns upon itself, compromising what it seems to approve. Howells sometimes allows his narrator, a popular novelist named Mr Twelvemough, to perceive the gulf between the ideals of equality Americans celebrate and the class prejudices that rule their actions. More often the narrator unthinkingly reveals the self-serving disposition of his class as he confidently repeats its favourite shibboleths: 'We are all free, now, black and white'; Americans are 'equal in opportunities'; 'people naturally despise a dependent.'[20] Letting his narrator call the exclusive hotel 'a microcosm of the American republic' (AR, 28), Howells invites the reader to see in the comparison both truth and falsity unperceived by the character. A source of unconscious irony, the narrator's obtuseness renders suspect the sincerity of the Altrurian's assurances that he will approach American life 'so much more intelligently' with Mr Twelvemough's instruction (AR, 14). Even the narrator soon experiences 'a cold doubt of something ironical in the man' (AR, 25). Dr Leete never creates such doubt in the minds of his listeners.

For all their irony, however, Howells's utopian novels support male dominance as staunchly as Bellamy's. The hotel piazza, where most of the extended conversations take place, is like a men's club; generic figures, including a banker, a minister, a doctor, a manufacturer, and a professor of political economy, discuss labour unions, business practices and other subjects women are presumed to know or care nothing about. The banker, the privileged speaker who voices many of Howells's ideas, acknowledges the existence of 'society-women' 'whose graciousness and refinement of presence are something of incomparable value' (AR, 40). But he refers slightingly to a 'woman's logic' and like the other men he regards 'a woman's reasoning' as a fit subject for humour. He quotes the motto, *Parole femmine, fatti maschi* (AR, 130) (women's words, men's deeds), but in the conversations that develop the important ideas of the novel even women's words have no place.

Given the banker's tribute to the grace and refinement of 'society-women', one might have expected Howells to model his chief female speaker along the lines of the conventional heroine such as Edith Leete – beautiful, charming, tactful, content to be an agreeable presence in a man's world. Instead, Howells cast his representative of genteel womanhood in the contrasting stereotype, the self-important busybody who never knows when to keep still. Named Mrs Makely (socially on the make) she exhibits the snobbery of well-to-do Americans in its most voluble form. She interrupts other speakers, patronizes everyone, and misses the shades of feeling in others' words. Her style of argument (for example, without poverty there would be no charity) would seem to justify the men's scorn of a 'woman's logic.'

Howells not only lets Mrs Makely's words condemn her; his narrator repeatedly emphasizes her deficiencies, calling her words 'fatuous' (AR, 94) and 'offensive' (AR, 61). The way the narrator polarizes the sexes – 'the ladies with their gossip and the gentlemen with their cigars' (AR, 24) – is consistent with his habit of noting the defects of the woman's speech but never commenting on the men's speech. He tags Mrs Makely's remarks – 'as she would say', 'as she would call it'; notes her pretentious pronunciation of *God* (AR, 138) and her imitation of British usage when she calls the Altrurian 'a dear' (AR, 137); he reveals her ignorance of words such as *incivism* and *black-listed* that male characters must define for her (AR, 87, 100). He notes that she is given to exaggeration and screaming intensity, that she is not satisfied to have her plan praised as 'good', but must have it 'magnificent' (AR, 133). The novel does portray in the country woman, Mrs Camp, a female character who is sensitive and intelligent, but she appears in only one scene, and significantly she is an invalid, partly paralysed by a stroke.

Naturally the American men at the hotel assume the masculine nature of the human race and its higher functions in such phrases as 'the essential equality of men' (AR, 13) and 'brotherliness between the rich and poor' (AR, 126). But the Altrurian speaks just as they do, with no more awareness of sexism in his pronouncements: the old cities were not 'fit dwelling-places for men' (AR, 159); 'a man is born and lives and dies among his own kindred' (AR, 162);

'we do not like to distinguish men by their callings' (AR, 161). He makes no reference to any women with callings; the artist, the scientist, the writer are always *he*, never *she*. He attributes the progress of civilization to 'men's minds and men's hands' (AR, 147) and defines the Altrurian ideal as 'the artist, the man of genius, who worked from the love of his work' (AR, 158). He claims 'the greatest advantage' to Altruria of 'the influence of women . . . in public affairs' (AR, 26), but in his lecture he says nothing at all of women's life in Altruria – their occupations, rights and privileges.

The epistolary sequel, *Through the Eye of the Needle*, incorporates the traditional romance missing from *A Traveler from Altruria*. Mr Homos, the writer of the letters in the first half of the sequel, courts and marries a wealthy American widow, Eveleth Strange, whose letters in the second half recount the first months of her married life in Altruria. Before the impending marriage becomes the subject of his letters, Mr Homos, writing to a friend in Altruria, dwells on the pretentions and snobbery of the well-to-do American, namely Mrs Makely, who entertains him in New York. The irony of the Altrurian's satirizing the hostess whose hospitality he repeatedly enjoys was probably unintended. Howells uses Mr Homos not to undercut Altruria but to expose the inequities of American capitalism from the outsider's perspective.

Injustice and inequality in nineteenth-century America were the products of economic conditions, Howells argued, conditions for which women, who remained outside the man's world of business, were not primarily responsible. But because almost all the evidence of inequity that Mr Homos retails in his letters is provided by Mrs Makely while her husband merely listens, she appears more guilty than he of the class prejudice and exploitation the novel satirizes. Unlike the banker and the lawyer in *A Traveler from Altruria*, who emphasize the contradictions between ideals and conditions in America, Mrs Makely approves the inequalities her household exemplifies. Unconscious of the irony, she assures the Altrurian that her maids' room, although 'always dark', is 'very pleasant', then proudly shows him her room, which has a 'perfect gush of sun from morning till night' (AR, 286). A kitchen, where the cook might work all day, can be put 'in any sort of hole', 'for you can keep on the electrics' (AR, 286). She prides herself on believing that her servants 'are human beings as we are' (AR, 286) but insists that they are 'different from us in *every* way' (AR, 288) when the Altrurian asks why she and they can't use the same elevator. As if these remarks, 'shrieked', 'screamed' and 'shouted', did not sufficiently discredit Mrs Makely, the Altrurian tags her speech ('as she would have said') and calls it 'incoherent jargon' (AR, 312). He not only reproduces her lapse from perfect breeding when she starts to say *parlor* and corrects herself: 'now we'll go back to the pa – drawing room' (AR, 287); he later calls attention to the lapse, making the correction seem more vulgar than the error.

Eveleth Strange, in contrast, is the gracious and compassionate embodiment of Howells's own troubled social conscience. Like Annie Kilburn and Margaret Vance, she yearns to alleviate suffering, is oppressed by the privileges of wealth but hesitates to renounce them. The corrective to Mrs Makely, she would seem to create a balance between male and female perspectives in her role as letter-writer. But her position as the outsider in Altruria reinforces her habitual impulse to doubt herself and seek the guidance of enlightened authority. Her letters are even more compelling indicators of the power of patriarchy than the Altrurian's in that she, a thoughtful and intelligent woman, unquestioningly uses the words and embraces the views that reflect the superior status of men.

Like all the characters, male and female, Altrurian and American, she uses the generic *he, man*, and *mankind* without apparent awareness of gender bias. She asserts that 'women are on an entire equality with the men here' (AR, 369); then, without irony, she describes a political meeting where women participate equally with men, then conclude by singing the Altrurian anthem, 'Brothers All' (AR, 379). She approvingly describes the Altrurian newspapers which often include 'the story of some good man or woman's life, ended at the patriarchal age they reach here' (AR, 431). Only once does she seem aware of the insufficiency of standard English, when she describes boats 'not *manned* but *girled*' by six young Altrurian women (AR, 367).

Not surprisingly, she accepts, even insists upon, the subordinate status to which the speech of the Altrurians relegates women. She emphasizes her defects as a public speaker – 'I have always shrunk from any sort of public appearances' (AR, 269) – and is happy to let her husband speak for her. She depends on him to translate her words into Altrurian and to take charge in a crisis because 'I couldn't ask any coherent questions' (AR, 407). The Altrurians she likes best are 'the wives of the artists and literary men' (AR, 403); if any women artists or writers live in Altruria she never mentions them. She admires her husband's 'manly gentleness' (AR, 410), sympathizes with the male Altrurians' efforts to control 'feminine curiosity', and compromises the women of Altruria when she compares them to 'the undergraduate maidens' in Tennyson's 'The Princess' (AR, 370).

But one must always ask whether any narrator of Howells is as innocent as she or he might appear. Howells's characters often mock what they approve and satirize a position by assuming it. The unnamed narrator who introduces *Through the Eye of the Needle* appears to indulge in conscious irony when he declares that the Altrurian's letters have greater 'sociological value' than his wife's letters because 'a woman's hand . . . is not to be credited with the firm and unerring touch of a man's' (AR, 273). But whether Howells is using the narrator to satirize the critics of women's writing, or masking a judgement by appearing to ridicule it, or disclaiming responsibility for a narrative 'not absolutely logical in its events' (AR, 273) is hard to say. Nor can the reader be sure that when Eveleth Homos declares that she will respond to questions only if 'ask[ed] . . . to speak' by one who 'represents the authorities' (AR, 422) she is not exaggerating her deference to make it seem ridiculous. If she writes with irony, however, she can be sure that her correspondent will not detect it, for the person she addresses is Mrs Makely.

III

Neither Julian nor the Altrurian traveller is handicapped by being a man in a civilization alien to him. In marked contrast, not only are the male narrators of Phelps's *The Gates Between* and Gilman's *Herland* introduced to unsettling new ideas; their sense of identity and their behaviour undergo radical modifications. In particular, their relation to women is transformed. Whereas the male narrators of the male writers lose no status in courtship and marriage, the male narrators of the female writers are themselves subjected to conditions which in their own worlds men had imposed on women. The male narrators suffer as women have suffered; they discover themselves silenced, bereft of power and authority, dependent upon the offices of the opposite sex. The three male visitors who invade Herland are actually imprisoned and anaesthetized when they persist in futile resistance to their female captors. Finally, both Phelps and Gilman, unlike Bellamy and

Howells, make language a central concern, showing far more sensitivity than the male writers to the power of language to oppress women and reinforce gender bias.

Elizabeth Stuart Phelps first dramatized the inadequacies of male discourse in the immensely popular novel *The Gates Ajar*, an allegory of Christian redemption narrated by a young New England woman named Mary Cabot whose brother has died in the Civil War. She is saved from despair by the ministry of her aunt, Winifred Forceythe, whose words work within her after the orthodox theology preached by the men of the church has failed to move her. Before her aunt arrives to comfort her, the narrator listens to the minister, Dr Bland, preach sermons filled with 'glittering generalities' and 'cold commonplace' that 'bewildered and disheartened me'.[21] What gives her 'the first faint hope' is her aunt's letter which quickens her spirit and prompts her to wonder 'What makes the words chase me about' (GA, 23). When her aunt arrives to console and guide her, the narrator feels that God 'has provided a voice to answer me out of the deeps' (GA, 51).

In portraying the male preacher and the female saviours Phelps reinforces some gender stereotypes and overturns others. Dr Bland's syllogisms and 'grand abstractions' illustrate the formal logic conventionally identified as masculine. Winifred Forceythe, who 'reason[s] from analogy' (GA, 96), offers not dogma and theory but *'pictures* of truth' (GA, 123), often drawn from the woman's sphere of everyday domestic life. But Dr Bland, who 'cannot seem to think outside of the old grooves' (GA, 50), exhibits the conservatism traditionally identified with women. Winifred is more innovative than Dr Bland because she enjoys the advantage conventionally assigned to men – the broader experience of life. The minister is unable to animate 'his old dry bones of metaphysics and theology' (GA, 74) because he has yet to suffer the 'intense pain' (GA, 75) of loss which alone inspires the imagination and sympathy that imbue words with the power to move others. In preaching of death and heaven he 'speaks a foreign tongue' (GA, 75). Winifred, no stranger to death, teaches 'through the kinship of her pain' (GA, 37) and comforts Dr Bland, when, after his wife's death, he discovers the inadequacy of his 'polished dogma' and his 'stereotyped logic' (GA, 143) and turns to her for solace.

Unlike conventional Victorian heroines, such as Edith Leete and Eveleth Strange, Winifred Forceythe displays the erudition traditionally considered the privilege of men. She deals not only in

'pictures of truth' but in the ideas of Plato, Tacitus, Augustine and
the German theologians. But like all Phelps's women of intellect
she has the traditional feminine virtues, apparent as soon as she
speaks, in a voice 'low and very sweet' (GA, 28). She can surpass
Dr Bland on his own metaphysical ground 'yet never speak[s]
an accent above that essentially womanly voice of hers' (GA, 74).
As in Howells's fiction, *womanly* connotes the breeding and refinement of the cultivated class. Winifred's spirituality is a mark of
caste as is evident when the narrator describes her in conversation
with Deacon Quirk, another male exponent of lifeless dogma. The
man, who has an 'animal mouth' and 'coarse hands' and says
'spiritool', 'speckylate', 'you was' and 'had ought', is by birth and
training both the spiritual and the social inferior of the woman,
'white, finely cut' (GA, 104), who speaks perfect English.

Phelps most fully dramatized male abuse of language in *The Gates
Between*, published in 1887, a year before *Looking Backward*. What
interests her in this novel, as in *The Gates Ajar*, is not gender bias
inscribed in the language but the importance of language as the
chief agent through which men's misuse of power is manifested.
This is the central insight reached by the narrator, Dr Esmerald
Thorne, whose narrative of his marriage and quarrel with his wife,
his death in a carriage accident, and his transformation in the land
of spirits is presented retrospectively. He recalls himself as he was
before his death, a prominent successful doctor whose medical
training and authority over his patients abnormally developed his
will, 'like a prize-fighter's bicipital muscle'.[22] He and his devoted
wife, Helen, replicate the behaviour of his parents: 'My mother
never spoke one irritated word to [my father] in all his life: he had
chafed and she had soothed; he had slashed and she had healed'.
Naturally the narrator assumes that 'the liberty to say what one felt
like saying appeared to me a mere identification of sex' (GB, 29),
and he acts accordingly.

Before his death, the narrator considers his exercise of the 'liberty
to say what one felt like saying' to be the exercise of power, but he
is to learn that it is a sign of weakness, a failure of control which
leads directly to his fatal accident. 'I am driven to death' (GB, 41),
he shouts to his wife in his last hour, when he vents his frustrations
by berating her for her supposed faults. He charges furiously from
the house to drive to the hospital, and unable to control his unruly
horse he dies in the overturned carriage, an age-old symbol of the
ungoverned will.

In life, the narrator unknowingly was the slave of a 'terrible master' – 'the ungoverned lip' (GB, 34); in death, initially, he is literally imprisoned, subject to the will of an unseen power, unable to make his body visible or his voice heard. He has become a 'dumb thing in a deaf world' (GB, 98), silenced in 'this mute life wherein there was neither speech nor language' (GB, 144). What most torments him is the memory of his cruel outburst to his wife, but he cannot 'give [his] sealed lips the power to say, "forgive" ' (GB, 144). Salvation comes only through divine grace acting upon the man's spirit, which must be utterly humbled and purified of worldly ambition.

The spirit world in which Thorne is transformed is sketched in the barest outline. We learn only that the inhabitants, freed of imperfection, live and work in this ideal realm where 'spiritual character formed the sole scale of social position' (GB, 186). The subject of the novel is not the utopian vision but the transformation of the narrator, who discovers his mission to be a mediator between two worlds – 'the bearer of a message to many men' (GB, 2). Here *men* does refer to the male sex. It is men like himself who must learn to honour 'the sacred graces of human speech', to recognize 'the preciousness and the poignancy of *words*', to understand that 'an irritable scene in loving homes' is 'as degrading as a blow' (GB, 214).

The humbling of Dr Thorne in the afterlife is in marked contrast to the liberation in *Beyond the Gates* of the female narrator, Mary, who during a near fatal illness dreams of her escape from earthly constraints to the perfect society in heaven. Like Esmerald Thorne, she feels unworthy of divine love but for Phelps's women heaven means new freedom and strength, not impotence. Dr Thorne's patient, Mrs Faith, a chronic invalid in life, rejoices when she meets him after death, 'I never knew what it was to be *alive* before' (GB, 152). Likewise, the narrator of *Beyond the Gates* at once enjoys in heaven 'sensations of pleasure', 'splendid strength', and 'a superabundance of vitality'.[23] Dr Thorne laments the loss of former power: 'I am shorn of it. It has all gone from me, like the strength of Samson' (BG, 138). Mary knows the 'acquisition of a fresh power' which she can best compare to the sense of mastery she enjoyed on earth in 'conquer[ing] a new language' (BG, 63). For Dr Thorne, heaven requires the unlearning of old habits and attitudes. For Mary, heaven promises intellectual growth, 'the command of unknown languages, arts, and sciences, and knowledges manifold'

(BG, 181). For the first time, she understands the words *freedom*, *health*, and *liberty*, as the 'poetical phrases' become for her 'attainable facts' (BG, 45).

Phelps's utopian heaven promises women power and knowledge denied them on earth. But traditions elevating men above women were too powerful for this descendant of Calvinist ministers and teachers to resist altogether. The religion celebrated in all three Gates books is patriarchal Christianity, in which women and men alike seek the supreme wisdom and love of God the Father and Christ His Son. In *Beyond the Gates*, Mary is guided to heaven by her father, a commanding figure of authority and omniscience. In *The Gates Between*, the habits of deference and submissiveness still cling to Mrs Faith and Helen Thorne, the spiritual guides of Dr Thorne. Female self-abnegation is likewise celebrated in *Beyond the Gates*, when heaven welcomes two new arrivals: a railroad engineer who became a national hero by dying to save the lives of hundreds of passengers, and a woman whose immolation on the altar of unregarded service to others is recognized only in heaven.

In her autobiography, *Chapters from a Life*, Phelps recalled one motive for writing *The Gates Ajar*: to comfort women grieving for the loss of loved ones in the Civil War but denied consolation from orthodox religion preached in the Christian churches. 'Creeds and commentaries and sermons were made by men', she observed. Their dogmas were 'chains of rusty iron eating into raw hearts'.[24] The painful image was perhaps also evoked by her memory of her father's public rejection of her views in his anti-feminist essays of the 1870s.[25] But she makes no complaint of him in her autobiography. And it was to her father, Professor of Rhetoric and Homiletics in the Andover Seminary, that she declared herself indebted for the writer's legacy: 'His appreciation of the uses and graces of language very early descended like a mantle upon me' (CL, 17). Her mother, whose 'simple home stories' sold hundreds of thousands of copies, exemplified the woman of genius 'torn by the civil war of the dual nature which can be given to women only' (CL, 12). Her father's was the vital influence, essential as 'sunshine or oxygen'; his example and teachings created 'my climate', 'the atmosphere I breathed' (CL, 17). That this atmosphere was often oppressive her novels indirectly confess, but the heavenly utopias she created to counter the authority of men such as her father also attest to the power of their example.

It may be incidental that only the male narrator in *The Gates Between* presents a vision of heaven as a reality in the world of the work. The female narrator of *Beyond the Gates* awakens at the end to discover that her vision of heaven was only a dream. Winifred Forceythe describes to Mary Cabot the heaven she imagines but cannot know as 'attainable fact'(BG, 45). The reader may ask whether for Phelps the positing of a utopian world as a reality required the authority of a male narrator, or whether she feared to undermine her criticism of male authority by presenting the liberation of women as an accomplished fact, or whether, because she felt women to be in closer touch than men with the essence of everyday life, she could not allow female narrators to turn visions into fictional reality. The novels, with their commingling of elements traditional and anti-traditional, can be read to support each of these views.

IV

In the ideal worlds imagined by Bellamy, Howells and Phelps, women may achieve economic equality with men, but the structures of their societies continue to sustain men in their positions of authority. Charlotte Perkins Gilman departs from the traditional pattern in creating Herland, an all but inaccessible kingdom hidden by cliffs and forests, where for two thousand years only women have lived. Here they command every power and hold every office and depend on men for nothing, not even the conceiving of children. Soon after the narrator, Vandyck Jennings, and his two male friends invade Herland, the omnipotence of their female captors subjects them to a humiliating reversal of gender roles. 'Struggling manfully, but held secure most womanfully',[26] the men are given their first lesson in the capacities of the sexes.

For *Herland*'s narrator, the transforming insight is the revelation that all his ideas and assumptions about men and women rest not upon fact but upon traditions perpetuated by a patriarchal society whose assumptions he had never questioned. He discovers the artificial basis of his whole structure of belief when in Herland he discovers that language is an expression of culture, of its values, codes and institutions that determine the meaning of words. We are told that Herland has its own language, 'an absolutely phonetic system . . . as scientific as Esperanto' (H, 31), but Gilman never reproduces it, for what interests her are the ideas attached to words, the different conceptions that the women of Herland and the men of Ourland associate with such words as *home, mother, feminine, love, wife, family, education, patriotism,* and above all, the word *woman.* (Recalling that in Esperanto feminine nouns, such as *virino* (woman), *patrino* (mother), and *edzino* (wife), are diminutives of masculine forms, one wonders whether Gilman imagined the process reversed in Herland's language.)

To demonstrate the power of language to veil and to reveal social realities, Gilman creates in Jennings a narrator who readily learns the lessons of Herland, who embraces new ideas almost as easily as he dons the new clothes provided by his captors. Whereas his male chauvinist friend, Terry Nicholson, will never acknowledge Herland realities or accept Herlanders as women (they remain to him 'Neuters, epicenes, bloodless, sexless creatures' (H, 133)), the narrator marvels at their achievements, admits the error of his original view of women as weak, timid, passive and conservative, and accepts a new definition of *women* – 'not as females, but as people, people of all sorts, doing every kind of work' (H, 137). He moves from his outer darkness in Chapter 1, when he says of Herland, 'why, this is a *civilized* country . . . there must be *men*' (H, 11), to enlightened recognition that the words *man* and *woman* do not signify unchanging realities; to the narrator, *man* and *manhood* had evoked 'a huge vague crowded picture of the world' filled with men marching, sailing, exploring, mining, farming, building. *Woman* had meant only 'female – the sex'. To the Herlanders, he realizes, the word *woman* 'called up all that big background . . . and the word *man* meant to them only *male* – the sex' (H, 137). What Gilman had argued four years before, in *The Man-Made World,* her narrator learns in the woman-made world of Herland. When his friends complain that the Herland women are not 'feminine' he perceives that the so-called 'feminine charms' are actually 'mere reflected masculinity' (H, 57) – what women think they must be to please men.

The narrator's education continues in the sequel, *With Her in Ourland,* published as was *Herland* in 12 instalments in Gilman's magazine, the *Forerunner.* In this narrative, more tract than novel, the narrator takes his wife Ellador to America, but he remains the pupil as her probing questions reveal to him the shams, injustices and hypocrisies of his American society. Merely her presence, which moves him to 'adopt her point of view',[27] is instructive. For instance, he feels more keenly the ugliness of the 'slang, profanity, obscenity' familiar to Americans when he imagines the effect upon his Herland wife accustomed to the 'loving use of language as an art' (WHO, 39).

In contrast to Eveleth Strange, who extols the virtues of Altruria and feels herself deficient, Ellador dwells on the failure of her husband's country to realize its ideals of unity and equality. Among the targets of her scrutiny is language which exalts men over women and denies women their humanity. She observes to her husband that Americans talk about the 'brotherhood of man' but apparently haven't considered 'the possibilities of a sisterhood of women' (WHO, 155). She asks why bearing children is called 'woman nature' when making war is called 'human nature', although only men fight (WHO, 11). She refuses to allow men to arrogate to themselves the identity of an entire nation, especially when they would impose their evil acts upon a whole people. She insists on distinctions: 'Male Scandinavians continually indulged in piracy'; 'the male Spaniards practiced terrible cruelties' (WHO, 69). When a male passenger on the ship to America tells Ellador that 'other peoples' razed Near Eastern cities, she asks, 'Do you mean other peoples or just other men?' and reminds him that 'people are men, women, and children' (WHO, 70).

Thus Ellador leads the narrator to articulate the conclusion of *Man-Made World* for himself: 'Wherever men had been superior to women we had proudly claimed it as a sex-distinction. Wherever men had shown evil traits, not common to women, we had serenely treated them as race-characteristics' (WHO, 70). Pressing the argument further, Ellador shows her receptive husband that the patriarchal principle, in its anti-democratic character, has victimized men as well as women, subjecting both sexes, throughout the centuries, to the rule of 'Kings and Fathers, Bosses, Rulers, Masters, Overlords', and behind them all 'that old Boss Father' – the 'Hebrew Deity' (WHO, 181).

V

Unlike the fiction of Bellamy, Howells and Phelps, *Herland* and *With Her in Ourland* received no attention in the press when they were published, generated no debate in newspapers or periodicals, and had no commercial book sale until a paperback edition of *Herland* was published in 1979. Before then, the audience for

Gilman's utopian fiction was limited to readers of the *Forerunner*, which, according to the author, never attracted more than 1500 subscribers a year during the seven years of its life.[28] The novels, virtually ignored in Gilman's lifetime, now seem remarkable in their revelation of a kind of gender bias unnoted in other utopian novels of the period. Indeed, in 1915, when Gilman published *Herland*, the reader was unlikely to have read *any* work of fiction which so pointedly exposed sexism in the language and revealed the assumptions underlying it.

The exceptional nature of Gilman's novels becomes more apparent when one considers other utopian fiction by women published in the half century after the Civil War. For instance, one might expect Gilman's observations about language to be anticipated in Mary Bradley Lane's *Mizora: A Prophecy* (1880–81), the first novel by a woman to portray an all-female utopia. Words such as *workwoman* and *stateswoman* remind the reader that in Mizora, as in Herland, women fill every office. The narrator, a Russian princess in exile, notes that the Mizoran women were 'frank to singularity'[29] in conversation. But nothing else suggests that the women, whose blonde beauty of 'the highest type' signifies both racial and moral purity, fail to exemplify Victorian ideals of womanhood as completely as they embody Anglo-Saxon racist ideology. All that the culture exacts of them as speakers is conformity to a standard that conventionally defines the conduct of ladies: 'Correct language, refined tastes, dignified, and graceful manners were the common requirements of all' (M, 65). Their voices are 'softer and sweeter than the strains of an eolian harp' (M, 17). But what most impresses the narrator upon her arrival is not their speech but the 'singular silence that pervaded everything' (M, 17), silence expressive of the same convention that obliges the narrator to begin her story by minimizing her literary skill – 'having little knowledge of rhetorical art' – and by apologizing for '[coming] before the public in the character of an author' (M, 7).

Bradley Lane's *Mizora* imposes on an all-female world the conventions confining women in a male-dominated society. These conventions operate even more potently in *Unveiling a Parallel: A Romance* by 'Two Women of the West' (1893), in which a male narrator discovers on Mars a society where women and men are assumed to share a common nature and women exercise the prerogatives earthly society grants only to men. Women not only vote, hold political office and head corporations; they propose to men, maul each other in prize fights, take lovers as men take mistresses, and roister at all-female dinners where they drink wine and tell coarse jokes. By insisting that equality demands for women no less than for men the privilege 'to indulge in vice',[30] the novel undermines its attack on the double standard that condemns in women what it condones in men; it compromises its satire of the narrator, who thinks women should confine themselves to 'feminine occupations' and cultivate 'the softer graces' pleasing to men (UPR, 110). Like the narrator, many readers were probably most repelled not by the 'vices' themselves but by the spectacle of women indulging in them. The novel endorses the narrator's pleasure in meeting (in a neighbouring kingdom) the perfect woman, Ariadne, chaste and beautiful, 'a white and slender lily' (UPR, 249), who restores his faith in womanhood 'as the highest and purest thing under heaven' (UPR, 182).

Utopian fiction offers further evidence, if it were needed, that women writers can defend the patriarchal status quo as firmly as men. Mary Agnes Tincker, in *San Salvador* (1892) puts in her utopia the communal kitchens and nurseries advocated by Charlotte Perkins Gilman, but concludes the novel with a plea that women seeking male privileges 'return . . . to their quiet homes' where they can best perform their highest duty: 'To make a race of noble men'.[31] The example of true womanhood is set by the heroine who journeys to a Christian utopia, 'The City of the Holy King', marries the noble ruler and bears a son. Her name, *Tacita*, signifies the mute perfection that pleases her first admirer who observes her sitting submissively attentive in a shadowy background, 'silent as any lily' (SS, 29).

Even when women are given authoritative voices in utopias where they discourse on the ideals and history of their society, the language of the novel belies radical departure from tradition. For instance, M. Louise Moore's *Al-Modad or Life Scenes Beyond the Polar Circumflex* (1892) depicts an island utopia where the principle of equality purportedly informs every institution including religion. Here the male narrator, chided for speaking of God as *He*, is told that the creator 'possesses the attributes of both sexes equally'.[32] He also reads in a history of the island about the 'compassionate Father-Creator' (AL, 181) and listens to a female teacher of physics lecture on the universal principle of polarity, according to which *'attraction* and *repulsion'* and 'Positive and Negative' are 'identical with the sex-principle – masculine and feminine' (AL, 127).

Al-Modad is but one of scores of novels that posit radical change but in language that often reinforces the old structures supposedly abolished. Writers could more easily imagine characters acting in non-traditional ways than they could relinquish generic male pronouns and dispense with binary forms that invariably elevate *man* above *woman*. Gilman's Ellador observes that 'ideas stay fixed in people's minds long after the facts have changed' (WHO, 241). Utopian fiction shows that linguistic forms have even greater powers of survival.

Even the language of Herland reinforces as well as subverts traditional concepts of gender. In Gilman's utopia, motherhood is exalted as a religion, 'the highest social service' (H, 69). *Motherhood* is 'the highest, holiest word' (WHO, 41); the Herland women have '[made] over the entire language in the interests of childhood' (WHO, 267). Although her effort to fulfil her role as mother caused Gilman great anguish and ultimately led to her separation from her husband and her daughter, she did not propose to diminish the importance of motherhood. Indeed, her belief in eugenics as the means to regeneration led her in *Herland* to celebrate the power of women as 'Conscious Makers of People' (H, 69). But when the paean to motherhood is removed from its radical context, in a book about a nation of women, it might do as good service as *Looking Backward* in the cause of separate spheres and traditional gender roles.

Indeed, writers of utopian fiction who constructed plots of courtship and marriage probably did more to support than to subvert tradition, even when they used the courtship plot, as Gilman and Phelps did, to expose bias and inequality by reversing the places of men and women. The happy marriages promised or realized in *Looking Backward, Through the Eye of the Needle, The Gates Between* and *Herland* all imply that heterosexual love assures characters their greatest happiness, that the family created by marriage is the essential unit of an ideal state.

Gilman anticipated by more than fifty years the observations of recent critics of sexist language. But given the traditional values affirmed in even her utopian fiction, it is not surprising that neither she nor her contemporaries proposed new linguistic forms or imagined societies that transcended altogether distinctions based on gender. Not until the 1970s, which produced more feminist utopias than any other decade, did novelists imagine societies where institutions are transformed and language is remade.

Conclusion

Near the end of Thomas Hardy's early novel *Far From the Madding Crowd* (1874), the protagonist Bathsheba Everdene observes to one of her suitors: 'It is difficult for a woman to define her feelings in language which is chiefly made by men to express theirs.'[1]

Bathsheba was not the first nineteenth-century heroine to assert men's appropriation of language for their own ends. More than fifty years earlier, Jane Austen's Anne Elliot explains why books confirm nothing about women's nature: 'Men have had every advantage of us in telling their own story. Education has been theirs in so much higher a degree; the pen has been in their hands. I will not allow books to prove any thing.'[2]

Jane Austen's heroine and her narrator are of one mind. In *Far From the Madding Crowd*, Hardy's narrator is at odds with the heroine. The narrator is sympathetic to Bathsheba, and yet he repeatedly reinforces the gender bias of the system she resists, especially when he voices commonplace criticisms of women's speech. He undermines Bathsheba even when he makes her the exception to the unflattering rule: she is 'that novelty among women – one who finished a thought before beginning the sentence which was to convey it'. Elsewhere the narrator makes her conform to the stereotype: she speaks when she should say nothing, the narrator says, because she has 'too much womanly redundance of speech' to remain silent.[3]

In these passages, Hardy pits his protagonist against his narrator. He created a heroine who refuses to be regarded as a man's property, who exposes the sexist bias in common assumptions,[4] and chafes at being forced to use a language she feels is not hers. But her story is told by a narrator who embodies the ideology of the patriarchal system so oppressive to her.

Conflicting voices such as these, suggestive of conflicting sympathies within the novelist, reveal similar tensions and contradictions in American realist fiction. Howells, James, Wharton and Cather all characterize female speech and language in ways that relegate women to a subclass, inferior to men. But, like Hardy,

184

these novelists, in their fiction, created women who belie the negative characterizations, women whose forthright speech exposes hypocrisy and self-delusion in male speakers. Forces more potent than gender stereotypes created characters such as Lily Bart, Penelope Lapham, Isabel Archer and Ántonia Shimerda. The more powerful the novelist's imagination, the greater the power of the fictional characters to transcend ideology and so to free their creator from the constraints of gender bias.

But escape is never complete. The characters of Howells, James, Wharton and Cather cross gender boundaries but the boundaries always remain, defining as exceptional the characters who cross them. Qualities traditionally defined as masculine or feminine commingle in the individual character, notably in the novels of James and Cather. The womanly nature of such characters as Alexandra Bergson and Ántonia Shimerda is fully realized only as they assume roles and achieve success traditionally identified with men. The 'subtlety and pliability' James defined as feminine in an essay on Sainte-Beuve are as essential to the genius of James's male artists as Sainte-Beuve's 'faculties of the masculine stamp' such as 'solid sense', 'constant reason' and 'copious knowledge'.[5] But the polarities survive intact; the constructs of gender – masculine and feminine – remain essential elements of definition.

Of the four writers, Cather goes furthest in transposing traditional gender roles. James, in writing of male artists (other than Roderick Hudson), does most to invest the word *feminine* with positive meaning. But gendered constructs bisect the fictional worlds of *My Ántonia* and *The Wings of the Dove* as strikingly as they do in *The Rise of Silas Lapham* and *The House of Mirth*. And in the fiction of all four novelists, the pen that writes masterpieces of literary art is always held by men.

Paradoxically, utopian fiction, which depicts societies reformed to eradicate inequities, often shows traditional gender bias at its most firmly entrenched. In Howells's Altruria and Bellamy's futuristic Boston, habitual usage which subordinates women to men and affirms men as the superior sex seems all the more resistant to change when no one observes the failure of language to accompany social and economic reform. Even in Herland, where men and women assume each other's roles, the reversal requires the perpetuation of binary systems. *Herland* does, however, destroy the illusion that polarities such as *masculine* and *feminine* signify the balance of equals. The violence erupting in Gilman's utopia proves that yoked opposites perpetuate imbalance, investing one side with superior value and power, at the expense of the other.

When the subject is language and gender, realist and utopian fiction tell essentially the same story. So long as the polarities remain, so long as *feminine* and *masculine* are set in opposition, the binary form, so irresistible in its rhetorical effect, will itself promote oppression and strife. Gilman's proposal of a third category, *human*, has yet to be embraced. But when novelists create characters aware of the inequities their language perpetuates, then fiction gives hope for change.

Notes

Introduction

1. The number includes at least three pseudonyms: Sherwood Bonner (Virginia MacDonald), Charles Egbert Craddock (Mary Noailles Murfree) and Saxe Holm (Helen Hunt Jackson). Three stories and two serials were published anonymously.
2. James Fullarton Muirhead, *America, the Land of Contrasts: A Briton's View of His American Kin* (London: John Lane, 1898), p. 186.
3. *Henry James: The Future of the Novel*, edited and with an introduction by Leon Edel (New York: Vintage Books, 1956), pp. 6, 14.

1 Language and Gender in Victorian America

1. Casey Miller and Kate Swift, *Words and Women* (Garden City, NY: Anchor Press, 1976), p. 69.
2. Introduction to *The Biglow Papers, Second Series: The Writings of James Russell Lowell in Prose and Poetry*, Vol. IX (Boston: Houghton Mifflin Company, 1894), 158.
3. 'Literary Notices', *Harper's Magazine*, 7 (1853), 715.
4. 'Americanism in Literature', *Atlantic Monthly*, 25 (1870), 58.
5. 'Editor's Easy Chair', *Harper's Magazine*, 29 (1864), 676; 50 (1875), 757.
6. *Atlantic Monthly*, 22 (1868), 127; 'Editor's Easy Chair', *Harper's Magazine*, 131 (1915), 635; Letter of January 27, 1902, *Selected Letters of W. D. Howells*, Vol. 5, ed. William C. Fischer (Boston: Twayne, 1983), p. 13.
7. 'Some Recent Women Poets', *Scribner's Monthly*, 10 (1875), 100–6.
8. 'Editor's Study', *Harper's Magazine*, 77 (1888), 966.
9. 'Editor's Study', *Harper's Magazine*, 82 (1891), 319; 77 (1888), 964.
10. Ralph Waldo Emerson, *Essays: First Series* (New York: Clarke, Given & Hooper, n.d.), p. 88.
11. James Lane Allen, 'Two Principles in Recent American Fiction', *Atlantic Monthly*, 80 (1897), 436–7.
12. Philip Rahv, 'Paleface and Redskin' (1939), *Essays on Literature and Politics, 1932–1972*, ed. Arabel J. Porter and Andrew J. Dvosin (Boston: Houghton Mifflin Company, 1978), pp. 3–7.
13. Sarah Josepha Hale, *Woman's Record; or, Sketches of All Distinguished Women* (New York: Harper & Brothers, 1853), p. 793; 'New England in the Short Story', *Atlantic Monthly*, 67 (1891), 847.
14. Charles W. Coleman, 'The Recent Movement in Southern Literature', *Harper's Magazine*, 74 (1887), 851; *Ladies' Home Journal*, 5 (1887), 2.

15. 'Editor's Study', *Harper's Magazine*, 121 (1910), 801.

16. *Lippincott's Magazine*, 44 (1889), 869.

17. 'Müller's Chips from a German Workshop', *North American Review*, 123 (1876), 208; 'Poems by W. D. Howells', 118 (1874), 191; 'Their Wedding Journey', 114 (1872), 444.

18. George Parsons Lathrop, 'Audacity in Women Novelists', *North American Review*, 150 (1890), 613–14.

19. Grant Allen, 'Women's Intuition', *Forum*, 9 (1890), 339.

20. 'Two Principles in Recent American Fiction' (see n. 11), 439.

21. Lester F. Ward, 'Genius and Woman's Intuition', *Forum*, 9 (1890), 405–6.

22. James S. Metcalfe, 'The Silent Revolution', *Cosmopolitan*, 21 (1890), 100.

23. H. H. Gardner, 'The Immoral Influence of Women in Literature', *Arena*, 1 (1890), 323, 327, 328.

24. Helen Watterson, 'Women's Excitement over "Woman,"' *Forum*, 16 (1893), 81.

25. Helen Gray Cone, 'Woman in American Literature', *Century Magazine*, 40 (1890), 928, 921.

26. Charlotte Perkins Gilman, *The Man-Made World or, Our Androcentric Culture* (New York: Charlton Company, 1911; Johnson Reprint Corporation, 1971), p. 22. Hereafter abbreviated MMW, with page numbers given in the text.

27. 'Genius and Woman's Intuition' (see n. 21), 408.

28. For instance, the reviewer in the *Independent* found the book 'witty and sensible in many of its contentions', 70 (13 April 1911), 793; 'a highly provocative book', according to *Current Literature*, 50 (May 1911), 548; in the *New York Times Review of Books*, the book was praised for its 'vigorous arguments', 'its clear and logical thinking and precise and forceful exposition' (26 February 1911, p. 111). Gary Scharnhorst quotes from a number of reviews in *Charlotte Perkins Gilman* (Boston: Twayne Publishers, 1985), p. 80.

29. Review of *A Woman's Poems*, *Atlantic Monthly*, 27 (1871), 774; Foster Coates, 'Women in Journalism', *Ladies' Home Journal*, 9 (1892), 18; Abram S. Isaacs, 'The Jewess in Authorship', *Ladies' Home Journal*, 9 (1892), 17.

30. Henry James, 'An Animated Conversation', *Scribner's Magazine*, 5 (1889), 372.

31. 'Editor's Easy Chair', *Harper's Magazine*, 102 (1901), 481.

32. 'The Immoral Influence of Women in Literature' (see n. 23), 327.

33. Elizabeth L. Post, *The New Emily Post's Etiquette* (New York: Funk & Wagnalls, 1975), p. 37.

34. George Wakeman, 'Verbal Anomalies', *Galaxy*, 2 (1866), 36; Richard Grant White, *Words and Their Uses* (New York: Sheldon & Company, 1872), p. 162; Frederic Bird, 'Paralyzers of Style', *Lippincott's Magazine*, 57 (1896), 282.

35. Elsie Clews Parsons, *The Old-Fashioned Woman* (New York: Arno Press, 1972; reprint of the 1913 edition), p. 159.

36. Otto Jespersen, *Language: Its Nature, Development and Origin* (London: George Allen & Unwin, 1922), pp. 247, 250, 251.

37. Elizabeth Stuart Phelps, 'The Décolleté in Modern Life', *Forum*, 9 (1890), 676.
38. Amelia Barr, 'Conversational Immoralities', *North American Review*, 150 (1890), 460–61.
39. Florence Kingsland, *Correct Social Usage*, Tenth revised edition (New York: New York Society of Self-Culture, 1908), p. 48.
40. *Ladies' Home Journal*, 7 (1890), 10; 4 (1887), 14.
41. *Language: Its Nature, Development and Origin* (see n. 36), p. 247.
42. *The Old-Fashioned Woman* (see n. 35), pp. 149–56.
43. H. C. Cooper, 'Light or Shadow?', *North American Review*, 151 (1890), 127.
44. *Language: Its Nature, Development and Origin* (see n. 36), p. 247.
45. 'Light or Shadow?' (see n. 43), 128.
46. Dennis Baron, *Grammar and Gender* (New Haven: Yale University Press, 1986), Chapters 2, 3, 6.
47. Huber Gray Buehler, *A Modern English Grammar* (New York: Newson & Company, 1900), p. 151.
48. G. P. Quackenbos, *An English Grammar* (New York: Appleton, 1862), p. 45.
49. Peter Bullions, *Practical Grammar of the English Language*, revised edition (New York: Sheldon & Company, 1870), p. 30.
50. Simon Kerl, *A Common-School Grammar of the English Language* (New York: Ivison, Phinney, Blakeman, 1868), pp. 81, 82.
51. George W. Carpenter, *English Grammar* (New York: Macmillan Company, 1920), p. 5; William Chauncey Fowler, *English Grammar: The English Language in Its Elements and Forms* (New York: Harper & Brothers, 1871), p. 67; Goold Brown, *The Institutes of English Grammar*, new edition (New York: William Wood, 1863), p. 51.
52. 'Contributors' Club', *Atlantic Monthly*, 42 (1878), 639–40; 43 (1879), 258. The item on *hesh, hizer, himer* is identified as Horace E. Scudder's by Philip B. Eppard and George Monteiro, *A Guide to the Atlantic Monthly's Contributors' Club* (Boston: G. K. Hall, 1983), p. 16.
53. See *Grammar and Gender* (n. 46), Chapter 10.
54. *The Commercial Advertiser*, 7 August 1884, quoted in Dennis E. Baron, 'The Epicene Pronoun: The Word that Failed', *American Speech*, 56 (1981), 88.
55. 'Table Talk', *Appleton's Magazine*, 2 (1869), 26.
56. *Words and Their Uses* (see n. 34), pp. 241–2. For a list of coinages from 1850 to 1985, see *Grammar and Gender* (n. 46), pp. 205–9.
57. Edwin Berck Dike, 'The Suffix -ess, etc.', *Journal of English and Germanic Philology*, 36 (1937), 29.
58. See for instance Francine Wattman Frank and Paula A. Treichler, *Language, Gender, and Professional Writing: Theoretical Approaches and Guidelines for Nonsexist Usage* (New York: Modern Language Association of America, 1989), pp. 208–10; Carolyn Korsmeyer, 'The Hidden Joke: Generic Use of Masculine Terminology', *Feminism and Philosophy*, ed. Mary Vetterling-Braggin, Frederick A. Elliston and Jane English (Totowa, NJ: Littlefield, Adams, 1977), pp. 144–5; Ethel Strainchamps, 'Our Sexist Language', *Woman in Sexist Society: Studies*

in Power and Powerlessness, edited and with an introduction by Vivian Gornick and Barbara K. Moran (New York: New American Library, 1971), p. 352.

59. For other examples, see Mamie Meredith, ' "Doctresses", "Authoresses", and Others', *American Speech,* 5 (1930), 476–81.

60. *Words and Their Uses* (see n. 34), p. 205; *North American Review,* 112 (1871), 474.

61. Gilbert Tucker, *Our Common Speech* (New York: Dodd, Mead & Company, 1895), p. 14; Simon Kerl, *A Common-School Grammar of the English Language,* pp. 314, 82; Philip Krapp, *The Elements of English Grammar* (New York: Charles Scribner's Sons, 1908), p. 45; Edward S. Gould, *Good English; or Popular Errors in Language* (New York: W. J. Widdleton, 1867), pp. 22–3.

62. *Words and Their Uses* (see n. 34), pp. 140, 205, 174.

63. Austin Phelps, *English Style in Public Discourse* (New York: Charles Scribner's Sons, 1883), p. 152.

64. Lindley Murray, *English Grammar Adapted to the Different Classes of Learners* (Philadelphia: J. B. Lippincott & Company, 1866), pp. 70, 175, 194.

65. Thomas W. Harvey, *An Elementary Grammar of the English Language* (Cincinnati: Wilson, Hinkle & Company, 1869), p. 68; George Lyman Kittredge and Sarah Louise Arnold, *The Mother Tongue: An Elementary English Grammar* (Boston: Ginn & Company, 1900), p. 140.

66. *Grammar and Gender* (see n. 46), p. 68.

67. Max Müller, *Lectures on the Science of Language,* Second Series (London: Longman, Green, Longman, Roberts & Green, 1864), p. 176.

68. James Russell Lowell, *Among My Books,* Second Series (Boston: Houghton Mifflin & Company, 1883), p. 23.

69. Otto Jespersen, *Growth and Structure of the English Language* (Leipzig: B. G. Teubner, 1905), p. 67.

70. *The Literary History of the United States,* fourth edition, revised, ed. Robert E. Spiller, Willard Thorp, Thomas H. Johnson, Henry Seidel-Canby and Robert M. Ludwig (New York: Macmillan, 1974), p. 675.

71. Thomas R. Lounsbury, 'Is English Becoming Corrupt?' *Harper's Magazine,* 108 (1904), 194.

72. *The Revolution in Words: Righting Women, 1868–1871,* ed. Lana F. Rakow and Cheris Kramarae (New York: Routledge, 1990). Hereafter abbreviated RW, with page numbers given in the text.

73. *Woman's Journal,* published from 1870 to 1917. Hereafter abbreviated WJ, with volume and page numbers given in the text.

74. Frances Willard, 'The Woman's Cause is Man's', *Arena,* 5 (1892), 725.

75. White, *Words and Their Uses* (see n. 34), p. 180; Mark Twain, 'Fenimore Cooper's Literary Offenses', *North American Review,* 161 (1895), 4; Thomas Lounsbury, 'On the Hostility to Certain Words', *Harper's Magazine,* 113 (1906), 366.

76. Alfred Bendixen, 'Introduction: The Whole Story Behind *The Whole Family',* *The Whole Family: A Novel by Twelve Authors* (New York: Ungar Publishing Company, 1986), pp. xxii–xxv.

77. 'An old maid is now thought such a curse, as no poetic fury can exceed; lookt on as the most calamitous creature in nature', Richard Allestree, *The Ladies Calling* (Oxford, 1673), Part II, Section I, p. 3.
78. 'Philology', *Godey's Lady's Book*, 82 (1871–72), 475; *Ladies' Home Journal*, 4 (1887), 8.
79. Amelia E. Barr, 'The Decline of Politeness', *Lippincott's Magazine*, 48 (1892), 87; 'Editor's Drawer', *Harper's Magazine*, 75 (1887), 807; Eugene Benson, 'A Lost Art – Conversation', *Appleton's Journal*, 2 (1869), 308.
80. 'Editor's Table', *Harper's Magazine*, 12 (1856), 557.
81. Henry James, *French Writers and American Women: Essays*, ed. Peter Buitenhuis (Branford, Conn.: Compass, 1960), pp. 38–40.
82. 'Editor's Easy Chair', *Harper's Magazine*, 55 (1877), 303; 'Editor's Drawer', *Harper's Magazine*, 78 (1889), 78; Fletcher Osgood, 'Why the American Conversational Voice is Bad', *Forum*, 19 (1895), 501; 'The Point of View', *Scribner's Magazine*, 25 (1899), 379; 'Editor's Drawer', *Harper's Magazine*, 79 (1889), 157; 'Are We a Polite People?' *Harper's Magazine*, 15 (1857), 527.
83. Interview, *Lamp*, 28 (February 1904), 27–31, in Ulrich Halfmann, 'Interviews with William Dean Howells', *American Literary Realism*, 6 (1973), 356.

2 The Voices of Men and Women in Howells's Fiction and Drama

1. Robert Frost to Hamlin Garland, 4 February 1921. *Selected Letters of Robert Frost*, edited by Lawrence Thompson (New York: Holt, Rinehart & Winston, 1965), p. 265.
2. 'Editor's Study', *Harper's Magazine*, 78 (1889), 492.
3. 'Editor's Study', *Harper's Magazine*, 76 (1887), 154.
4. *Atlantic Monthly*, 37 (1876), 372–3.
5. *Through the Eye of the Needle*, in *The Altrurian Romances*, Introduction and Notes to the Text by Clara and Rudolf Kirk (Bloomington: Indiana University Press, 1968), p. 282.
6. *April Hopes*, Introduction and Notes to the Text by Kermit Vanderbilt (Bloomington: Indiana University Press, 1974), p. 231. Hereafter abbreviated AH, with page numbers given in the text.
7. 'Our Daily Speech', *Harper's Bazar*, 40 (1906), 931.
8. *Ibid.*
9. 'Minor Topics', *Nation*, 2 (1866), 325.
10. 'Editor's Easy Chair', *Harper's Magazine*, 134 (1917), 594.
11. *Imaginary Interviews* (New York: Harper & Brothers, 1910), p. 178.
12. For instance, in 'Woman's Limitations in Burlesque', *Harper's Weekly*, 46 (1902), 1465, and 'Editor's Easy Chair', *Harper's Magazine*, 103 (1901), 1004.
13. Ulrich Halfmann, 'Interviews with William Dean Howells', *American Literary Realism*, 6 (1973), 326–7.
14. *Ibid.*, 354.

15. *The Early Prose Writings of William Dean Howells*, ed. Thomas Wortham (Athens: Ohio University Press, 1990), pp. 243–4.
16. 'W. D. Howells and the "American Girl" ', *Texas Quarterly*, 19 (1976), 152. The following is a typical example of the narrator's identification of himself with men: 'The two men put on that business air with which our sex tries to atone to itself for having unbent to the lighter minds of the other.' *The Minister's Charge or the Apprenticeship of Lemuel Barker*, Introduction and Notes to the Text by Howard M. Munford (Bloomington: Indiana University Press, 1978), p. 272. Hereafter abbreviated MC, with page numbers given in the text.
17. *The Rise of Silas Lapham*, Introduction and Notes to the Text by Walter J. Meserve (Bloomington: Indiana University Press, 1971), p. 127. Hereafter abbreviated RSL, with page numbers given in the text.
18. *An Imperative Duty*, Introduction and Notes to the Text by Martha Banta (Bloomington: Indiana University Press, 1970), p. 17.
19. *The Complete Plays of W. D. Howells*, edited and with an introduction by Walter J. Meserve (New York: New York University Press, 1960), p. 35. Hereafter abbreviated CP, with page numbers given in the text.
20. *A Woman's Reason* (Boston: Osgood, 1883), p. 444.
21. *The Vacation of the Kelwyns: An Idyl of the Middle Eighteen-Seventies* (New York: Harper, 1920), p. 187. Hereafter abbreviated VK, with page numbers given in the text.
22. *Annie Kilburn* (New York: Harper, 1889), pp. 140–1, 258. Hereafter abbreviated AK, with page numbers given in the text.
23. 'At the Sign of the Savage', in *A Fearful Responsibility and Other Stories* (Westport, Conn.: Greenwood Press, 1970), p. 175.
24. *The Son of Royal Langbrith*, Introduction and Notes to the Text by David Burrows (Bloomington: Indiana University Press, 1969), p. 84. Hereafter abbreviated SRL, with page numbers given in the text.
25. *A Hazard of New Fortunes*, Introduction and Notes to the Text by Everett Carter (Bloomington: Indiana University Press, 1976), p. 16. Hereafter abbreviated HNF, with page numbers given in the text.
26. Howells's phrase in 'Editor's Study', *Harper's Magazine*, 72 (1886), 484.
27. Letter of 2 February 1877. Houghton Library, Harvard University.
28. Howells's phrase in 'Editor's Study', *Harper's Magazine*, 72 (1886), 484. Edwin H. Cady recognized *April Hopes* as one of Howells's most important novels. *The Realist at War: The Mature Years, 1885–1920, of William Dean Howells* (Syracuse University Press, 1958), pp. 58–63. Recent studies of *April Hopes* are Paul John Eakin, *The New England Girl: Cultural Ideals in Hawthorne, Stowe, Howells, and James* (Athens: University of Georgia Press, 1976), pp. 124–9; Elizabeth Stevens Prioleau, *The Circle of Eros: Sexuality in the Work of William Dean Howells* (Durham, NC: Duke University Press, 1983), pp. 88–106; Kermit Vanderbilt, 'The Conscious Realism of Howells' *April Hopes*', *American Literary Realism*, 3 (1970), 53–66.
29. *Mrs Farrell*, with an introduction by Mildred Howells (New York: Harper and Brothers, 1921), p. 185. Hereafter abbreviated MF, with page numbers given in the text.

30. *The Landlord at Lion's Head* (New York: Harper & Brothers, 1887), pp. 3, 57. Hereafter abbreviated LLH, with page numbers given in the text.
31. Mary Suzanne Schriber, in *Gender and the Writer's Imagination: From Cooper to Wharton* (Lexington: University Press of Kentucky, 1987), pp. 86–116, examines the effects of Howells's conservative views on his portrayal of women characters.
32. 'Interviews with William Dean Howells' (see n. 13), 297.
33. *Doctor Breen's Practice* (Boston: Osgood, 1881), p. 126. Hereafter abbreviated DBP, with page numbers given in the text.
34. *The Story of a Play* (New York: Harper & Brothers, 1898), p. 54. Hereafter abbreviated SP, with page numbers given in the text.
35. *The Day of Their Wedding* (New York: Harper & Brothers, 1896), p. 16.
36. *Ragged Lady* (New York: Harper & Brothers, 1899), p. 45.
37. 'Editor's Easy Chair', *Harper's Magazine*, 113 (1906), 637.
38. *Selected Letters of William Dean Howells*, V, 1902–11, ed. William C. Fischer with Christoph K. Lohmann (Boston: Twayne, 1983), pp. 124.
39. *The American Language: An Inquiry into the Development of English*, Supplement, fourth edition (New York: Knopf, 1961), p. 418.
40. *Miss Bellard's Inspiration* (New York: Harper & Brothers, 1905), pp. 28, 32.
41. *The Quality of Mercy*, Introduction and Notes to the Text by James P. Elliott (Bloomington: Indiana University Press, 1979), p. 103.
42. *The Lady of the Aroostook* (Boston: Houghton, Osgood, 1879), pp. 55, 59. Hereafter abbreviated LA, with page numbers given in the text.
43. *The Coast of Bohemia* (New York: Harper & Brothers, 1893), p. 199.
44. Howells's phrase in a review of Henry Ward Beecher's *Norwood*, *Atlantic Monthly*, 21 (1868), 761.
45. Habegger has made the fullest study of Penelope Lapham's humour in *Gender, Fantasy, and Realism in American Literature* (New York: Columbia University Press, 1982), pp. 184–95.
46. *The Circle of Eros* (see n. 28), p. 151.
47. Edwin H. Cady, *The Road to Realism: The Early Years, 1837–1885, of William Dean Howells* (Syracuse: Syracuse University Press, 1956), pp. 206–7, 233–5; Sidney H. Bremer, *Invalids and Actresses: Howells's Duplex Imagery for American Women'*, *American Literature*, 47 (1976), 599–614.
48. John W. Crowley, 'W. D. Howells: The Ever-Womanly', in *American Novelists Revisited: Essays in Feminist Criticism*, edited by Fritz Fleischmann (Boston: G. K. Hall, 1982), pp. 170–88; Gail Thain Parker, 'William Dean Howells: Realism and Feminism', in *Harvard English Studies 4: The Uses of Literature*, ed. Monroe Engel (Cambridge: Harvard University Press, 1973), pp. 133–61.

3 Masculine and Feminine in James's Criticism and Fiction

1. William Dean Howells, *Heroines of Fiction*, 2 vols (New York: Harper & Brothers, 1901), II, 168, 164.

2. *Notes on Novelists with Some Other Notes* (New York: Charles Scribner's Sons, 1914), p. 214. Hereafter abbreviated NN, with page references given in the text.

3. *Notes and Reviews* (Cambridge, Mass.: Dunster House, 1921), p. 116. Hereafter abbreviated NR, with page numbers given in the text. That James himself, in his early novels, frequently resorted to the hyperbole and sentimental clichés and epithets he condemned in women's fiction is amply demonstrated by William Veeder, *Henry James: The Lessons of the Master: Popular Fiction and Personal Style in the Nineteenth Century* (Chicago: University of Chicago Press, 1975), pp. 22–35, 56–65 and *passim*.

4. *Literary Reviews and Essays*, ed. Albert Mordell (New York: Grove Press, 1957), p. 289. Hereafter abbreviated LRE, with page references given in the text.

5. Letter of 17 November 1905, to Mary Cadwalader Jones, Houghton Library, Harvard University.

6. *Partial Portraits* (London: Macmillan & Company, 1911), p. 62. Hereafter abbreviated PP, with page references given in the text.

7. *French Poets and Novelists* (London: Macmillan & Company, 1893), pp. 161, 181. Hereafter abbreviated FPN, with page references given in the text. For fuller discussion of James's gender-biased criticism of George Sand, see Sarah B. Daugherty, 'Henry James, George Sand, and *The Bostonians*: Another Curious Chapter in the Literary History of Feminism', *Henry James Review* 10 (1989), 42–9.

8. *The Future of the Novel*, ed. Leon Edel (New York: Vintage Books, 1956), p. 40.

9. *Essays in London and Elsewhere* (New York: Harper & Brothers, 1893), p. 255. Hereafter abbreviated ELE, with page references given in the text.

10. *Scribner's Magazine*, 5 (1889), 372.

11. *Watch and Ward* (London: Macmillan & Company, 1923), p. 24. Hereafter abbreviated WW, with page references given in the text.

12. Margaret Fuller, 'Woman in the Nineteenth Century', *The Writings of Margaret Fuller*, selected and edited by Mason Wade (New York: Viking Press, 1941), p. 179.

13. For readings of Roger Lawrence as an exemplary, morally irreproachable guardian, see Robert Emmet Long, *Henry James: The Early Novels* (Boston: Twayne Publishers, 1983), pp. 21–2; J. A. Ward, *The Search for Form: Studies in the Structure of James's Fiction* (Chapel Hill: University of North Carolina Press, 1967), pp. 68–70.

    Roger Lawrence emerges as a morally flawed and self-deluded character in Lee Ann Johnson, 'A Dog in the Manger: James's Depiction of Roger Lawrence in *Watch and Ward*, *Arizona Quarterly*, 29 (1973), 176; Leo B. Levy, 'The Comedy of *Watch and Ward*', *Arlington Quarterly* 1 (1968), 87.

    Alfred Habegger argues that James in making Roger Lawrence a prosaic, unromantic, self-effacing figure consciously rejected the aggressive masculine hero idealized in women's novels. *Henry James and the 'Woman Business'* (Cambridge: Cambridge University Press, 1989), pp. 75–80.

14. *The Novels and Tales of Henry James* (New York: Charles Scribner's Sons, 1907–9), I, 49. All citations by volume and page number are to this edition.
15. For James's harsh criticism of the London stage and the speech of its leading actors, see *The Scenic Art: Notes on Acting and the Drama, 1872–1901*, edited by Allan Wade (New Brunswick: Rutgers University Press, 1948), pp. 139–46 and *passim*.
16. *The Collected Tales of Henry James*, 12 vols, ed. Leon Edel (Philadelphia: J. B. Lippincott Company, 1961–64), II, 346. Hereafter abbreviated CT, with volume and page references given in the text.
17. *The Europeans* (Boston: Houghton, Osgood & Company, 1878), p. 185. Hereafter abbreviated E, with page references given in the text.
18. Leon Edel, *Henry James: The Conquest of London: 1870–1881* (Philadelphia: J. B. Lippincott Company, 1962), pp. 106–13.
19. *The Sacred Fount* (New York: Charles Scribner's Sons, 1901), pp. 52, 9.
20. George Bishop, *When the Master Relents: The Neglected Short Fiction of Henry James* (Ann Arbor, Mich.: UMI Research Press, 1988), p. 25.
21. S. Gorley Putt, *Henry James: A Reader's Guide* (Ithaca, NY: Cornell University Press, 1966), p. 270.
22. Quoted in Jean Strouse, *Alice James: A Biography* (Boston: Houghton Mifflin Company, 1980), p. 206.
23. Letter of 25 July 1900, to James B. Pinker, *Henry James Letters: 1895–1916*, Vol. III, ed. Leon Edel (Cambridge: Harvard University Press, 1984), 154–5.
24. E. A. Sheppard, *Henry James and The Turn of the Screw* (London: Auckland University Press, 1974), pp. 54, 57.
25. Page references in parentheses are to *Joseph Conrad, Heart of Darkness: A Study in Contemporary Criticism*, ed. Ross C. Murfin (New York: St Martin's Press, 1989).
26. *The Notebooks of Henry James*, ed. F. O. Matthiessen and Kenneth B. Murdock (New York: George Brazillier, 1955), pp. 93, 310.
27. Millicent Bell, *Meaning in Henry James* (Cambridge: Harvard University Press, 1991), p. 228; Roslyn Jolly, *Henry James: History, Narrative, Fiction* (Oxford: Oxford University Press, 1993), p. 99.
28. Anne Robinson Taylor, *Male Novelists and Their Female Voices: Literary Masquerades* (Troy, NY: Whitston Publishing Company, 1981), p. 185.
29. Oscar Cargill, 'Henry James as Freudian Pioneer', *A Casebook on Henry James's 'The Turn of the Screw'*, ed. Gerald Willen (New York: Crowell, 1960), p. 237.
30. Tony Tanner, *The Reign of Wonder: Naivety and Reality in American Literature* (Cambridge: Cambridge University Press, 1965), pp. 325, 324. Extended analyses of *The Sacred Fount* as a parable of the creative process include Susanne Kappeler, *Writing and Reading in Henry James* (New York: Columbia University Press, 1980), pp. 118–59; Dorothea Krook, *The Ordeal of Consciousness in Henry James* (Cambridge: Cambridge University Press, 1962), pp. 167–94; Donna Przybylowicz, *Desire and Repression: The Dialectic of Self and Other in the Late Works of Henry James* (University, Ala: University of Alabama Press, 1986), pp. 48–87.

31   Jean Frantz Blackall, 'The Experimental Period', A Companion to
     Henry James Studies, ed. Daniel Mark Fogel (Westport, Conn.: Green-
     wood Press, 1993), p. 168.
32   The Notebooks of Henry James (see n. 26), p. 196.
33   James's satiric portrayal of Mrs Stringham is analysed by Jonathan
     Freedman, Professions of Taste: Henry James, British Aestheticism and
     Commodity Culture (Stanford: Stanford University Press, 1990), pp.
     207–9.
34   The Bostonians (New York: Dial Press, 1945), p. 24. Hereafter abbrevi-
     ated B, with page references given in the text.
35   Lillian Faderman argues that Verena has more to gain with Olive
     than with Basil Ransom, that during her months with Olive she is
     'happy, active, fruitful'. 'Female Same-Sex Relationships in Novels
     by Longfellow, Holmes, and James', New England Quarterly, 51 (Sep-
     tember 1978), 309–32.
36   Elizabeth Allen, A Woman's Place in the Novels of Henry James (New
     York: St Martin's Press, 1984), p. 80.
37   W. R. Martin, 'The Use of the Fairy Tale', English Studies in Africa, 2
     (1959), 98–109. For similar views of Ransom as the hero who rescues
     Verena from a morbid relationship, see Charles Anderson, 'James's
     Portrait of the Southerner', American Literature, 27 (November 1955),
     309–31; Robert Emmet Long, 'The Society and the Masks: The Blithe-
     dale Romance and The Bostonians', Nineteenth-Century Fiction, 19
     (1968), 105–22; Theodore C. Miller, 'The Muddled Politics of Henry
     James's The Bostonians', Georgia Review, 26 (1972), 336–46.
38   Graham Burns, 'The Bostonians', Critical Review, 12 (1969), 45–60. See
     also Judith Fetterley, The Resisting Reader: A Feminist Approach to
     American Fiction (Bloomington: Indiana University Press, 1978), pp.
     101–53; Michael Kreyling, 'Nationalizing the Southern Hero: Adams
     and James', Mississippi Quarterly, 34 (1981), 383–402. Elizabeth
     McMahan, 'Sexual Desire and Illusion in The Bostonians', Modern
     Fiction Studies, 25 (1979), 241–51.
39   The Scenic Art (see n. 15), p. 120.
40   The American Scene, edited and with an introduction by W. H. Auden
     (New York: Charles Scribner's Sons, 1946), pp. 67, 25, 127, 167.
41   Ibid., pp. 65, 64.
42   Ruth Bernard Yeazell, Language and Knowledge in the Late Novels of
     Henry James (Chicago: University of Chicago Press, 1976), p. 69.
43   The transposition or fusion of gender roles in James's fiction has
     been extensively analysed by a number of critics. See, for instance,
     Lynda S. Boren, Eurydice Reclaimed: Language, Gender, and Voice in
     Henry James (Ann Arbor, Mich.: UMI Research Press, 1989), pp. 21–39
     and passim; David McWhirter, Desire and Love in Henry James: A Study
     of the Late Novels (Cambridge: Cambridge University Press, 1989),
     especially pp. 49–53, 59–63; Julie Olin-Ammentorp, ' "A Circle of
     Petticoats": The Feminization of Merton Densher', Henry James Re-
     view, 15 (1994), 38–54; Philip Sicker, Love and the Quest for Identity in
     the Fiction of Henry James (Princeton: Princeton University Press,
     1980), pp. 120 ff.

4 Language and Convention in Wharton's Hieroglyphic World

1. *A Backward Glance* (New York: D. Appleton-Century Company, 1934), p. 144. Hereafter abbreviated BG, with page numbers given in the text.
2. See Hilda M. Fife, 'Letters from Edith Wharton to Vernon Lee', *Colby Library Quarterly*, Series III, No. 9 (February 1953), 139–44.
3. An excellent analysis of Wharton's view of other women writers is Amy Kaplan, 'Edith Wharton's Profession of Authorship', *ELH*, 53 (Summer 1986), 435–57.
4. Edith Wharton, 'George Eliot', *Bookman*, 15 (May 1902), 248.
5. See for instance Woolf's essay, 'Women and Fiction' (1929). On the difficulties facing women writers she states: 'The very form of the sentence does not fit her. It is a sentence made by men; it is too loose, too heavy, too pompous for a woman's use.' *Women and Writing*, edited and with an introduction by Michèle Barrett (New York: Harcourt, Brace, Jovanovich, 1979), p. 48.
6. 'The Spark', *Novellas and Other Writings* (New York: Library of America, 1990), p. 465.
7. 'The Great American Novel', *Yale Review*, NS 16 (July 1927), 647, 650.
8. *The Collected Short Stories of Edith Wharton*, 2 vols, edited and with an introduction by R. W. B. Lewis (New York: Charles Scribner's Sons, 1968), I, 21. References to this edition will be made in the text by volume and page numbers.
9. *The Custom of the Country* (New York: Library of America, 1985), p. 669. Hereafter abbreviated CC, with page numbers given in the text.
10. A number of critics view Ralph as a victim seemingly powerless to avert his fate. Geoffrey Walton states that Ralph is 'predestined to be a victim of Undine', because of his temperament and upbringing. *Edith Wharton: A Critical Interpretation* (Rutherford, NJ: Fairleigh Dickinson University Press, 1970), p. 115. Louis Auchincloss analyses *The Custom of the Country* as a 'determinist novel in the manner of Zola', its characters victims of 'ineluctable circumstances'. *Edith Wharton: A Woman in Her Time* (New York: Viking Press, 1971), pp. 88, 104.
11. *The Age of Innocence* (New York: Library of America, 1985), p. 1050. Hereafter abbreviated AI, with page numbers given in the text.
12. See Nina Baym, 'Melodramas of Beset Manhood: How Theories of American Fiction Exclude Women Authors', *American Quarterly*, 33 (1981), 123–39.
13. *Twilight Sleep* (New York: D. Appleton & Company, 1927), p. 324. Hereafter abbreviated TS, with page numbers given in the text.
14. *The House of Mirth* (New York: Library of America, 1985), p. 239. Hereafter abbreviated HM, with page numbers given in the text.
15. The importance of Newland Archer as the embodiment of his society's codes and the speaker of its language is most fully analysed by David A. Godfrey, 'The Full and Elaborate Vocabulary of Evasion: The Language of Cowardice in Edith Wharton's Old New York',

Midwest Quarterly, 30 (1988), 27–44; Gary H. Lindberg, *Edith Wharton and the Novel of Manners* (Charlottesville: University Press of Virginia, 1975), pp. 101 ff., 128–37.

16. *The Children* (New York: D. Appleton & Company, 1928), p. 234. Hereafter abbreviated C, with page numbers given in the text. An illuminating analysis of Martin Boyne, which compares him to John Marcher in 'The Beast in the Jungle', is developed by Judith L. Sensibar, 'Edith Wharton Reads the Bachelor Type: Her Critique of Modernism's Representative Man', *American Literature*, 60 (December 1988), 575–90.

17   *The Glimpses of the Moon* (New York: D. Appleton & Company, 1922), p. 72. Hereafter abbreviated GM, with page numbers given in the text.

18. Dale M. Bauer's analysis of *The House of Mirth* reveals the power of the dominant language to suppress resisting voices within individual characters of privileged society, such as Lily Bart. *Feminist Dialogics: A Theory of Failed Community* (Albany: State University of New York Press, 1988), pp. 89–127.

19. *A Son at the Front* (New York: Charles Scribner's Sons, 1923), p. 32. Hereafter abbreviated SF, with page numbers given in the text.

20. *The Mother's Recompense* (New York: D. Appleton & Company, 1925), p. 135. Hereafter abbreviated MR, with page numbers given in the text.

21. *The Marne* (New York: D. Appleton & Company, 1918), p. 113.

22. *Hudson River Bracketed* (New York: D. Appleton & Company, 1929), p. 113. Hereafter abbreviated HRB, with page numbers given in the text.

23. *The Gods Arrive* (New York: D. Appleton & Company, 1923), p. 178. Hereafter abbreviated GA, with page numbers given in the text.

24. The composition of 'Literature' is documented by Nancy R. Leach, 'Edith Wharton's Unpublished Novel', *American Literature*, 25 (November 1953), 334–53.

25. *French Ways and Their Meaning* (New York: D. Appleton & Company, 1919), p. 117. Hereafter abbreviated FWM, with page numbers given in the text.

26. Alan Price, 'War as Editor: Edith Wharton in 1914–15', presented at the annual meeting of the Northeast Modern Language Association, 5 April 1991.

27. Letter of 6 March [1911?] (University of Virginia).

28. Edith Wharton, 'The Three Francescas', *North American Review*, 175 (July 1902), 19.

29. Letter of 14 October 1914. Quoted by Clare Colquitt, 'Unpacking Her Treasures: Edith Wharton's "Mysterious Correspondence" with Morton Fullerton', *Library Chronicle of the University of Texas*, NS 31 (1985), 103.

30. The Commonplace Book is in the Barrett Collection at the University of Virginia.

31. *The Reef* (New York: Library of America, 1985), p. 368.

32. *The Buccaneers* (New York: D. Appleton-Century Company, 1938), p. 245. Hereafter abbreviated B, with page numbers given in the text.

33. Susan Goodman, *Edith Wharton's Women: Friends and Rivals* (Hanover, NH: University Press of New England, 1990), Chapter 3. Wharton's importance as a critic of the cultural ideology that confines women is also emphasized by Elizabeth Ammons, *Edith Wharton's Argument with America* (Athens: University of Georgia Press, 1980) and by Mary Suzanne Schriber, *Gender and the Writer's Imagination: From Cooper to Wharton* (Lexington: University Press of Kentucky, 1987), Chapter 5.

5 Singers, Writers and Storytellers in Cather's America

1. Bernice Slote, 'Writer in Nebraska', *The Kingdom of Art: Willa Cather's First Principles and Critical Statements, 1893–1896*, selected and edited by Bernice Slote (Lincoln: University of Nebraska Press, 1966), p. 4. Hereafter abbreviated KA, with page numbers given in the text.
2. 'Professions for Women', in *Women and Writing*, edited and with an introduction by Michèle Barrett (New York: Harcourt, Brace, Jovanovich, 1979) p. 59.
3. *Ibid.*, p. 60.
4. Sharon O'Brien, *Willa Cather: The Emerging Voice* (New York: Oxford University Press, 1987), p. 122.
5. *The World and the Parish: Willa Cather's Articles and Reviews*, 2 vols., selected and edited by William M. Curtin (Lincoln: University of Nebraska Press, 1970), I, 146. Hereafter abbreviated WP, with volume and page numbers given in the text.
6. Theodore Dreiser, *Sister Carrie* (New York: Modern Library, c. 1900), p. 208.
7. See for instance reviews of Eugene Field, Rudyard Kipling and Robert Louis Stevenson in *The Kingdom of Art*, pp. 332–3, 310–318.
8. *Willa Cather: The Emerging Voice* (see n. 4), pp. 155–60.
9. Sandra M. Gilbert and Susan Gubar, *No Man's Land: The Place of the Woman Writer in the Twentieth Century*, Vol. II, *Sexchanges* (New Haven: Yale University Press, 1989), p. 203.
10. *The Song of the Lark*, 1915 edition (Lincoln: University of Nebraska Press, 1978), pp. 489–90. Hereafter abbreviated SL, with page numbers given in the text.
11. *Willa Cather: The Emerging Voice* (see n. 4), p. 167.
12. The importance in the novel of the Orpheus myth and Gluck's opera, *Orpheus and Eurydice*, is discussed by Richard Giannone, *Music in Willa Cather's Fiction* (Lincoln: University of Nebraska Press, 1968), pp. 88–90, and by Erik Ingvar Thurin, *The Humanization of Willa Cather: Classicism in an American Classic*, Lund Studies in English 81 (Lund, Sweden: Lund University Press, 1990), pp. 191–2.
13. Hermione Lee, *Willa Cather: Double Lives* (New York: Pantheon Books, 1989), p. 127. The importance of Thea's female sexuality is also emphasized by Susan J. Rosowski, *The Voyage Perilous: Willa Cather's Romanticism* (Lincoln: University of Nebraska Press, 1968), pp. 70–2.

14. *Willa Cather on Writing: Critical Studies on Writing as an Art*, with a foreword by Stephen Tennant (New York: Alfred A. Knopf, 1953), p. 62.

15. *Ibid.*, p. 64. For discussion of Thea as a Wagnerian singer and the importance of Wagner in Cather's fiction, see Giannone (n.12), pp. 97–9; Lee (n. 13), pp. 129–32; Susie Thomas, *Willa Cather* (Savage, Md.: Barnes & Noble Books, 1990), pp. 20–53.

16. Many examples from literature and art are analysed by Susan Gubar, ' "The Blank Page" and the Issues of Female Creativity', *Writing and Sexual Difference*, ed. Elizabeth Abel (Chicago: University of Chicago Press, 1982), pp. 73–93.

17. 'Three American Singers', *McClure's Magazine* 13 (December 1913), 38. In a letter to Dorothy Canfield Fisher, 15 March 1916, Cather explained that she dropped the German part of the novel because in its difference from the Moonstone sections it seemed to destroy the unity of the novel. In a review in the *Nebraska State Journal*, 29 March 1896, Cather praised James's *The Tragic Muse*, 'so perfect a novel that one does not realize what a masterly study it is of the life and ends and aims of the people who make plays live' (KA, 362).

18. Most prominent are Carl Linstrum in *O Pioneers!*, Jim Burden in *My Ántonia* and Claude Wheeler in *One of Ours*.

19. Masculine mistrust of the spoken vernacular or 'the mother tongue', identified with women, is discussed by Sandra M. Gilbert and Susan Gubar in *The War of the Words*, Vol. I of *No Man's Land: The Place of the Woman Writer in the Twentieth Century* (New Haven: Yale University Press, 1988), pp. 254 ff.

20. *The Voyage Perilous* (see n. 13), p. 73.

21. 'The Best Stories of Sarah Orne Jewett', *Willa Cather on Writing* (see n. 14), pp. 56–7.

22. *Uncle Valentine and Other Stories: Willa Cather's Uncollected Short Fiction, 1915–1929*, edited and with an introduction by Bernice Slote (Lincoln: University of Nebraska Press, 1973), pp. 102, 104. Hereafter abbreviated UV, with page numbers given in the text.

23. *Willa Cather's Collected Short Fiction, 1892–1912*, Introduction by Mildred R. Bennett (Lincoln: University of Nebraska Press, 1965), p. 117. Hereafter abbreviated CSF, with page numbers given in the text.

24. *My Ántonia* (Boston: Houghton Mifflin Company, 1918), pp. 294–5. Hereafter abbreviated MA, with page numbers given in the text.

25. Walter J. Ong, *Interfaces of the Word: Studies in the Evolution of Consciousness and Culture* (Ithaca: Cornell University Press, 1977), p. 25.

26. *Shadows on the Rock* (New York: Alfred A. Knopf, 1931), p. 40.

27. See for instance, L. V. Jacks, 'The Classics and Willa Cather', *Prairie Schooner* 35 (1961), 289–96; Paul A. Olson, 'The Epic and Great Plains Literature: Rolvaag, Cather, and Neihart', *Prairie Schooner*, 55 (1981), 263–85; Susan J. Rosowski, 'Willa Cather – A Pioneer in Art: *O Pioneers!* and *My Ántonia*', *Prairie Schooner*, 55 (1981), 141–54; Mary Ruth Ryder, *Willa Cather and Classical Myth: The Search for a New Parnassus*, *Studies in American Literature*, Vol. 11 (Lewiston, NY: Edwin Mellen Press, 1990); Donald Sutherland, 'Willa Cather: The

Classic Voice', *The Art of Willa Cather*, ed. Bernice Slote and Virginia Faulkner (Lincoln: University of Nebraska Press, 1974), pp. 156–79; Thurin, *The Humanization of Willa Cather* (see n. 12).

28. *The Professor's House* (New York: Alfred A. Knopf, 1925), p. 257. Hereafter abbreviated PH, with page numbers given in the text.

29. *Interfaces of the Word*, (see n. 25), p. 252.

30. *Willa Cather and Classical Myth*, (see n. 27), p. 228.

31. *One of Ours* (New York: Alfred A. Knopf, 1922), p. 420.

32. Letter of 10 June 1876, *Selected Letters of W. D. Howells*, Vol. 2, ed. George Arms and Christoph K. Lohmann (Boston: Twayne Publishers, 1979), p. 130.

33. Letter of 27 November 1908, *Letters of Sarah Orne Jewett*, ed. Annie Fields (Boston: Houghton Mifflin Company, 1911), p. 246.

34. Mildred Bennett, in a letter to Dorothy Canfield Fisher (19 March 1951), explained why she believed that Cather had helped write the autobiography of Ellen Terry: 'The opening pages of the Terry book have a definite Cather flavor and later comes the thesis that first impressions are the deepest – a prominent Cather belief.' Bailey/Howe Library, University of Vermont.

35. The Willa Cather Collection, Manuscripts Department, Alderman Library, University of Virginia.

36. Willa Cather, Preface to 'Alexander's Bridge', in *Willa Cather: Stories, Poems, and Other Writings* (New York: Library of America, 1992), p. 942.

37. Edith Wharton, *The Writing of Fiction* (New York: Charles Scribner's Sons, 1925), p. 46.

38. H. L. Mencken, 'Four Reviews', *Willa Cather and Her Critics*, ed. James Schroeter (Ithaca, NY: Cornell University Press, 1967), pp. 10, 8.

39. Letter of 21 November 1917, Houghton Library, Harvard University.

40. E. K. Brown, *Willa Cather: A Critical Biography* (New York: Alfred A. Knopf, 1953), pp. 204, 201.

41. Grant Overton, *The Women Who Make Our Novels* (Freeport, NY: Books for Libraries Press, c. 1928, reprinted 1967), p. 84.

42. Patrick W. Shaw, '*My Ántonia*: Emergence and Authorial Revelation', *American Literature*, 56 (December 1984), 536, 537.

43. *Willa Cather: Double Lives* (see n. 13), p. 153.

44. Sharon O'Brien, ' "The Thing Not Named": Willa Cather as a Lesbian Writer', *Signs*, 9 (1984), 597, 593.

45. *Sexchanges* (see n. 9), p. 201.

46. Anne Robinson Taylor, *Male Novelists and Their Female Voices: Literary Masquerades* (Troy, NY: Whitston Publishing Company, 1981), p. 5.

47. *My Mortal Enemy* (New York: Alfred A. Knopf, 1926), p. 11. Hereafter abbreviated MME, with page numbers given in the text.

48. *The Voyage Perilous* (see n. 13), p. 146.

49. Marilyn Berg Callander, *Willa Cather and the Fairy Tale* (Ann Arbor, Mich.: UMI Research Press, 1988), p. 44.

50. Janis P. Stout, *Strategies of Reticence: Silence and Meaning in the Works of Jane Austen, Willa Cather, Katherine Anne Porter, and Joan Didion* (Charlottesville: University Press of Virginia, 1990), p. 84.

51. *Willa Cather: Double Lives* (see n. 13), p. 212.
52. *Willa Cather and the Fairy Tale* (see n. 49), p. 44.
53. Theodore S. Adams, 'Willa Cather's *My Mortal Enemy*: The Concise Presentation of Scene, Character, and Theme', *Colby Library Quarterly*, Series X (September 1973), 138.
54. *Willa Cather on Writing* (see n. 14), p. 41.
55. Blanche H. Gelfant, 'Art and Apparent Artlessness: Self-Reflexivity in *My Ántonia*', *Approaches to Teaching My Ántonia*, ed. Susan J. Rosowski (New York: Modern Language Association of America, 1989), p. 127.
56. Ann Romines, *The Home Plot: Women, Writing and Domestic Ritual* (Amherst: University of Massachusetts Press, 1992), p. 143.
57. Deborah Carlin, *Cather, Canon, and the Politics of Reading* (Amherst: University of Massachusetts Press, 1992), p. 29.
58. Susan J. Rosowski, 'Writing Against Silences: Female Adolescent Development in the Novels of Willa Cather', *Studies in the Novel*, 21 (Spring 1989), 68.
59. Virginia Woolf, *A Room of One's Own* (New York: Harcourt, Brace, Jovanovich, 1929), p. 103.
60. Merrill Maguire Skaggs, *After the World Broke in Two: The Later Novels of Willa Cather* (Charlottesville: University Press of Virginia, 1990), p. 181.
61. *Sapphira and the Slave Girl* (New York: Alfred A. Knopf, 1940), p. 5. Hereafter abbreviated SSG, with page numbers given in the text.
62. Letter of 14 October 1940, Bailey/Howe Library, University of Vermont.
63. Letter of 9 November 1940, The Willa Cather Collection, Manuscripts Department, Alderman Library, University of Virginia.
64. Elizabeth Shepley Sergeant, *Willa Cather: A Memoir* (Philadelphia: J. B. Lippincott Company, 1953), p. 270.
65. Henry Seidel Canby, 'Conversation Piece', *Saturday Review of Literature*, 23 (14 December 1940), 5. Cather praised Canby's review in a letter to Viola Roseboro, 20 February 1941. Alderman Library, University of Virginia.
66. Eugénie Lambert Hamner, 'The Unknown, Well-Known Child in Cather's Last Novel', *Women's Studies*, 11 (1984), pp. 347–57.
67. *Willa Cather: The Emerging Voice* (see n. 4), pp. 30, 29.

6 Illusions of Change in Utopian Fiction

1. *Harper's Magazine*, 77 (June 1888), 154–5.
2. Lucy M. Freibert, 'World Views in Utopian Novels by Women', *Women and Utopia: Critical Interpretations*, ed. Marlene Barr and Nicholas D. Smith (Lanham, Md: University Press of America, 1983), p. 67.
3. These include the following novels reprinted by the Arno Press in 1971: W. W. Satterlee, *Looking Backward and What I Saw* (1890); Richard Michaelis, *A Sequel to Looking Backward; or 'Looking Further Forward'* (1890); Ludwig A. Geissler, *Looking Beyond: A Sequel to Look-*

ing Backward by Edward Bellamy and an Answer to Looking Further Forward by Richard Michaelis (1891); Solomon Schindler, *Young West: A Sequel to Edward Bellamy's Celebrated Novel, Looking Backward* (1894). For other titles, see Nancy Snell Griffin, *Edward Bellamy: A Bibliography* (Metuchen, NJ: Scarecrow Press, 1986), pp. 112–18.

4. Arthur E. Morgan, *Edward Bellamy* (New York: Columbia University Press, 1944), p. 275.
5. 'World Views in Utopian Novels by Women' (see n. 2), p. 67.
6. Sylvia E. Bowman, *The Year 2000: A Critical Biography of Edward Bellamy* (New York: Bookman Associates, 1958), pp. 269–97; 'Bellamy's Missing Chapter', *New England Quarterly*, 31 (March 1958), 47–65. See also Sylvia Strauss, 'Gender, Class, and Race in Utopia', in *Looking Backward, 1988–1888: Essays on Edward Bellamy*, ed. Daphne Patai (Amherst: University of Massachusetts Press, 1988), pp. 68–90.
7. Quoted in 'Gender, Class, and Race in Utopia' (see n. 6), p. 68.
8. Edward Bellamy, *Looking Backward 2000–1887* (Boston: Houghton Mifflin Company, 1898), p. 45. Hereafter abbreviated LB, with page numbers given in the text.

    Bellamy's portrayal of women in *Looking Backward* is discussed by Jean Pfaelzer, 'A State of One's Own: Feminism as Ideology in American Utopias, 1880–1915', *Extrapolation*, 24 (Winter 1983), 311–28; Kenneth Roemer, 'Sex Roles, Utopia and Change: The Family in Late Nineteenth-Century Utopian Literature', *American Studies*, 13 (Fall 1972), 33–47; Sylvia Strauss, 'Gender, Class, and Race in Utopia' (see n. 6), pp. 77–80, and 'Women in "Utopia" ', *South Atlantic Quarterly*, 75 (Winter 1976), 115–31.
9. Edward Bellamy, *Equality* (New York: D. Appleton & Company, 1897), p. 257. Hereafter abbreviated E, with page numbers given in the text.
10. Charles Lotin Hildreth, review of *Looking Backward* in *Belford's Magazine*, January 1890. Quoted in Richard Toby Widdicombe, *Edward Bellamy: An Annotated Bibliography of Secondary Criticism* (New York: Garland Publishing, 1988), p. 144.
11. 'Gender, Class, and Race in Utopia' (see n. 6), pp. 76, 75.
12. Mary H. Ford, 'A Feminine Iconoclast', *Nationalist*, 1 (November 1889), 254.
13. Abby Morton Diaz, 'The Why and Wherefore', *Nationalist*, 2 (December 1889), 8.
14. See for instance Mary Livermore, *The Story of My Life* (Hartford: A. D. Worthington & Company, 1897), pp. 598 ff.
15. *Edward Bellamy*, (see n. 4), p. 252.
16. John L. Thomas, Introduction, *Looking Backward 2000–1887* (Cambridge: Harvard University Press, 1967), p. 61.
17. Letter of 31 December 1889, to John S. Wood, *Selected Letters, Volume 3: 1882–1891*, edited and annotated by Robert C. Leitz III with Richard H. Ballinger and Christoph K. Lohmann (Boston: Twayne Publishers, 1980), 268.
18. Letter of 27 April 1890, to William C. Howells, *Selected Letters* (see n. 17), 3: 28; Letter of 6 November 1892, to William C. Howells, *Selected*

Letters, Volume 4: 1892–1901, edited and annotated by Thomas Wortham with Christoph K. Lohmann, David J. Nordloh and Jerry Herron (Boston: Twayne Publishers, 1981), 29.

19. 'Edward Bellamy', *Atlantic Monthly*, 82 (August 1898), 255–6.
20. *The Altrurian Romances*, Introduction and Notes to the Text by Clara and Rudolf Kirk (Bloomington; Indiana University Press, 1968), pp. 14, 17, 18. Hereafter abbreviated AR, with page numbers given in the text.
21. *The Gates Ajar*, ed. Helen Sootin Smith (Cambridge: Harvard University Press, 1964), pp. 51, 49. Hereafter abbreviated GA, with page numbers given in the text
    The fullest analysis of Phelps's utopian fiction is Carol Farley Kessler, *Elizabeth Stuart Phelps* (Boston: Twayne Publishers, 1982), Chapter 2, pp. 20–42.
22. *The Gates Between* (Boston. Houghton Mifflin Company, 1887), p. 22. Hereafter abbreviated GB, with page numbers given in the text.
23. *Beyond the Gates* (Boston: Houghton Mifflin Company, 1886), pp. 44, 54. Hereafter abbreviated BG, with page numbers given in the text.
24. *Chapters from a Life* (Boston: Houghton Mifflin Company, 1896), p. 98. Hereafter abbreviated CL, with page numbers given in the text.
25. These included 'Woman-Suffrage as Judged by the Working of Negro-Suffrage' and 'Reform in the Political Status of Women'. See *Elizabeth Stuart Phelps* (n. 21), pp. 71–2, 85.
26. *Herland*, with an introduction by Ann J. Lane (New York: Pantheon Books, 1979), p. 23. Hereafter abbreviated H, with page numbers given in the text.
27. *With Her in Ourland*, *Forerunner*, 7 (1916), 44. Hereafter abbreviated WHO, with page numbers given in the text.
28. *The Living of Charlotte Perkins Gilman; An Autobiography* (New York: Arno Press, 1972), pp. 305–6.
29. Mary E. Bradley Lane, *Mizora: A Prophecy*, with introductions by Stuart A. Teitler and Kristine Anderson (Boston: Gregg Press, 1975), p. 27. Hereafter abbreviated M, with page numbers given in the text.
30. Alice Ilgenfritz Jones and Ella Merchant, *Unveiling a Parallel: A Romance* (Boston: Arena Publishing Company, 1893), p. 132. Hereafter abbreviated UPR, with page numbers given in the text.
31. Mary Agnes Tincker, *San Salvador* (New York: Arno Press, 1978), p. 302. Hereafter abbreviated SS, with page numbers given in the text.
32. M. Louise Moore, *Al-Modad; or, Life Scenes beyond the Polar Circumflex. A Religio-Scientific Solution of the Problems of Present and Future Life* (Shell Bank, Cameron Parish, LA: Moore & Beauchamp, 1892), p. 302. Hereafter abbreviated AL, with page numbers given in the text.

Conclusion

1. *Far from the Madding Crowd*, New Wessex Edition, Introduction by John Bayley (London: Macmillan, 1974), p. 376.

2.   *Persuasion*, ed. John Davie, Introduction by Claude Rawson, World's Classics (Oxford; Oxford University Press, 1992), p. 221.

3.   *Far from the Madding Crowd*, pp. 58, 227.

4.   For instance, when Bathsheba's servant Liddy says of their neighbour Farmer Boldwood. 'A woman jilted him, they say', Bathsheba corrects her: 'People always say that – and we know very well women scarcely ever jilt men; 'tis the men who jilt us' (p. 127).

5.   'Sainte-Beuve', *North American Review*, 130 (January 1880), 53.

Index